NEW DIRECTIONS IN COMPUTATIONAL ECONOMICS

Advances in Computational Economics

VOLUME 4

The titles published in this series are listed at the end of this volume.

New Directions in Computational Economics

edited by

W. W. Cooper and A. B. Whinston

University of Texas at Austin, U.S.A.

KLUWER ACADEMIC PUBLISHERS

DORDRECHT / BOSTON / LONDON

Library of Congress Cataloging-in-Publication Data

New directions in computational economics / edited by William W. Cooper and Andrew B. Whinston.
p. cm. -- (Advances in computational economics ; v. 4)
Includes index.
ISBN 0-7923-2539-7 (HB)
1. Economics, Mathematical--Congresses. 2. Econometrics--Congresses. I. Cooper, William W. (William Wager), 1914- . II. Whinston, Andrew B. III. Series.
HB135.N476 1994
330'.01'51--dc20 93-23548

ISBN 0-7923-2539-7

Published by Kluwer Academic Publishers,
P.O. Box 17 3300 AA Dordrecht, The Netherlands.

Kluwer Academic Publishers incorporate
the publishing programmes of
D. Reidel, Martinus Nijhoff, Dr. W. Junk and MTP Press.

Sold and distributed in the U.S.A. and Canada
by Kluwer Academic Publishers,
101 Philip Drive, Norwell, MA 02061, U.S.A.

In all other countries, sold and distributed
by Kluwer Academic Publishers Group,
P.O. Box 322, 3300 AH Dordrecht, The Netherlands.

Printed in the Netherlands (on acid-free paper)

Table of Contents

Part Three: Economic Modeling and Computational Systems

Preface

The National Science Foundation recently compiled contributions from a select group of leading scholars into a report entitled 'Research Opportunities in Computational Economics'. This report provided the basis for discussions predicting the future course of the computational economics field. In order to sustain and further foster the current high level of interest in this topic, a conference was held around the themes outlined in that report of March 6, 1991.

The conference was divided into nine sessions, each consisting of three of four presentations focusing on one of the topics that had been identified as providing potential research opportunities in the computational economics area. A common theme underlying the diverse collection of topics in the sessions was the application of computing technology as a tool for achieving solutions to realistic problems in computational economics and related areas in the environmental, ecological and energy fields in both developing and developed countries.

The diversity of the specified topics brought together – often for the first time – researchers from all specialities in this broad field to interact in a small conference setting. Thus, in addition to being a forum for the presentation and discussion of important papers, this conference provided an opportunity to lay the foundation for the creation of continuing intellectual exchanges in this field.

New Directions in Computational Economics presents a selection of papers by the conference participants. Part One of this volume addresses experimental and computational issues in auction mechanisms. Gerry Thompson's paper presents a survey of recent results for sealed bid auctions. He develops various characterizations of the auction mechanism using techniques from game theory. Dorsey, Johnson and Van Boening use neural networks as the basis for estimating bid functions for first price sealed bid auctions. They explore different ways of designing and training the neural network and of estimating the resulting form of the bid function. Finally, based on experimental results, researchers of the Economic Science Laboratory at the University

W.W. Cooper and A.B. Whinston (eds.), New Directions in Computational Economics, vii–ix.

of Arizona have developed a computational mechanism which they refer to as a 'smart market' to better match bids and offers for natural gas. They describe the tests of their mechanism using laboratory experiments.

Part Two consists of papers that formulate and solve models of economic systems. Hans Amman and David Kendrick's paper explores adaptive control models and the computational difficulties that result from nonconvexities. However, they are still able to present methods that can find global optima. Using goal programming, Nagurney, Thore and Pan formulate spatial resource allocation models that they use to analyze various policy issues. Thompson and Thrall next present a rigorous mathematical analysis of the relationship between efficiency and profitability, drawing up recent mathematical developmens in Data Envelopment Analysis and finally, the problem of matching uncertain streams of assets and liabilities is solved using stochastic optimization techniques described in the paper by John Mulvey. He indicates that the nature of the computations would suggest the use of parallel computing systems.

The last section of the book applies economic concepts to issues in computer science in addition to using computational techniques to solve economic models. Moore, Richmond and Whinston explore the application of economic criteria in the evaluation of algorithms. Instead of basing algorithmic complexity on a measure of the expected cost of computing a solution, they extend the measure to include the value or utility of the solution and determine the degree of solution precision to maximize the overall objective function. Stahl and Whinston present a model of distributed computing, such as the Internet, and propose a pricing mechanism to allocate processors to different users of the distributed network. They show that there exist prices that lead to an efficient allocation of computational resources and suggest various ways of approximating these prices. Manne and Rutherford present a general equilibrium model to analyze issues of international trade, capital flows and sectional analysis. Solutions are obtained using optimization techniques which provide guidance on important political issues. And finally, several algorithms have been proposed for solving stochastic control models applied to economics. A model of the Austrian economy is used to evaluate a model proposed by the authors, Neck and Matuhlo.

An important purpose of the conference was to provide a forum for the informal discussions that took place. One evening after dinner, for example, a spirited discussion on the future of computational economics took place. Issues ranged from the potential for theoretical advances to research funding questions and to the possibilities of solving radically different applications based on future breakthroughs in parallel computing. We were fortunate to have Dan Newlan of the National Science Foundation and Al Brenner, head of the IEEE Technical Committee on Supercomputing, moderating the discussion. The meeting and this volume are evidence of the rapid and continued growth of the computational economics field.

We are indebted to the members of the organizing committee for their substantial help in all phases of the conference: David Kendrick, George Kozmetsky, Alan Manne, Gerald Thompson, Stan Thore and Leon Lasdon. The conference would not have been possible without the strong support of George Kozmetsky and the financial backing of the RGK Foundation. The fact that the organization and execution of the conference was flawless was due to RGK Foundation staff, especially Cynthia Smith and Jami Hampton.

The National Science Foundation provided financial support through travel grants to speakers and participants. We are indebted to Dan Newlan for making the arrangements on behalf of the Foundation. The IEEE Computer Society through the office of its President, Bruce Shriver, provided financial support and connections to researchers outside of economics who were doing large-scale computations. This allowed us to add a dimension to the program that we would not have been able to achieve. We extend our thanks and appreciation to all of these individuals and organizations.

William W. Cooper & Andrew B. Whinston
IC^2 Institute
Graduate School of Business
The University of Texas at Austin

List of Contributors

Hans M. Amman
Department of Economics, University of Amsterdam, Amsterdam, The Netherlands

Mark V. Van Boening
School of Business, University of Mississippi, MS, U.S.A.

Robert E. Dorsey
School of Business, University of Mississippi, MS, U.S.A.

John D. Johnson
School of Business, University of Mississippi, MS, U.S.A.

David Kendrick
Department of Economics, University of Texas at Austin, Austin, TX, U.S.A.

Alan S. Manne
Department of Operations Research, Stanford University, Stanford, CA, U.S.A.

Josef Matulka
Department of Economics, University of Bielefeld, Bielefeld, Germany

Kevin McCabe
Department of Accounting, Carlson School of Management, University of Minnesota, Minneapolis, MN, U.S.A.

W.W. Cooper and A.B. Whinston (eds.), New Directions in Computational Economics, xi–xiii.

James C. Moore
Krannert School of Management, Purdue University, West Lafayette, IN, U.S.A.

John J. Mulvey
School of Engineering and Applied Science, Department of Civil Engineering and Operations Research, Princeton University, Princeton, NJ, U.S.A.

Anna Nagurney
School of Management, University of Massachusetts at Amherst, Amherst, MA, U.S.A.

Reinhard Neck
Department of Economics, University of Bielefeld, Bielefeld, Germany

Jie Pan
Department of Mathematics and Computer Science, St. Joseph's University, Philadelphia, Pennsylvania, U.S.A.

Stephen J. Rassenti
Economic Science Laboratory, University of Arizona, Tucson, AZ, U.S.A.

William Richmond
School of Business, George Mason University, Fairfax, VA, U.S.A.

Thomas Rutherford
Department of Economics, University of Colorado, Boulder, CO, U.S.A.

Vernon Smith
Economic Science Laboratory, University of Arizona, Tucson, AZ, U.S.A.

Dale Stahl
Department of Economics, University of Texas at Austin, Austin, TX, U.S.A.

Gerald L. Thompson
Carnegie Mellon University, Graduate School of Industrial Administration, Pittsburgh, PA, U.S.A.

Russel G. Thompson
College of Business Administration, Decision and Information Sciences Department, University of Houston, Houston, TX, U.S.A.

Sten Thore
IC^2 Institute, University of Texas at Austin, Austin, TX, U.S.A.

Robert M. Thrall
Jones School of Administration, Rice University, Houston, TX, U.S.A.

PART ONE

Experimental and Computational Methods for Auction Mechanisms

GERALD L. THOMPSON

Sealed Bid Auctions and Economic Market Games*

ABSTRACT. In this paper a survey is given of some recent results concerning the solutions and applications of sealed bid auctions, which are also called market games by economists. A historical discussion of the problem is given followed by the formulation of the problem as a maximizing linear program. Economic interpretations of the solution to the linear program are made with the interpretations of the dual variables being seller prices and buyer surpluses. The *core* of the game is defined to be the set of all solutions to the dual of the linear program. Two distinguished core extreme points, the MaxSeller–MinBuyer and MinSeller–MaxBuyer points are defined. It is then shown how to calculate these two points by solving suitable perturbed variations of the original linear program. The *fair division point* is defined to be the average of the two core points. Several structure theorems are given that characterize the core. Finally, a discussion of how sealed bid auctions can be used to settle real life auctions is presented.

1. INTRODUCTION

Auctions of various kinds have been and are being used throughout the world to decide on how goods should be exchanged between sellers and buyers. Some auction mechanisms are well known, such as the English verbal auction in which the highest bidder gets the object. Another is the silent Dutch auction which operates as follows: the price (represented by a clock mechanism) starts high and falls steadily; each buyer has a concealed button and the first buyer to push his button gets the object, but its price is determined by the price on the clock when the second buyer pushes his button. Besides these two there are thousands of other auction mechanisms in use [1, 6, 8, 11, 14] to exchange billions of dollars worth of goods each year.

In this paper we survey some recent work by various authors on *sealed bid auctions*, which are also called *market games* in the economics literature.

* This report was prepared as part of the activities of the Management Science Research Group, Carnegie Mellon University, under Contract No. N00014–85-K–0198 NR 047–048 with the Office of Naval Research.

W.W. Cooper and A.B. Whinston (eds.), New Directions in Computational Economics, 3–17.

The nice thing about these auctions is that they can be represented by a mathematical model which can be quickly solved on a computer, even if they have many buyers and sellers. Hence sealed bid auctions are capable of being used in real applications.

The sealed bid auction to be discussed here is applicable to the exchange of discrete indivisible objects such as paintings, houses, cars, furniture, etc. It is assumed that sellers arrive at an auction house with a number of objects that they wish to sell. They put these objects on display where buyers evaluate them and submit a sealed bid for each of the objects they wish to purchase. This bid is the *maximum* amount that the buyer is willing to pay for one unit of the seller's good. The seller is also permitted to make a reservation bid for his own good, that is, the *minimum* price at which he is willing to sell it. The auctioneer then collects all of the bids and, by some process, determines which seller should sell his good to which buyer, and what the price should be for it. The requirement is that the exchange price must be less than or equal to the buyer's concealed bid, and greater than or equal to the seller's reservation price, in order for the transaction to take place. Of course, it is possible that some of the sellers can't sell all of their goods if their reservation prices are too high, and also that some of the buyers may not be able to buy all that they want to if their bids are too low.

The question is: what is the best way of determining the prices for the goods that are exchanged and the identities of the specific sellers and the buyers to whom they sell. The sealed bid mechanism removes emotional, impulsive, and time pressures from the winning bid determination which is prevalent in English and Dutch auctions. On the other hand, to be useful, any auction mechanism must work relatively quickly, and must be able to provide answers in a few seconds or minutes after all bids have been collected.

In this paper we shall discuss a mathematical model of the bid setting process that provides a solution in which the total bid value of all goods exchanged is maximum, and, at the same time, provides outcomes in which each buyer and seller is treated equally fairly (in a sense to be defined). The model to be described is also called a *market game* by economists.

The first discussion of an economic market game was given by Böhm-Bawerk in his *Positive Theory of Capital* [3]. He described a horse auction in there was one buyer who wanted to buy a horse and 7 sellers. He gave a discussion of the problem which was surprisingly complete but was not very well accepted by economists of his time. Although this example was widely discussed in the economic literature, no satisfactory solution was found for it. In 1944, von Neumann and Morgenstern discussed it in their famous book *Theory of Games and Economic Behavior*, [7] where they classified it as a market game. Later Shapley and Shubik [9, 10] narrowed its definition to an assignment market game, which made use of the well-known assignment linear programming model.

Vickery [21, 22] discussed the idea of price setting in a sealed bid auction by using the bid of the second highest bidder, which is like the method mentioned above used in the Dutch auction. He showed that its solution was pareto optimal for the buyers. Barr and Shaftel [2] showed that Vickery's work could be extended to the case of several buyers and sellers and non homogeneous goods by using an assignment model.

In [16] the author remarked that the Barr-Shaftel model was actually an assignment market game which they solved for a special core point, the *maximum buyer surplus* point. The set of all possible solutions to a sealed bid auction (or market game) is called the *core* of the auction (or market game). It can be shown to be a convex set having a finite number of extreme points. In [18] the author extended the definition of assignment market games to transportation market games, and gave a constructive algorithm for computing all of the extreme points of their cores. He also showed how to compute another distinguished extreme point of the core, the *maximum seller surplus* point. The midpoint of the line segment connecting the maximum buyer and seller surplus points was defined in [16] to be the *fair division point*. This point is especially interesting as a candidate for the solution to a sealed bid auction because at the fair division point, *every* player receives exactly the average of his maximum and his minimum return in *any* other core solution. Since one of the points of the core must be selected as the solution to the auction, other things being equal, the fair division point seems to be a good choice. Various properties of these points and other extreme points are discussed in this paper.

We also summarize a number of results relating to the core of a sealed bid auction and to its possible applications. The first set of results has to do with the effect on the core when the numbers of buyers or sellers are increased or decreased. It is shown in [17] that if the number of buyers is held fixed and the number of sellers goes up, prices will go down or stay the same, but if the number of sellers goes down, prices will go up or stay the same. The reverse holds if the number of sellers is held fixed, and the number of buyers changes. In [17] the author describes a recursive or auction method for solving assignment problems which starts with all of the buyers and one dummy seller, and adds the sellers one by one until finally the original problem is found. The algorithm turns out to be a very efficient way to solve assignment problems.

Other results concerning cores are discussed in Section 5. It is noted that the maximum number of extreme points in the seller core of a transportation game is equal to the binomial coefficient $2m$ by m. This is a huge number that increases exponentially as m becomes large. An example of a small game having the maximum number of extreme points is given. It is noted that the number of core extreme points increases with the degeneracy of the problem, being largest for an assignment market game and least for a nondegenerate transportation game. The size of a core also increases when the tastes of the buyers become more diverse, but decreases when tastes become less diverse.

In a new paper [20], the author and Sten Thore will discuss the use of sealed bid auction models to characterize economic organizations such as firms, industries, or even countries. It thus appears that the idea of using sealed bid auctions to model the exchanges of economic goods will turn out to be very useful in economic theory.

2. NOTATION FOR A SEALED BID AUCTION

The notation will be the same as that in the previous papers [15, 16, 17, 18] and in the book [19].

The index set of the m sellers is denoted by

$$I = \{1, 2, \ldots, m\} \tag{1}$$

and the index set of the n buyers is denoted by

$$J = \{1, 2, \ldots, n\}. \tag{2}$$

It is assumed that seller $i \in I$ has

$$a_i > 0 \tag{3}$$

units of a good to sell, and that buyer $j \in J$ wants to buy

$$b_j > 0 \tag{4}$$

units of that good. For $i \in I$ and $j \in J$ let

$$c_{ij} \geq 0 \tag{5}$$

be the (sealed) bid of buyer j which is the maximum amount j is willing to pay for one unit of seller i's goods. Let

$$p_i \geq 0 \tag{6}$$

be the *reservation price* of seller i, i.e., the minimum price he is willing to take for one unit of his good. The nonnegativity requirement in (6) means that seller i can dispose of or repossess his goods without charge if he cannot sell them.

In order to consider this problem as an economic market game we make the following economic assumptions (see [9] and [10]):

a) Utility is identified with money.
b) Side payments are permitted.
c) The goods being traded are indivisible.
d) Supply and demand functions are inflexible.

Given these assumptions, it follows that the only profitable coalitions are those containing positive numbers of both buyers and sellers. Because of assumption (6) and the side payment condition (b), the only important coalition is the all player coalition $S = I \cup J$. We concentrate on evaluating the value $v(S)$ for this coalition only, since the other coalitions are not interesting.

Let x_{ij} be the number of units that seller i sells to buyer j, and let y_i be the quantity of unsold goods of seller i. The value $v(I \cup J)$ can be obtained as the maximum possible sum of (buyer) evaluations of all transactions, which in turn, can be found by solving the following linear program (see [19]):

$$\begin{aligned}
&\text{Maximize} \quad && f = \sum_{i\in I}\sum_{j\in J} c_{ij}x_{ij} + \sum_{i\in I} p_i y_i \\
&\text{Subject to} \quad && \sum_{j\in J} x_{ij} + y_i = a_i \quad \text{for } i \in I \\
& && \sum_{i\in I} x_{ij} \le b_j \quad \text{for } j \in J \\
& && y_i, x_{ij} \ge 0 \quad \text{for } i \in I \text{ and } j \in J. \qquad (7)
\end{aligned}$$

Notice that the objective function counts all "true" sales x_{ij}, with value $c_{ij}x_{ij}$, from seller i to buyer j together with the "reservation sales" y_i, with value $p_i y_i$, of seller i to himself. The first set of constraints says that all of the amount a_i of seller i's goods are either sold or retained by him. The second set of constraints in (7) requires the total purchases of buyer j to be less than or equal to his demand, b_j. The nonnegativity requirement on x_{ij} means that the exchange of property is from seller i to buyer j. The nonnegativity requirement on y_i means that seller i can "retain" only a zero or positive amount of his own goods.

Problem (7) can be shown to be equivalent to a classical transportation problem, which implies that its basic solutions have integral values, provided the a_i's and b_j's are integer.

The dual linear program to (7) can be constructed by associating the m dual variables u_i to the first set of constraints in (7), and associating the n dual variables v_j to the second set of constraints in (7). The dual problem then is:

$$\begin{aligned}
&\text{Minimize} \quad && z = \sum_{i\in I} u_i a_i + \sum_{j\in J} v_j b_j \\
&\text{Subject to} \quad && u_i + v_j \ge c_{ij} \quad \text{for } i \in I \text{ and } j \in J \\
& && u_i \ge p_i \quad \text{for } i \in I
\end{aligned}$$

$$v_j \geq 0 \quad \text{for } j \in J. \tag{8}$$

The dual variable for the first set of constraints in (8) is x_{ij}. Using it we can write the first dual complementary slackness condition as:

$$x_{ij}^0 \left(u_i^0 + v_j^0 - c_{ij} \right) = 0 \quad \text{for all } i \in I, j \in J \tag{9}$$

(the superscript 0 on a variable will always mean an optimal value of that variable). From (9) we can derive the *first exchange rule*:

$$x_{ij}^0 > 0 \quad \text{implies} \quad u_i^0 + v_j^0 = c_{ij}. \tag{10}$$

Similarly, the dual variable for the second set of constraints in (8) is u_i. Using it we can write the second dual complementary slackness condition as:

$$y_i^0 \left(u_i^0 - p_i \right) = 0. \tag{11}$$

From (11) we can derive the *second exchange rule*

$$y_i^0 > 0 \quad \text{implies} \quad u_i^0 = p_i. \tag{12}$$

We are going to interpret an optimal value of dual variable u_i^0 as the *selling price* that seller i receives in that solution, and an optimal value of the dual variable v_j^0 as the buyer surplus in that solution. Hence using these interpretations we can give the economic interpretation to the above exchange rules as follows:

> *First Exchange Rule.* If in a given solution of the dual linear programs (7) and (8) seller i sells a positive amount of his good x_{ij}^0 to buyer j at a price u_i then *buyer j's surplus* is $v_j^0 = c_{ij} - u_i^0$ (see (10)).
> *Second Exchange Rule.* If in a given solution of the dual linear programs (7) and (8) seller i retains a positive amount y_j^0 of his good then he obtains exactly his reservation price, i.e., $u_i^0 = p_i$ (see (12)). Also, we define *seller i's surplus* to be $u_i^0 - p_i$, that is the difference between the actual price he receives and his reservation price.

The solution to the primal problem (7) always gives a unique value for f^0 and usually (but not always) gives unique values for x_{ij}^0 and y_i^0. However, we will see in the next section that there are many solutions to the dual problem (8).

In order to illustrate these ideas we will solve a simple house auction due to L.S. Shapley and M. Shubik, see [10]. It is an example of a sealed bid auction concerning three sellers each of whom has a house to sell, and three buyers, each of whom wants to buy a single house. The evaluations of the buyers and sellers for these houses (made circa 1955) are given in Table I.

TABLE I

Evaluations of buyers and sellers in the house auction

		Buyers' Evaluations		
Houses	Sellers Evaluations	Buyer 1	Buyer 2	Buyer 3
Seller 1	\$18,000	\$23,000	\$26,000	\$20,000
Seller 2	15,000	22,000	24,000	21,000
Seller 3	19,000	21,000	22,000	17,000

TABLE II

Initial tableau for (7) using the house auction data in Table I

	x_{11}	x_{12}	x_{13}	x_{21}	x_{22}	x_{23}	x_{31}	x_{32}	x_{33}	y_1	y_2	y_3	
u_1	1	1	1	0	0	0	0	0	0	1	0	0	≤ 1
u_2	0	0	0	1	1	1	0	0	0	0	1	0	≤ 1
u_3	0	0	0	0	0	0	1	1	1	0	0	1	≤ 1
v_1	1	0	0	1	0	0	1	0	0	0	0	0	≤ 1
v_2	0	1	0	0	1	0	0	1	0	0	0	0	≤ 1
v_3	0	0	1	0	0	1	0	0	1	0	0	0	≤ 1
	23	26	20	22	24	21	21	22	17	18	15	19	

If we set up the linear programming problem (7) using the data given in Table I we will obtain the initial tableau shown in Table II. The problem in Table II was solved by a computer which gave the answers shown in Table III. Note that all of the answers are in integers, as expected.

If you try solving this problem with different linear programming software, you will certainly obtain the same solution for the primal problem x_{ij}^0 and the objective function f^0. However you will not necessarily get the same solution for the dual problem variables u_i^0 and v_j^0. The reason for this is given in the next section.

3. THE CORE OF A SEALED BID AUCTION

As noted in the previous section, the linear program of a sealed bid auction may have many dual solutions, each of which can be used as a way of exchanging goods in the auction. For some of these autions the outcomes are more favorable to the buyers and less favorable to the sellers, and for other solutions it is the other way around. In this section we show first how to

TABLE III

Solution to linear program in Table II

Seller i	Price Received	Seller's Evaluation	Seller's Surplus
1	23	18	5
2	21	15	6
3	19	19	0
	63	52	11
Buyer j	**Price Paid**	**Buyer's Evaluation**	**Buyer's Surplus**
1	19	21	2
2	23	26	3
3	21	21	0
	63	68	5

$x_{12}^0 = 1$ meaning that seller 1 sells his house to buyer 2
$x_{23}^0 = 1$ meaning that seller 2 sells his house to buyer 3
$x_{31}^0 = 1$ meaning that seller 3 sells his house to buyer 1
f^0 = \$26,000 + \$21,000 + \$21,000 = \$68,000

calculate two distinguished extreme points of the core, the maximum seller surplus point, and the maximum buyer surplus point. Then a brief discussion is given of how the other extreme points of the core are found. The fair division point is defined and interpretations for various points of the core are given.

Definition 1. The *core* of the sealed bid auction is defined to be the set of all solutions to the dual problem (8). The core is denoted by $C = (C(U), C(V))$, where $C(U)$ is the set of dual solutions u_i, which is called the *seller core*, and $C(V)$ is the set of solutions v_j, which is called the *buyer core.*

It can easily be shown that the core is nonempty. From well-known results in linear programming, the core can be shown to be a bounded convex polyhedral set having a finite number of extreme points.

Definition 2. For a given auction, the *maximum seller surplus* u_i^* for seller i is given by

$$u_i^* = \max_{U \in C(U)} u_i. \tag{13}$$

The *minimum seller surplus* u_{*i} for seller is given by replacing max by min in (19). Using these we can define vectors u^* and u_* as:

$$\begin{aligned} u^* &= (u_i^*, \ldots, u_m^*) \text{ the maximum seller surplus vector} \\ u_* &= (u_{*i}, \ldots, u_{*m}) \text{ the minimum seller surplus vector} \end{aligned}$$

Definition 3. For a given auction, the *maximum buyer surplus* for buyer j is given by

$$v_j^* = \max_{v \in C(v)} v_j. \tag{14}$$

The *minimum buyer surplus vector* is given by replacing max by min in (14). Using these we can define vectors v^* and v_* as:

$$\begin{aligned} v^* &= (v_i^*, \ldots, v_n^*) \text{ the maximum buyer surplus vector} \\ v_* &= (v_{*i}, \ldots, v_{*n}) \text{ the minimum buyer surplus vector} \end{aligned}$$

Using these four vectors we define the following two larger vectors:

(u^*, u_*) the MaxSeller–MinBuyer surplus point

(u_*, v^*) the MinSeller–MaxBuyer surplus point.

Next we assert that these two vectors belong to the core.

Theorem 1. For any sealed bid auction the vector pairs (u^*, v_*) and (u_*, v^*)

a) belong to the core C;
b) are the farthest distance apart of any two vectors in C;
c) individually and collectively maximize, or minimize, buyer or seller surpluses.

A proof of this is contained in [15].

Surprisingly it is easy to calculate these two points of the core by solving just two linear programs.

Theorem 2. Given a sealed bid auction the vectors (u^*, v_*) and (u_*, v^*) can be calculated as follows:

a) Replace b_j by $b_j + \varepsilon$, for $j \in J$, and ε a small number, in (7) and (8) and solve the resulting linear program; then the optimal dual solutions u^0 and v^0 have the property that $u^* = u^0$ and $v_* = v^0$.
b) Replace a_i by $a_i + \varepsilon$, for $i \in I$, and ε a small number, in (7) and (8) and solve the resulting linear program; then the optimal dual solutions u^0 and v^0 have the property that $u_* = u^0$ and $v^* = v^0$.

The computational importance of this theorem is immediately evident. Special algorithms exist which can solve these problems in a few seconds or minutes on a PC or a workstation, even if they have hundreds of thousands or millions of variables. Any other core point (u, v) in C satisfies the inequalities $u_* \leq u \leq u^*$ and $v_* \leq v \leq v^*$, so that the core C is contained within the hyper parallelpiped P which consists of all vectors (x, y) satisfying

$$(u_*, v_*) \leq (x, y) \leq (u^*, v^*).$$

The line segment L connecting the distinguished points (u^*, v_*) and (u_*, v^*) is a main "diagonal" of P. The core is a subset of P which contains L.

Definition 4. The *fair division point* (u^f, v^f) of an auction is the mid point of line segment L, that is

$$(u^f, v^f) = \frac{1}{2}\left[(u_*, v^*) + (u^*, v_*)\right]$$

where (u_*, v^*) and (u^*, v_*) are the two distinguished core points mentioned above.

Theorem 3. The amount received from the fair division point (u^f, v_f) by each buyer and seller is exactly half way between the maximum and the minimum each can obtain from any core solution.

We illustrate these definitions and theorems by showing in Table IV the MaxSeller–MinBuyer and the MinSeller–MaxBuyer surplus points for the example of the previous section. We also exhibit all extreme points for this example in Table IV. In the calculations for the house auction we used $\varepsilon = 0.001$, but any other small value could have been used. So, for example, to find the MaxSeller–MinBuyer surplus solution make the right hand sides of constraints 4, 5, and 6 of Table II be 1.001 instead of 1. The dual solution of that linear program will give the surpluses shown in row 6 of Table IV. Similarly, making the right hand sides of constraints 1, 2, and 3 of Table II be 1.001 instead of 1 (and returning the right hand sides of constraints 4, 5, and 6 to 1) gives the MinSeller–MaxBuyer surplus solution shown in row 1 of Table IV.

We do not go into the (rather complicated) details of how the other 4 points of the core shown in Table IV were calculated. An algorithm for finding them is given in [15].

A picture of the buyer core is shown in Figure 1. Obviously, we could not draw the whole core C which is six-dimensional. However, the picture of the buyer core $C(U)$ gives a good idea of what the core C looks like. The seller core $C(V)$ has a picture that is essentially like that in Figure 1.

By similar perturbations of the right hand sides of some of constraints of Table II it is possible to maximize or minimize the sum of the returns to any coalition of just buyers or just sellers. These solutions will also be found at the MaxSeller–MinBuyer or the MinSeller–MaxBuyer points. It thus appears that the points on line L of the core are the most important, with the fair division point being (to the author) the most important point in the core.

It is remarkable that by carrying out the very simple calculations outlined above on a PC, workstation or other computer, it is possible to easily solve auctions involving hundreds or thousands of participants and use the results in real bargaining applications.

TABLE IV

Shown are all the extreme points of the core of the house auction of Section 2

Core Extreme Point	Buyer Surpluses 1	2	3	Selling Prices 1	2	3	Seller Surpluses 1	2	3
1*	1	3	0	23	21	20	5	6	1
2	2	3	0	23	21	19	5	6	0
3	1	4	0	22	21	20	4	6	1
4	2	5	0	21	21	19	3	6	0
5	2	4	1	22	20	19	4	5	0
6**	2	5	1	21	20	19	3	5	0
Fair Division Point	1.5	4	0.5	22	20.5	19.5	4	5.5	0.5

* This is the Seller maximum surplus point
** This is the Buyer maximum surplus point

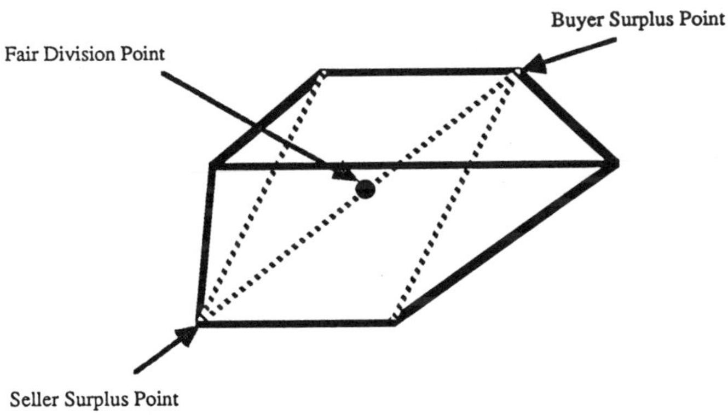

Fig. 1. Buyer core of the house auction.

4. GENERAL RESULTS ON CORES

We present here a brief summary of recent results of the sizes of the cores of market games. Only a general discussion of these results is given, but interested readers may find more details by consulting the references.

One special class of market games are *assignment games* in which $m = n$, $a_i = 1$ for all i in I, and $b_j = 1$ for all j in J. In other words the number of buyers equals the number of sellers and each seller wants to sell exactly one object and each buyer wants to buy exactly one object. Such games always have many core extreme points, and the maximum possible number of such extreme points is characterized by the following theorem, see [18].

Theorem 4. For an assignment game with $m = n$ the maximum number of extreme points is given by the binomial coefficient $N = \binom{2n}{n}$.

This binomial coefficient increases very rapidly with n. For instance for n = 1, 2, 3, 4, 5, and 6 the values of N are: 2, 6, 20, 70, 252, and 924. For this reason it is unlikely that all of extreme points will ever be computed for instances of assignment games much larger than 3 or 4. An example of an assignment auction with $n = 3$ and the maximum number of 20 extreme core points has the following bid matrix:

$$C = \begin{pmatrix} 32 & 8 & 4 \\ 8 & 20 & 2 \\ 4 & 2 & 17 \end{pmatrix}.$$

On the other hand the fewest number of extreme points in a core for any market game is 1, which happens when the matrix C consists of all zeros.

For a positive market game without seller reservation bids it can be shown that there is always an even number of extreme core points. In this case the smallest number of extreme points for a positive market game is two.

The tastes of the buyers and sellers, as indicated by the sizes of the bids, is also important in determining the number of extreme core points as the following theorem indicates, see [18].

Theorem 5. If C is the bid matrix of a positive $n \times n$ assignment market game without seller reservation prices, and either

1. $c_{ij} = c_j$ for $j = 1, \ldots, n$, that is, if the sellers goods are equally attractive to all the buyers, or
2. $c_{ij} = c_i$ for $i = 1, \ldots, n$, that is, if the buyers have identical tastes,

or both, then the core of the game has exactly two extreme points.

Clearly Theorem 5 would apply only to very utilitarian kinds of goods which are easily grown or made by a seller, and which buyers need, but do not particularly care about their quality or appearance.

The main reason that assignment market games have so many extreme core points is that they have many submarkets, where a *submarket* is a subset of sellers and a subset of buyers (with at least one of the subsets being proper) having the property that the subset of sellers can satisfy *exactly* the demands of the subset of buyers. In the assignment market game it is clear that any subset of k sellers can satisfy *exactly* the demands of any subset of k buyers, where $k < n$. When a problem has submarkets it is said to be *degenerate*. It can be shown that the larger the degeneracy, that is the larger the number of submarkets a problem has, the larger the number of possible core extreme points it has. Since assignment market games have the maximum degeneracy, they also have the maximum number of possible core extreme points.

Turning now to transportation market games, we discuss similar results. The first remark is that transportation market games may have none, some, or many submarkets. In the case it has no submarkets, it is called a *nondegenerate market game.*

Theorem 6. A primal nondegenerate positive market game without seller reservation prices has a core containing exactly two extreme points.

This theorem, see [18], characterizes the minimum number of core extreme points. The next theorem, see [18], does the same for the maximum number of extreme points.

Theorem 7. Let C be the bid matrix of an $m \times n$ (where $m < n$) transportation market game without seller reservation prices; then the maximum number of extreme points in its core is given by the binomial coefficient $M = \binom{2m}{m}$.

This result seems intuitively reasonable, given the previous result for assignment market games. Once again the binomial coefficient M increases rapidly with m, and the computational burden of computing all the core extreme points in this case is also prohibitive, except for small values of m.

5. CONCLUSIONS

The auction and market game models discussed in this paper are interesting from theoretical, computational and practical viewpoints. From a theoretical point of view it was shown how define the core of a market game and to give upper and lower bounds on the number of its extreme points. It was also stated that the size of the core increases as the tastes of the buyers, or abilities of the sellers increases. It was also stated that under certain conditions, adding sellers or dropping buyers tends to decrease prices, but dropping sellers or adding buyers tends to increase prices.

It was noted that there are algorithms for finding all of the core extreme points of a market game. Such algorithms are impractical for some market games that have too many core extreme points. However, the difficulty of computing the two distinguished core extreme points, the MaxSeller–MinBuyer point and the MinSeller–MaxBuyer point does not increase very rapidly with the size of the problem. Hence also, the difficulty of computing the fair division point does not increase very rapidly with the size of the problem.

Finally, it should be remarked that if one has chosen a certain core point, such as the fair division point, to be the solution for a sealed bid auction, then the computational difficulty of finding it is sufficiently small that the techniques outlined here, and given in more detail in the papers in the bibliography, can be used for practical solutions to sealed bid auctions in real time, even when the numbers of buyers and sellers is large. In fact in [18] the author shows that the MaxSeller–MinBuyer and the MinSeller–MaxBuyer solutions can be calculated by solving transportation problems instead of linear programs. References [4, 5, 12, 13 and 15] describe methods for solving transportation problems which are much faster than solving the corresponding linear programs.

BIBLIOGRAPHY

1. Amihud, Y. (Ed.), 1976, *Bidding and Auctioning for Procurement and Allocation*, Proceedings of a Conference at the Center for Applied Economics, New York University: New York University Press.
2. Barr, J. L. and T. L. Shaftel, 1976, 'Solution properties of deterministic auctions', *Journal of Financial and Quantitative Analysis* 11, 287–311.
3. Böhm-Bawerk, E. von, 1891, *Positive Theory of Capital*, translated by W. Smart, 1923. New York: G. E. Steckert.
4. Bradley, G. H., G. G. Brown, and G. W. Graves, 1977, 'Design and implementation of large scale primal transshipment algorithms", *Management Science* 24, 1–34.
5. Glover, F., D. Karney, D. Klingman, and A. Napier, 1974, 'A computational study on start procedures, basis change criteria, and solution algorithms for transportation problems', *Management Science* 20, 793–813.
6. Johnson, R. D., 1976, 'A perfectly competitive auction pricing alternative for agricultural products", in Y. Amihud (Ed.), *Bidding and Auctioning for Procurement and Allocation*, Proceedings of a Conference at the Center for Applied Economics, New York University: New York University Press, pp. 203–208.
7. von Neumann, J. and O. Morgenstern, 1953, *Theory of Games and Economic Behavior*, Third Edition, Princeton University Press.
8. Schotter, A., 1976, 'Auctions and economic theory', in Y. Amihud (Ed.), *Bidding and Auctioning for Procurement and Allocation*, Proceedings of a Conference at the Center for Applied Economics, New York University: New York University Press, pp. 3–12.
9. Shapley, L. S., 1955, 'Market as cooperative games', The Rand Corporation, P–629, March, manuscript.
10. Shapley, L. S. and M. Shubik, 1972, 'The assignment game I: The core', *International Journal of Game Theory* 1, 111–130.
11. Smith, V. L., 1976, 'Bidding and auctioning institutions: experimental results", in Y. Amihud (Ed.), *Bidding and Auctioning for Procurement and Allocation*, Proceedings of a Conference at the Center for Applied Economics, New York University: New York University Press, pp. 43–64.
12. Srinivasan, V. and G. L. Thompson, 1973, 'Benefit–cost analysis of coding techniques for the primal transportation problem', *Journal of the Association for Computing Machinery* 20, 194–213.
13. Srinivasan, V. and G. L. Thompson, 1977, 'Cost operator algorithms for the transportation problem', *Mathematical Programming* 12, 372–391.
14. Stark, R. M., 1971, 'Competitive bidding: A comprehensive bibliography', *Operations Research* 19, 484–490.
15. Thompson, G. L., 1980, 'Computing the core of a market game', in A. V. Fiacco and K. O. Kortanek (Eds.), *Extremal Methods and Systems Analysis*, New York: Springer Verlag, pp. 312–334.
16. Thompson, G. L., 1979, 'Pareto optimal, multiple deterministic models for the bid and offer auctions', *Methods of Operations Research* 35, 517–530.

17. Thompson, G. L., 1981, 'A recursive method for solving assignment problems', in P. Hansen (Ed.), *Studies in Graphs and Discrete Programming*, Amsterdam: North Holland Publishing Co., pp. 319–343.
18. Thompson, G. L., 1981, 'Auctions and market games', in R. J. Auman, *et. al.* (Eds.), *Essays in Game Theory and Mathematical Economics in Honor of Oskar Morgenstern*, Mannheim: Bibliographisches Institut, pp. 181–196.
19. Thompson, G. L. and S. Thore, 1992, *Computational Economics: Economic Modeling with Optimization Software*, San Francisco: The Scientific Press, 352 pp.
20. Thompson, G. L. and S. Thore, 'Exchanging heterogeneous good via sealed bid auctions', forthcoming.
21. Vickery, W., 1961, 'Counterspeculation, auctions and competitive sealed tenders', *Journal of Finance* 16, 8–37.
22. Vickery, W., 1976, 'Auctions, markets, and optimal allocation', in Y. Amihud (Ed.), *Bidding and Auctioning for Procurement and Allocation*, Proceedings of a Conference at the Center for Applied Economics, New York University: New York University Press, pp. 13–20.

ROBERT E. DORSEY, JOHN D. JOHNSON AND MARK V. VAN BOENING

The Use of Artificial Neural Networks for Estimation of Decision Surfaces in First Price Sealed Bid Auctions

ABSTRACT. Artificial neural networks, optimized using genetic algorithms, are used to estimate bid functions for first price sealed bid auctions. Data generated in experimental markets is used for two means of estimating the bid function. First, the neural network provides a best fit to the data, thus estimating the bid function that subjects were using. Alternative objective functions are used for the neural network to demonstrate the effect on the resultant bid function. Second, the neural network is optimized using profit maximization as the objective function to identify the optimal bid function given the bids of the experimental subjects.

1. INTRODUCTION

Artificial neural networks have qualities that in many ways parallel human decision processes and thus may provide insight into people's behavior in specific economic environments. "Neural nets" can learn associative patterns and approximate the functional relationship between the information provided to economic agents (the inputs) and agents' responses (the outputs). Much like nonlinear regression, the neural net can estimate complex decision surfaces. However, it does not require a pre-specified model and it can achieve a continuous approximation to any functional mapping between inputs and outputs. The neural network arrangement of simple nodes into multiple layers connected through nonlinear functions produces a mapping consistent with any underlying functional relationship, regardless of its complexity even in the presence of noise, distortion, and missing data.

In this study, neural networks, optimized using the genetic adaptive neural network algorithm (GANNT) of Dorsey *et al.* (1992b), are used to estimate bid functions of bidders in first price sealed bid auctions. The point of departure is the experimental markets reported in Cox *et al.* (1988). Although consistent patterns of behavior emerged in those markets, the behavior was sometimes at odds with the prevailing Nash equilibrium bidding theory. We

W.W. Cooper and A.B. Whinston (eds.), New Directions in Computational Economics, 19–40.

chose experimental market data since the primary inputs and outputs can be controlled via the institution and message space. However, rather than the standard approach of comparing theory with behavior, this paper uses the neural network to answer two questions. First, what is the form of the bidding function that best corresponds to the bids revealed by bidders given their values? Second, what is the best *ex post* bid function relative to the revealed bids? The objective of the paper is to explore the neural network as an aid in evaluating economic data.

An advantage of the neural network is that it does not require *a priori* restrictions that are assumed solely for tractability or estimation ease. These often accompany an economic theory or an estimation technique. Examples include assumptions about preferences, analytical skills or beliefs, or assumptions about error terms. A method that consistently provides researchers with close approximations of the underlying response function, even in the presence of substantial noise and/or nonspherical error terms, could prove to be a valuable tool in understanding economic behavior.

The next section examines the neural network in more detail and describes how the genetic algorithm is used to optimize the network. A discussion of the theory and data (Cox *et al.* 1988) is presented in Section 3. The results from this study are provided in Section 4 and the final section offers some concluding remarks.

2. NEURAL NETWORKS

Rosenblatt (1958) demonstrated that simple artificial neuron structures like that shown in Figure 1, called perceptrons, combined with a simple learning rule could solve interesting problems. This structured node sums the weighted inputs from its neighbors, compares this sum to its threshold value θ and passes the result through a function referred to as an interaction rule. The value of a typical node Y is given by:

$$Y = g(\cdot) = g\left(\sum_{k=1}^{n} \omega_k y_k - \theta\right). \tag{1}$$

The threshold value θ, also known as the offset, is the minimum activation level necessary for the node to transmit a positive signal to its neighbors.

Each node Y can be represented as a function of n weighted inputs. These perceptrons can be arranged in multiple, fully interconnected, layers producing a multi-layered perceptron as illustrated in Figure 2. In this network the input nodes are linked to the output nodes through one or more interconnected hidden layers. The multi-layered perceptron is referred to as a feed-forward network since inputs are fed into the bottom (or input) layer and are fed forward through the network topology to the output layer.

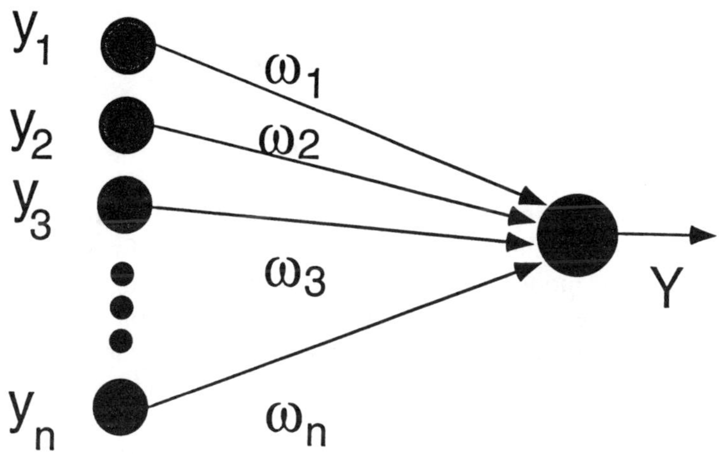

Fig. 1. A typical artificial neuron (perceptron).

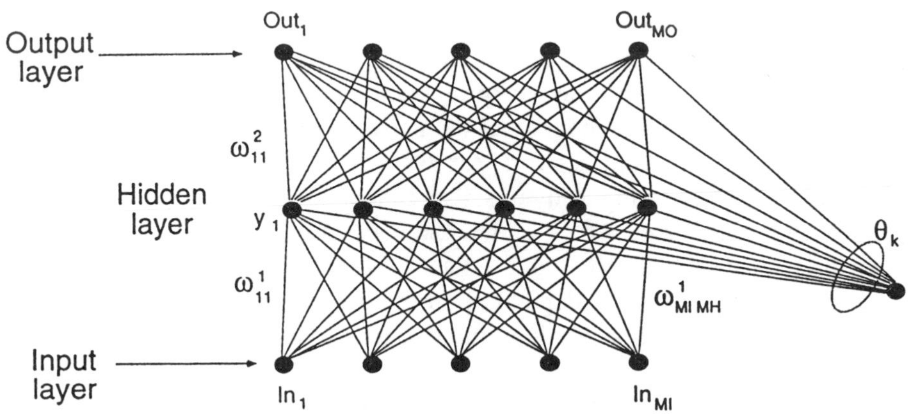

Fig. 2. A multi-layered perceptron.

Such multi-layered feedforward networks can provide a completely flexible mapping between inputs and outputs. The superposition theorem of Kolmogorov (1957) and recent improvements by Lorentz (1976), Hecht-Nielsen (1987), Irie and Miyake (1988) and Sprechter (1965) establish that a neural network as described above can approximate a perfectly general mapping from $\mathbf{R}^n \rightarrow \mathbf{R}^m$ as long as the correct nonlinearity, or "squashing function", $g(\cdot)$ is chosen.[1] Funahashi (1989) and Hornik *et al.* (1989) have

[1] In the case of the Irie and Miyake integral formulation the squashing function $g(\cdot)$ is known but an infinite number of hidden units are required.

shown that the squashing function can be specified *a priori* as the sigmoid function, shown in equation 2, without sacrificing flexibility.

$$g\left(\sum_{i=1}^{n} \omega_k y_k - \theta\right) = \frac{1}{1 + e^{-\sum_{i=1}^{n} \omega_k y_k - \theta}} . \tag{2}$$

They also show that the underlying "true" functional form need not be continuous. In fact, they show that standard multi-layer feedforward networks with as few as one hidden layer using arbitrary squashing functions can approximate any Borel measurable function. The implication of this research is that a perfectly general approximation to the true function can be achieved to any arbitrarily small error given a sufficient number of hidden layer neurons.

Although the neural network could theoretically obtain such general mappings, to do so requires the identification of the appropriate weights ω_i. The independent work of Werbos (1974), LeCun (1986), Parker (1985), and Rumelhart *et al.* (1986a) yielded the backpropagation training algorithm which is a commonly used method for establishing the appropriate weights for multi-layered feedforward networks. This process is frequently called training. Wasserman (1989) and Hecht-Nielsen (1990) however, have pointed out several problems with the backpropagation training algorithm. Included among these are: 1) the tendency of the network to become trapped in local optima; 2) to suffer from network paralysis as the weights move to higher values; 3) to become temporally unstable, that is, to forget what it has already learned as it learns a new fact; and 4) the necessity for the backpropagation algorithm to have a differentiable objective function. Since the aforementioned flexibility theorems depend upon the use of the correct weights, the utility of backpropagation as a learning rule for producing a flexible mapping is questionable.

In order to overcome these problems, weights in this study were obtained using the GANNT algorithm which employs a genetic search technique. The network does not become trapped on a local optimum since the genetic algorithm continues to search the full parameter space. Because the genetic algorithm does not use the derivative of the network output to proportionately adjust its weight matrices, as with gradient decent methods, the derivative (of the objective function) need not exist and the network can use any objective function (as long as its value can be computed in a finite amount of time).

This also implies that the network paralysis problem can be overcome. The paralysis problem occurs with backpropagation as the weights adjust to very large values, forcing the weight adjustments to become increasingly smaller (since these values are proportional to the network output) until the network is paralyzed. Temporal instability is overcome because the network is trained in a batch mode. That is to say weights are only changed at the end of each complete sweep through the data. In addition, Dorsey *et al.*

(1992a) empirically show that the genetic algorithm performs well on a large class of problems with generic network architectures. They demonstrated that each of the problems in Rumelhart *et al.* (1986a) could be solved using one hidden layer which contained six neurons, which may mean that the genetic algorithm based training method for the selection of the appropriate weight matrices can overcome many of the shortcomings of backpropagation, producing the desired flexibility.

3. FIRST PRICE AUCTION BID FUNCTIONS

Consider a first price sealed bid auction where $N = 4$ bidders are competing for $Q = 1$ unit of a commodity. Each bidder $i = 1, \ldots, 4$ has monetary valuation v_i for the unit being auctioned, and privately bids the monetary amount b_i for the unit. The bidder with the highest bid wins the auction, and pays the amount of his/her bid. All other bids are rejected. Thus the winning bidder has net monetary gain $(v_i - b_i)$, and the three other bidders have zero net monetary gain.

Let bidder i's preferences over the monetary gain be represented by the utility function

$$u_i(b_i) = (v_i - b_i)^{r_i} \tag{3}$$

when b_i is the winning bid, and $u_i(b_i) = 0$ if b_i is rejected or $b_i = 0$. The exponent r_i is bidder i's risk parameter, where $r_i \in (0, r_{\max})$ with $r_{\max} \geq 1$. If $0 < r_i < 1$, i is risk averse, if $r_i = 1$ then i is risk neutral, and if $r_i > 1$ then i is risk preferring.[2] The population from which the $N = 4$ bidders are independently drawn has a distribution of risk parameters represented by the integrable *cdf* $\Phi(r)$ with a continuous density function on $(0, r_{\max}]$. A bidder is assumed to know his/her own aversion towards risk but only the distribution from which rival r's are drawn, i.e., bidder i knows r_i and $\Phi(r)$. The individual v_i valuations are independently drawn from the *cdf* $H(v)$ with a continuous density function on $[0, v_{\max}]$. $H(v)$ and its parameters are common information, i.e., each bidder knows his/her own v_i but only knows the distribution from which rivals' values are drawn.

Cox *et al.* (1988) use the uniform distribution $H(v) = v/v_{\max}$ when inducing value on their experimental subjects. They show that for an expected utility maximizing bidder, the Nash equilibrium bid function is

$$b_i = \frac{N-1}{N-1+r_i} v_i \quad \text{for} \quad b_i \leq b^* = v_{\max} - r_{\max} \frac{G(b^*)}{G'(b^*)} \tag{4}$$

[2] That is, bidder i would require a positive, zero or negative Arrow-Pratt risk premium, respectively.

where $G(b)$ is the probability that bid b is the winning bid. Thus for $b \leq b^*$, b is linear in v. For $b > b^*$, the Nash equilibrium bid function cannot be expressed in closed form.

Using OLS regression of observed bids on values to estimate (4), Cox *et al.* (1988) find strong support for the linear bidding strategy. (A risk neutral bidder using (4) would have $\alpha = 0$ and $\beta = 0.75$.) Approximately 80% of 156 regressions have R^2 values exceeding 0.95, and over 90% of the bidders exhibit evidence of risk aversion ($\hat{\beta} < 0.75$). However, they also find a significant number of nonzero intercepts, which is inconsistent with the theory. They extend the theory to account for throwaway bids and utility of winning (which predicts nonzero intercepts), they also report subsequent experimental results.

In the next section, a subset of those results serve as a benchmark against which neural net estimations of the equilibrium bid function are compared. We think this is an interesting comparison for two reasons. First, we are interested to see if the neural net estimates conform to a theory with extensive assumptions. Second, the theoretical equilibrium bid function may be nonlinear, in which case a linear estimator like OLS would be inappropriate. We briefly summarize each situation.

Cox *et al.* (1988) make several explicit assumptions in the derivation of the bid function in (4). Bidders are assumed to maximize expected monetary payoffs with a utility function that is twice continuously differentiable and strictly increasing in monetary payoff. Furthermore, the utility function is strictly log-concave in net income $y = v_i - b_i$, so that a bidder's preferences for the risky monetary payoff can be risk averse, risk neutral, or risk preferring, but the preferences must by less convex than e^y. The derivation also assumes symmetric behavior by bidders, where each bidder believes that rivals will use a differential bid function $b(v, r)$ which is strictly increasing in v for all bidders. Finally, bidders are assumed to know $H(v)$ and $\Phi(r)$. In their experimental auctions, Cox *et al.* (1988) control $H(v)$ but not $\Phi(r)$.

These assumptions are made primarily for technical reasons, since they improve the tractability of the model. But when *a priori* restrictions are placed on a model, the likelihood that the model is "true" may be reduced. For example, Basmann *et al.* (1988, also see Johnson 1987) have shown that when testing certain utility functions against more general alternatives, traditional indicators of fit (e.g., F and t statistics) did not reject the models. But under a likelihood ratio test, each function was rejected as a suitable model. Imposing a simple model like a linear bid function upon observed bids and values may provide sufficient fit, but it may also provide little or no guidance for a researcher in the development of a more accurate model.

Secondly, it may be the case that the Nash equilibrium bid function is nonlinear. The value b^* is the maximum bid that can be made by the least

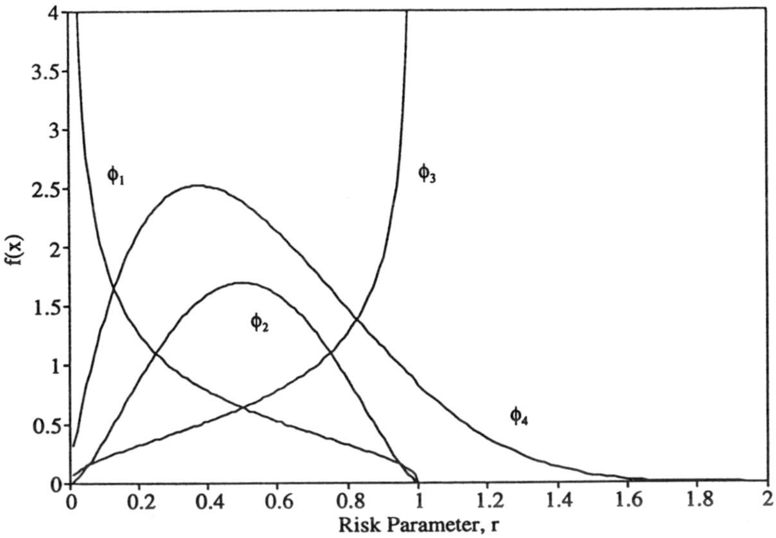

Fig. 3. Distribution of risk parameters.

risk averse bidder in the set over which $\Phi(r)$ is defined; it also determines how much of the equilibrium bid function can be expressed in closed form. If $r_{\max} = 1$, so that the least risk averse bidder is risk neutral, then when $N = 4$, $b^* = 0.75(v_{\max})$ and observed bids greater than b^* would not be applicable in testing (4) with OLS. When there are risk preferring bidders in the population (i.e., $r_{\max} > 1$) the problem is compounded. If $r_{\max} = 3$ then $b^* = 0.50(v_{\max})$ and 40% of the bid function cannot be expressed in closed form. When using a technique like OLS to test the theory, a researcher must know $r_{\max}$ in order know what range of data is applicable to the linear model. When $r_{\max}$ is not controlled by an experimental design, the value of $r_{\max}$ must be assumed.

Smith *et al.* (1992) numerically estimate the equilibrium bid function over $b > b^*$ for different values of $r_{\max}$. Their results suggest that above b^*, the bid function is nonlinear, but it is monotonically increasing in v. They find, however, that the nonlinear portion is affected not only by $r_{\max}$, but also by the shape of $\Phi(r)$. For the beta density functions shown in Figure 3, the corresponding effects are shown in Figure 4. The $\phi(r)$ distributions are beta density functions (recall $\Phi(r)$ is a *cdf*), and the notation b_k denotes the bid function estimated under the assumption that r is distributed as $\phi_k(r)$. Both b and v are normalized to $[0, 1]$, and in each of estimated bid functions, the bidder is risk averse with $r_i = 0.1$. In the first three $\phi(r)$ distributions, there are no risk preferring agents ($r_{\max} = 1$), but the central tendency varies. In $\phi_4(r)$, there is a 10% chance of observing a risk preferring agent ($r_{\max} = 2$ and $P(r > 1) = 0.10$).

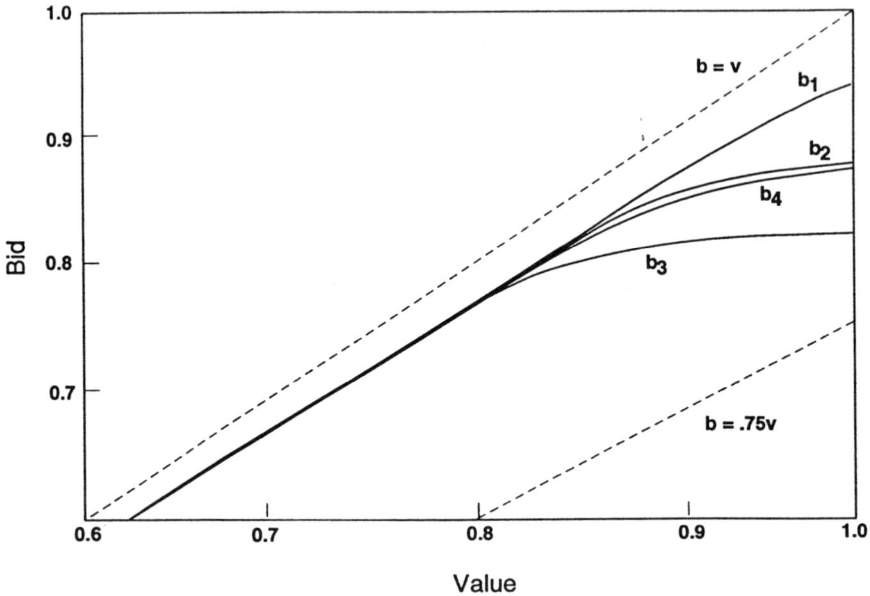

Fig. 4. Numerically estimated bid functions.

4. ESTIMATION BY NEURAL NETWORKS

In this section, the neural network is used to achieve an approximation of the underlying bid functions that best explain the observed bidding behavior. These approximated functions are used in two applications. First, we estimate bid functions by obtaining a mapping between bids and values that uses alternative objective functions. In this case the neural network was examined as an alternative to more conventional econometric techniques for identifying the locus of points that achieve a prespecified criterion for closeness of fit, such as sum of squared errors. Second, we estimate the *ex post* optimal bid function using profits as the optimizing criterion. The neural network was used to estimate the bid function for the 1000 values and bids revealed in this series of auctions.

The neural network uses the revealed data from the experiment and provides a flexible mapping between the inputs and outputs. The arrangement of the simple nodes into a multi-layer framework produces a mapping between inputs and outputs consistent with any underlying functional relationship regardless of its true functional form. For example, Caporaletti *et al.* (1992) have recently shown that the neural network can generate significantly more accurate in-sample forecasts for correctly specified simultaneous equation models than OLS, 2SLS or 3SLS. When predicting outside the sample, the neural net is no worse than the other techniques when the model is correctly specified and is clearly superior when the model is misspecified.

The importance of having a general mapping between the input and output vectors is evident since it eliminates the need for unjustified *a priori* restrictions so commonly used to facilitate estimation, (e.g., Gauss Markoff assumptions for ordinary least squares).[3] Experimental markets can accurately control and quantify the primary inputs and outputs so an estimation technique that will consistently provide the researcher with a close approximation to the underlying response function may significantly enhance understanding of subjects' behavior.

Estimation of Subject Bid Functions

To explore whether these flexible mappings actually provide any guidance to the researcher, a series of sealed bid auctions was examined using the neural network to demonstrate the relationship between the bids made by individual bidders and their values. The data used by the neural net for estimation was generated in experiments run at the University of Arizona. The ten experiments were four person first price auctions, each with twenty-five auctions. This data is a subset (series 4) of the experiments reported in Cox *et al.* (1988) in their Table II. All ten experiments used the same values for the bidders.

A typical example of the resultant bid functions that the neural network estimated is shown in Figure 5 (Experiment 2 bidder 2). The neural network architecture consisted of three layers. The input layer contained a single input node corresponding to the individuals's private value. Four nodes were used for the hidden layer and a single node, corresponding to the individual's bid, was in the output layer. A sigmoid function was used between the input and hidden layers but was not used between the hidden and output layers. Bias nodes were provided on the hidden and input layers.

The network was trained using the GANNT algorithm.[4] A population of twenty strings was used each with elements corresponding to the seven weights of the network. The starting values for the weights in the first generation strings were drawn uniformly over the range $[-200, 200]$. The mutation rate was 0.095. Each estimate was trained for 500,000 generations. All training was done in batch mode so that the fitness value was based on the fit of all the data for that specific estimation. Programs for the estimation

---

[3] It should be noted that if these assumptions hold, the neural network model will yield a similar solution, since the image of any underlying mapping can always be projected into a perfectly flexible mapping.The appropriateness of OLS is an empirical question which cannot be settled in general for any finite number of observations. Thus a test of the assumptions must become a routine part of any application.

[4] See Dorsey and Mayer (1992a, b) and Dorsey *et al.* (1992b) for a detailed discussion of the genetic algorithm optimization procedures.

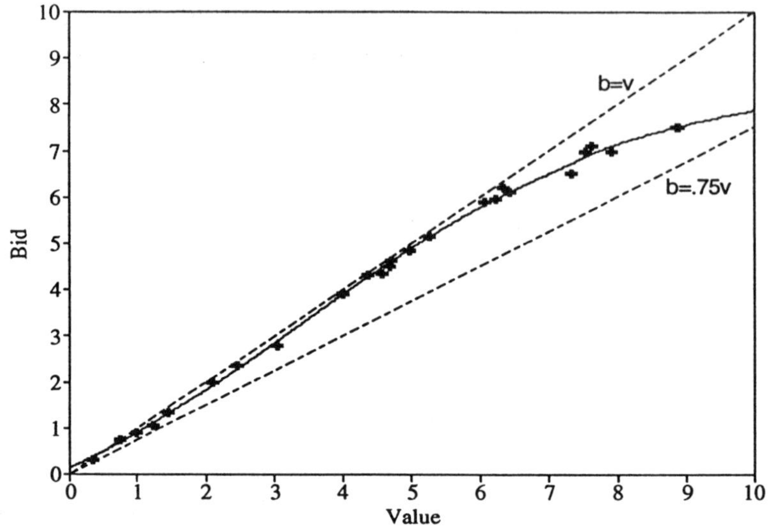

Fig. 5. Experiment 2 Bidder 2.

were written in Fortran and were run on the CRAY X-MP supercomputer at the Mississippi Center for Supercomputing Research.

Once the network was trained, bid functions were generated by submitting the 1000, one cent incremented values between 0.01 and 10.00 to the neural net. Bid function estimates were generated for each of the 40 subjects by training the neural net on their bids in the 25 auctions of their experiment. In addition, a composite bid function was estimated by training the neural net on all 1000 bids made by all subjects in all 10 experiments.

Two versions of this composite bid function were estimated. Figure 6 shows a bid function which was estimated using 2 nodes in the hidden layer and Figure 7 shows the bid function that results when 8 nodes were used in the hidden layer. Clearly the addition of nodes in the hidden layer allows the function to adjust more finely to the specific data points. The additional nodes did not make a substantial reduction in the sum of squared errors however.[5] The bid function in Figure 6 had a sum of squared errors of 502.18 while the one in Figure 7 had 497.62.

Table I shows the relative fit of the neural net compared to a corresponding fit of an OLS estimate on the same data. The sum of squared errors is shown for both neural net and OLS estimation techniques for each individual bidder

[5] The number of hidden layer nodes to include is a subject of current research. Too many nodes can cause overfitting and too few nodes can limit the flexibility of the mapping. White (1989) has proposed a test for a sufficient number of hidden nodes. An alternative criterion such as whether or not a significant improvement in likelihood is achieved may be an appropriate rule.

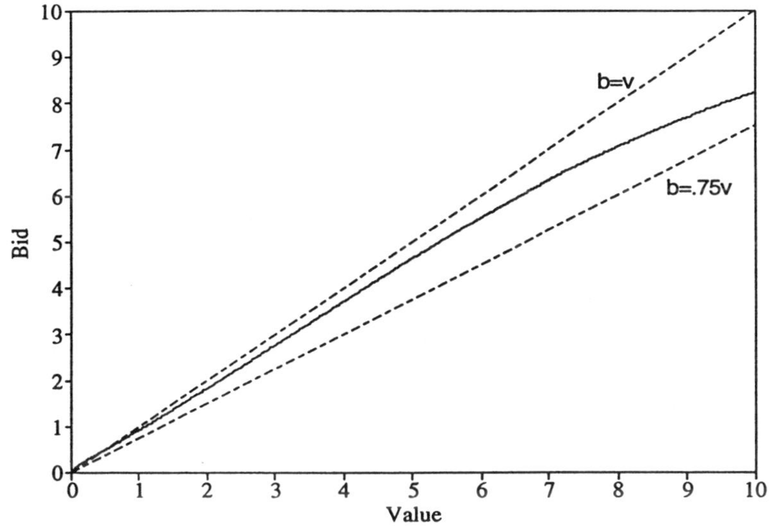

Fig. 6. Composite bid function – all bidders (two hidden layer nodes).

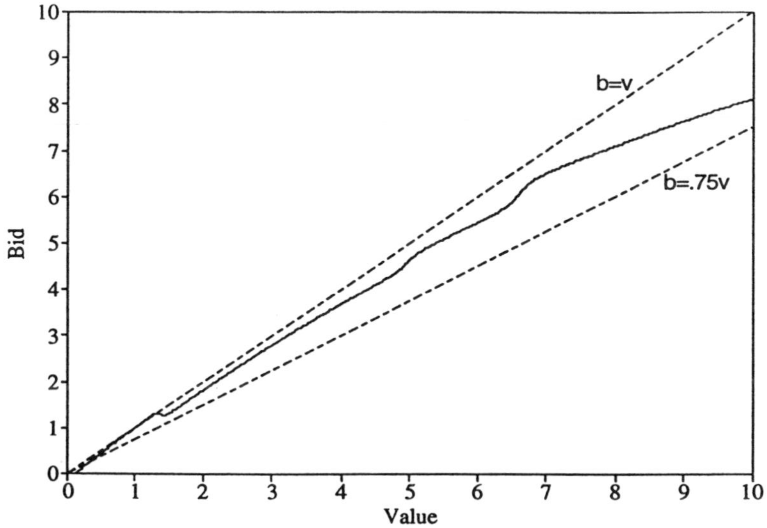

Fig. 7. Composite bid function – all bidders (eight hidden layer nodes).

as well as for the composite of all the data. Clearly, the neural net explains more of the error than OLS. In every estimation the neural net produced a lower sum of squared errors than did the OLS estimate. In ten of the forty estimates the neural network estimate reduced the SSE to less than half of the OLS estimate.

TABLE I

Comparison of neural net and OLS estimates

Experiment	Bidder	Number of Observations	OLS SSE	NN SSE	# of Observations Closest to Prediction OLS	NN
1	1	25	0.989	0.680	10	15
1	2	25	9.648	4.674	12	13
1	3	25	4.457	3.781	10	15
1	4	25	14.239	12.173	7	18 **
2	1	25	60.845	45.126	9	16
2	2	25	1.603	0.198	7	18 **
2	3	25	6.733	0.234	3	22 ***
2	4	25	0.427	0.276	9	16
3	1	25	4.931	3.226	6	19 ***
3	2	25	5.150	1.777	4	21 ***
3	3	25	2.785	1.789	8	17 *
3	4	25	16.413	14.331	9	16
4	1	25	2.372	0.612	6	19 ***
4	2	25	0.981	0.398	8	17 *
4	3	25	0.332	0.238	6	19 ***
4	4	25	49.254	36.259	10	15
5	1	25	4.460	1.941	8	17 *
5	2	25	1.034	0.565	6	19 ***
5	3	25	0.141	0.086	8	17 *
5	4	25	2.022	0.497	5	20 ***
6	1	25	1.796	1.676	9	16
6	2	25	3.240	2.785	9	16
6	3	25	36.499	28.673	12	13
6	4	25	6.257	2.946	5	20 ***
7	1	25	0.320	0.297	13	12
7	2	25	2.363	2.131	13	12
7	3	25	19.798	19.339	16	9
7	4	25	0.255	0.251	9	16
8	1	25	1.298	0.595	6	19 ***
8	2	25	9.199	8.576	10	15
8	3	25	1.022	0.573	12	13
8	4	25	29.835	29.798	15	10
9	1	25	5.014	2.852	6	19 ***
9	2	25	0.342	0.333	14	11
9	3	25	2.866	2.835	6	19 ***
9	4	25	0.294	0.294	13	12
10	1	25	19.504	14.606	9	16
10	2	25	2.170	2.133	14	11
10	3	25	1.225	1.046	15	10
10	4	25	12.673	11.336	8	17 *
Cumulative		1000	526.119	502.134	392	608 ***

Significance Levels: * 10%, ** 5%, *** 1%

This increase in fit would be anticipated if the underlying model is nonlinear since the neural net is not constrained to a linear model. When the true bid function is linear (Experiment 7 Bidder 1 may be such an example, shown in Figure 8), the neural net does not provide a significant improvement in the sum of squared errors and in fact produces a linear bid function consistent with the OLS estimate. Another example of this is shown in Figure 9 (Experiment 8 Bidder 4) where the OLS estimate and the neural net estimate of very noisy data are essentially identical. In both of these figures only the neural net function is shown since the OLS estimate is essentially collinear.

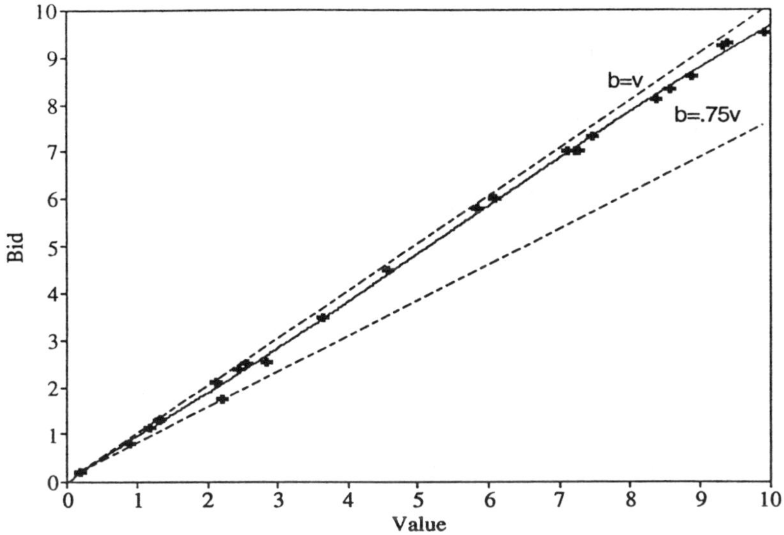

Fig. 8. Experiment 7 Bidder 1.

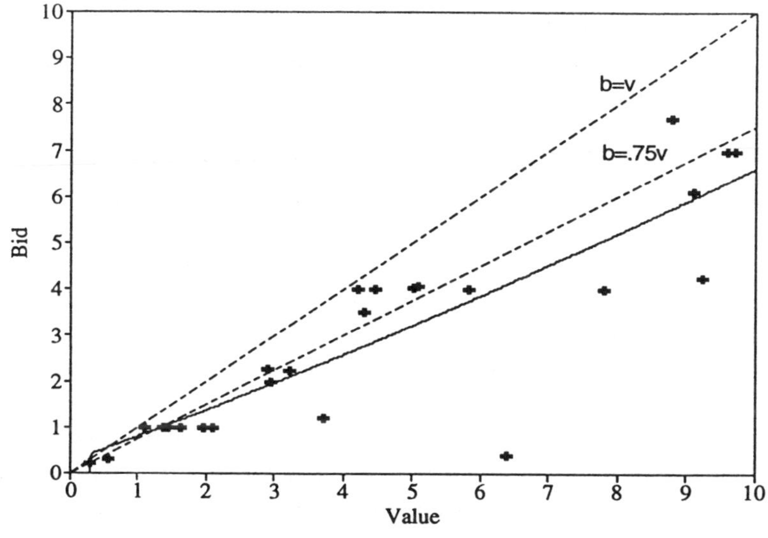

Fig. 9. Experiment 8 Bidder 4.

A pairwise comparison of the errors for each observation is also shown in Table I. As can be seen, the neural net also gets closer to more observations than does the OLS model. A nonparametric sign test is used for the comparison of the paired errors for the two estimation techniques (see Hoel 1971, p. 310). This test indicates that the median error arising from estimation with the neural net model when it is trained using a sum of squared errors optimization criterion is significantly smaller than the OLS median error in seventeen of the forty bid functions estimated.

The objective function used for optimizing the neural net was the sum of squared errors so that comparisons could be made with the OLS results. The sum of squared errors, although well behaved, is not necessarily the best criterion to use. An advantage of the neural net is that it is not constrained to have a well behaved objective function. Further, the objective function does not need to be differentiable or even continuous when optimized with the genetic algorithm.

Objective functions such as minimizing the sum of absolute errors or maximizing the number of observations within a prespecified error limit are alternative objective functions. However, they present significant computational difficulties to derivative-based optimization techniques. To see the effects of such objective functions on the resultant shape of the bid response function, the bid function for bidder 1 in Experiment 2 was reestimated using the sum of absolute errors. This bidder appeared to make two errors, one at a low value (bid = 5.00, value = 1.31) and one at high value (bid = 1.42, value = 9.92). With a sum of squared errors criterion, these "mistakes" heavily influence the resulting bid function. With the sum of absolute errors criterion however, Figures 10 and 11 show that the bid function is not nearly as prone to be affected by the outliers with this objective function as with sum of squared errors. Note that the low value "error" had very little influence on the bid function. The high value error, since it occurred at the highest value observation, still significantly affected the resultant bid function. If these errors occur within the interior of the range of observations they do not cause the extreme turns in the bid function. Other objective functions may even provide a superior estimation and will be explored in future research.

The figures demonstrate another characteristic of the neural net estimated bid function. Clearly the neural net provides a better fit to the observed data than does OLS. In addition, it appears to interpolate well. That is, within the range of the observed values for each subject, the neural net provides a bid function that appears reasonable and a likely predictor of potential bids should those values be chosen. However, the neural net does not always perform well in extrapolation. Outside the range of values that happened to be chosen the neural net tends to extrapolate in the direction of the bid function at the last data point. This can generate unreasonable forecasts for extremely low or high values. When neural nets are used to replicate bidders, care should be taken to ensure that the neural net is trained on observations of bids and values over their complete potential range.

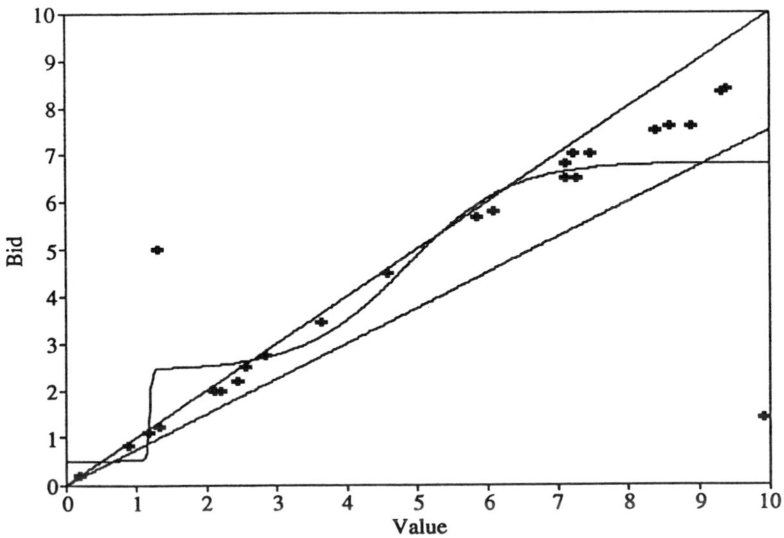

Fig. 10. Experiment 2 Bidder 1 (sum of squared errors).

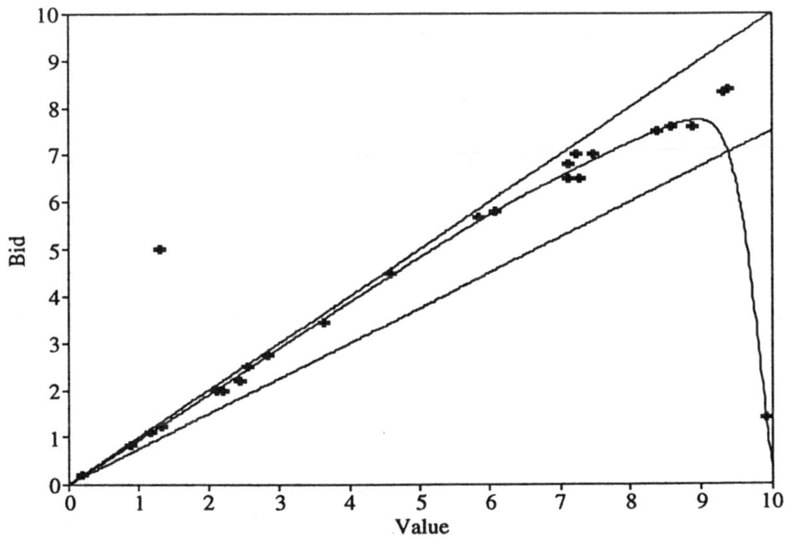

Fig. 11. Experiment 2 Bidder 1 (sum of absolute errors).

Estimation of Optimal Response Bid Function

The above subsection discussed the use of neural network to obtain a best approximation of bid functions used by individuals in experimental settings. An alternative approach to identifying an optimal bidding strategy for the sealed bid auction is to estimate *ex post* the bid function that would generate the highest profits given the bids of all other players. To estimate this

TABLE II

Distribution of the highest of three other bids $\hat{b}_i$

Range	Number of bids
\$0.00 to \$1.00	1
1.00 to 2.00	0
2.00 to 3.00	58
3.00 to 4.00	27
4.00 to 5.00	84
5.00 to 6.00	149
6.00 to 7.00	168
7.00 to 8.00	323
8.00 to 9.00	151
9.00 to 10.00	39

bid function, the objective function used for the optimization of the neural network was total profits earned across all auctions. The neural network sequentially took each of the four subject values in each auction and, using the candidate bid function, bid against the remaining three actual bids. In this manner the neural net used all one thousand values and competed in one thousand auctions. The total profit earned in all auctions was the criterion for optimization. Let $\hat{b}_i$ be the largest of the three other bids in each of the one thousand auctions.[6] The range of $\hat{b}_i$ that the neural network faced extended from a low value of \$0.97 to a high value of \$9.68. The number of $\hat{b}_i$s in each one dollar interval is shown in Table II.

The revealed bids did not provide the neural network with any significant information with which to optimize below a bid of \$2.00. Therefore, for the initial training an additional 10 auctions were created by randomly selecting bid-value pairs from the data where the value was \$1.00 or less. After the initial training run, only the actual auction data was used. Profit figures reported in Table III below include only earnings for the 10 actual experiments.

The neural network architecture consisted of three layers as before. However in this case the hidden layer consisted of 6 nodes. Again the neural network was optimized with the genetic algorithm. Once optimized, the plot of the bid functions shown in Figures 12 and 13 were generated by submitting the 1000 one cent increment values between 0.01 and 10.00 to the

[6] This objective function would pose a substantial difficulty for derivative based training algorithms such as backpropagation since the profit function is a non differentiable function of weights and since the profit maximizing bid function is not known *a priori*.

TABLE III
Comparison of profits earned

Participant	Subject Profit	Risk Neutral	NN SSE	OLS	Local Optimum	Profit Maximum
E1B1	5.69	9.26	9.96	7.73	12.05	9.62
E1B2	5.68	3.73	4.77	3.79	7.59	7.13
E1B3	3.62	1.21	4.34	5.05	1.83	7.69
E1B4	-1.41	5.17	3.13	3.36	3.07	3.73
E2B1	3.99	7.16	6.95	5.49	9.79	6.56
E2B2	5.21	7.79	5.38	5.56	7.02	9.04
E2B3	1.84	0.00	4.34	5.05	0.68	3.77
E2B4	4.62	8.29	7.63	6.24	9.56	10.65
E3B1	8.38	7.16	8.05	7.00	10.94	9.37
E3B2	7.49	7.62	4.77	4.69	9.08	8.04
E3B3	7.63	3.97	7.01	7.40	5.99	6.21
E3B4	7.93	10.57	7.80	6.29	12.79	15.05
E4B1	5.40	9.26	8.53	7.15	12.05	7.86
E4B2	2.86	3.73	4.04	3.79	7.59	7.13
E4B3	3.30	2.95	4.21	5.18	1.88	3.71
E4B4	3.66	8.29	4.69	6.29	9.56	12.96
E5B1	6.00	7.16	5.64	5.49	9.79	6.56
E5B2	2.93	5.96	4.77	3.79	5.80	7.13
E5B3	1.63	0.00	4.34	6.08	1.83	3.77
E5B4	7.25	5.98	6.37	5.17	9.56	8.30
E6B1	6.98	9.39	10.35	8.22	12.55	11.08
E6B2	3.10	7.55	4.56	3.57	6.38	8.51
E6B3	0.79	4.91	5.48	5.30	3.78	5.96
E6B4	7.03	8.26	9.06	7.35	12.56	12.70
E7B1	1.11	7.16	6.95	5.49	5.08	3.59
E7B2	5.50	3.73	4.04	3.79	7.59	7.13
E7B3	0.47	3.03	4.34	5.05	1.83	3.77
E7B4	2.54	8.29	4.69	5.17	12.79	12.96
E8B1	5.80	8.63	8.63	7.18	9.79	9.79
E8B2	6.54	5.96	4.77	4.69	7.59	8.04
E8B3	7.03	7.74	7.01	8.16	5.99	8.43
E8B4	7.62	8.29	7.80	7.35	9.56	12.96
E9B1	7.84	7.16	7.72	5.68	9.79	8.33
E9B2	5.66	5.96	4.77	4.69	10.05	8.04
E9B3	5.58	5.92	4.34	5.05	1.83	4.53
E9B4	0.45	10.49	9.06	7.35	9.56	14.62
E10B1	6.75	9.26	9.18	7.54	10.72	7.86
E10B2	0.64	5.96	4.77	4.69	6.99	5.40
E10B3	2.78	3.90	2.98	3.57	3.34	3.35
E10B4	6.21	10.58	7.63	6.24	9.56	12.27
TOTAL	184.12	257.41	244.86	226.69	305.72	323.57

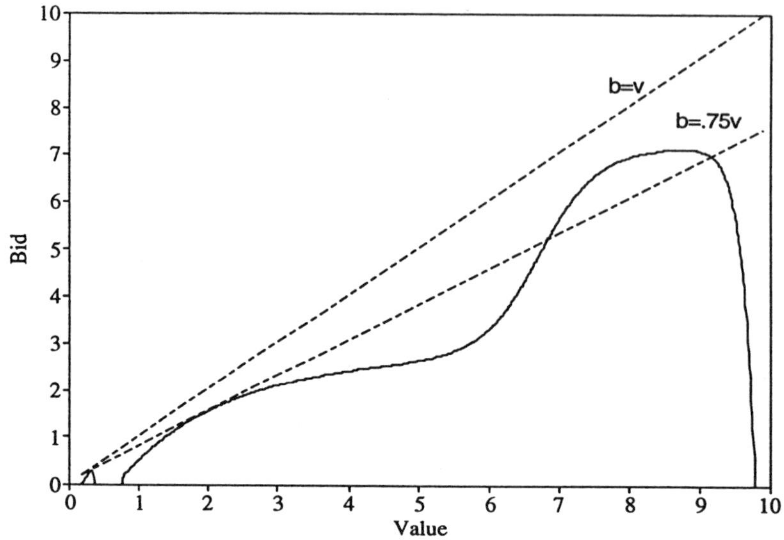

Fig. 12. Profit maximizing bid function.

neural network and plotting the corresponding bids generated by the neural net. Table III compares the profits earned by several different bid functions with the profits earned by the subjects. The total profits earned by all subjects was \$184.12. Each individual bidder's profits are shown in the first column. They ranged from a low of -\$1.41 to a high of \$8.38. The next column shows the profits that would have been made by each bidder had they used the risk neutral linear bid function, $b_i = 0.75v_i$. The total profit for the linear bid function was \$257.41 and ranged from a low of 0 to a high of \$10.58. The third column shows the profits that would have been made using the bid function shown in Figure 7. This bid function was the neural net's best fit of all subject's bid value pairs using sum of squared errors as the optimization criterion. This bid function generated a total profit of \$244.86. The profits for each individual bidder's values ranged from a low of \$2.98 to a high of \$10.35.

Profits are also shown for two other bid functions. The bid function shown in Figure 12, which was generated by optimizing the neural network using total profits as the objective function, is shown in the last column. This bid function generated a total profit of \$323.55. For the individual sets of values these ranged from \$3.71 to \$15.05. Although this was the maximum achieved by the neural network, another bid function that achieved nearly the same profit is shown in Figure 13. This bid function, which is a local optimum for the objective function of profit optimization, generated a total profit of \$305.72 with profits for individual values ranging from a low of 68 cents to a high of \$12.79. This local optimum is approximately a step function and

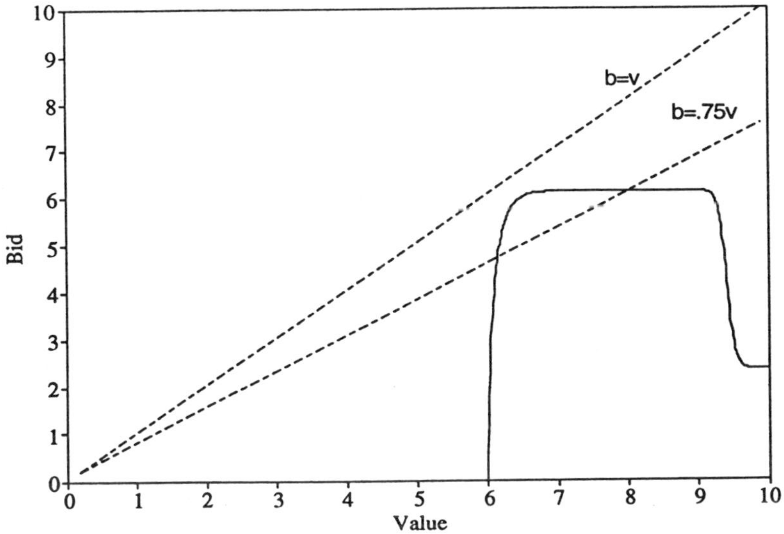

Fig. 13. Local optimum with profit maximization criterion.

thus represents a very simple strategy which, at least for this set of values and bids, performed nearly as well as the best bid function found, shown in the last column, and better than any of the others proposed.

Another comparison of the relative performance of these alternative bid functions is to examine how each bid function performs with only the subset of 25 values drawn by any one subject. Table III shows that when the six bid functions are compared, the profit maximizing bid function and the local optimum bid function would have each been the most profitable strategy for 16 of the forty sets of values. The OLS bid function would have been optimal for 4 sets of values and the linear (risk neutral) bid function would have been optimal for 4 sets of values. The strategy taken by bidder 3 in experiment 3 dominated the profits that would have been earned by all of the proposed bid functions. This was the only case in which a subject's strategy dominated the alternatives. The bid function shown in Figure 7, which was the neural net approximation of the bid function, was not the optimal strategy for any set of values.

5. SUMMARY

The artificial neural network optimized with the genetic algorithm is proposed as a tool for understanding the empirical response functions of economic agents. The neural net has the ability to approximate any functional relationship between the information provided to the agents and their response and thus may provide insight to the decision processes. Once optimized, the neural net can also replicate the behavior of agents. Simulated participants can be more accurately designed by using a neural net model. Neural networks can even be used in real time economic environments since, once trained, the process of generating a response from the neural net is virtually instantaneous no matter how complex the underlying model.

This paper uses data from experimental markets to investigate the effectiveness of the neural net in evaluating (estimating) response functions. The results provide general support for the models of Cox *et al.* (1988) and Cox *et al.* (1982) although there is a suggestion that behavior may not be consistent across values for certain bidders which would be inconsistent with current theories. Nonetheless, with an objective function based on the sum of squared errors, the neural net estimated bid function was monotonic in value for 36 of the 40 subjects. A common pattern in the bid functions was for the lower segment to be approximately linear and for the upper section to fall away from the 45-degree line. This pattern can also be observed in the bid function estimated over all 1000 observations. This is consistent with numerical estimation of bid function. Many of the bid function estimates imply that the expectations of the value of $r_{\max}$ might be quite large.

The neural network bid function estimated using the profit maximization optimization criterion provides an intriguing counterpoint to the previous estimates. This bid function is clearly not monotonic and provides some indication that a risk preferring strategy may be optimal. The bid function was optimized solely on in-sample data and has not been evaluated on out of sample data. The degree to which the shape of this bid function is due solely to this particular set of data will be the subject of future research. A revised profit optimizing bid function will be computed and will be tested on out of sample auctions.

This work suggests that the neural net may be a valuable tool to aid economists in evaluating data. The use of the GANNT algorithm will significantly increase the scope of the optimizing criteria that can be used to develop artificially intelligent players. Clearly, additional research must be done, however, to understand the complexities and potential of the neural net.

ACKNOWLEDGEMENTS

Drs. Dorsey and Johnson are supported in part by the U.S. Department of Education Fund for the Improvement of Post Secondary Education under grant #P116B00509. We would like to thank the Mississippi Center for Super Computing Research for the use of their Cray XMP supercomputer.

BIBLIOGRAPHY

Basmann, R. L., D. J. Slottje, K. Hayes, J. D. Johnson, and D. J. Molina, 1988, 'The generalized Fechner-Thurstone direct utility function and some of its uses', in *Lecture Notes in Economic and Mathematical Systems #316*, New York: Springer-Verlag.

Caporaletti, L. E., R. E. Dorsey, J. D. Johnson, and W. A. Powell, 'A decision support system for in-sample simultaneous equation systems forecasting using artificial neural systems', *Decision Support Systems*, forthcoming.

Cox, J. C., B. Roberson, and V. L. Smith, 1982, 'Theory and behavior of single object auctions', in V. L. Smith (Ed.), *Research in Experimental Economics*, Greenwich, CT: JAI Press.

Cox, J. C., V. L. Smith, and J. M. Walker, 1988, 'Theory and individual behavior of first price auctions', *Journal of Risk and Uncertainty* 1, 61–99.

Dorsey, R. E. and W. J. Mayer, 1992a, 'Optimization using genetic algorithms', in Andrew Whinston and John D. Johnson (Eds.), *Advances in Artificial Intelligence in Economics, Finance and Management*, Greenwich, CT: JAI Press.

Dorsey, R. E. and W. J. Mayer, 1992b, 'Genetic algorithms for estimation problems with multiple optima, non differentiability, and other irregular features', *Journal of Business and Economic Statistics*, forthcoming.

Dorsey, R. E., J. D. Johnson, and W. J. Mayer, 1992a, 'A genetic algorithm for the training of feedforward neural networks', in A. Whinston and J. D. Johnson (Eds.), *Advances in Artificial Intelligence in Economics, Finance and Management*, Greenwich, CT: JAI Press.

Dorsey, R. E., J. D. Johnson, and W. J. Mayer, 1992b, 'The genetic adaptive neural network training (GANNT) algorithm for generic feed forward artificial neural systems', Department Working Paper, University of Mississippi Department of Economics and Finance.

Funahashi, K., 1989, 'On the approximate realization of continuous mappings by neural networks', *Neural Networks* 2, 183–192.

Hecht-Nielson, R., 1987, 'Kolmogorov's mapping neural network existence theorem', *Proc. of the IEEE First Intl. Conf. on Neural Networks III*, June 21–24, pp. 11–14.

Hecht-Nielson, R., 1990, *Neurocomputing*, Reading, MA: Addison-Wesley.

Hoel, P. G., 1971, *Introduction to Mathematical Statistics*, 4th Edition, New York: John Wiley and Sons.

Hornik, K., M. Stinchcombe, and H. White, 1989, 'Multilayer feedforward networks are universal approximators', *Neural Networks* 2, 359–366.

Irie, B. and S. Miyake, 1988, 'Capabilities of three layer perceptrons", *Proc. of the IEEE Second Intl. Conf. on Neural Networks I*, pp. 641–648.

Johnson, J. D., 1987, 'The sensitivity of the cost of living to changes in the prices of monetary assets: A variable consumer preference approach', unpublished Ph.D. dissertation, College Station, TX: Texas A&M University.

Kolmogorov, A. N., 1957, 'On the representation of continuous functions of many variables by superposition of continuous functions of one variable and addition', *Doklady Akad. Nauk USSR* 114, 953–956.

LeCun, Y., 1986, 'Learning processes in an asymmetric threshold network', in E. Bienenstock, F. Fogelman Souli and G. Weisbuch (Eds.), *Disordered Systems and Biological Organization*, Berlin: Springer.

Lorentz, G. G., 1976, 'The 13th problem of Hilbert', *Proc. of Symposia in Pure Math* 28, American Mathematical Society.

Parker, D., 1985, 'Learning logic', Technical Report TR–87, Center for Computational Research in Economics and Management Science, MIT, Cambridge, MA.

Rosenblatt, F., 1958, 'The perceptron: A probabilistic model for information storage and organization in the brain', *Psychological Review* 65, 386–408.

Rumelhart, D.E., G. E. Hinton and R. J. Williams, 1986a, 'Learning internal representation by error propagation', in D. E. Rumelhart and J. L. McClelland (Eds.), *Parallel Distributed*

Processing: Exploration in the Microstructures of Cognition, Vol. I, MA: MIT Press, pp. 318–362.

Rumelhart, D. E., G. E. Hinton and R. J. Williams, 1986b, 'Learning representations by back-propagating errors', *Nature* 323, 533–536.

Smith, V. L., S. L. Rassenti, and M. V. Van Boening, 1992, 'Numerical estimation of equilibrium bid functions in first price auctions', working paper, University of Arizona.

Sprechter, D. A., 1965, 'On the structure of continuous functions of several variables', *Transactions of the American Mathematics Society* 115, 340–355.

Wasserman, P. D., 1989, *Neural computing: Theory and practice*, New York: Van Nostrand Reinhold, Chapters 2 and 3.

Werbos, P. J., 1974, *Beyond Regression: New Tools for Prediction and Analysis in the Behavioral Sciences*, Ph.D. thesis, Cambridge, MA: Harvard University.

White, H., 1989, 'An additional hidden unit test for neglected nonlinearity in multi-layer feedforward networks', *Proc. of the Intl. Joint Conference on Neural Networks*, Washington, D.C.

STEPHEN RASSENTI, VERNON SMITH AND KEVIN MCCABE

Designing a Real Time Computer Assisted Auction for Natural Gas Networks

ABSTRACT. In technologically interdependent economic systems inefficiencies can easily arise from allocations contrived through independent bilateral negotiations. We can challenge this problem with the 'smart market': a coordination center applies optimization algorithms to private bids and offers submitted by decentralized agents to compute prices and allocations. This paper presents the laboratory development of a market institution for trading natural gas in a pipeline network. The institution has evolved over the past five years through thousands of hours of cash-motivated subject participation, professional analysis and continuous reprogramming. It is not a trivial matter to engineer the most efficient market possible when subtle nuances in institutional rules can affect outcomes. Yet doing so in the laboratory is much less costly than a potentially failed field experiment.

1. INTRODUCTION

The political economy of the 1980's and 90's has been marked by the worldwide revolt against the central control and regulation of economic activity by governments. Neither national boundaries nor particular political systems have escaped these forces as both democratic and totalitarian regimes have succumbed intellectually to classical liberal concepts of economic organization based on decentralization. The trend to substitute market competition for economic regulation has motivated our interest in potential new institutions for exchange. We use the experimental economics laboratory to examine and improve the efficiency, price, and market tracking characteristics of institutional variants. We call this activity market engineering.

Particularly challenging are technologically interdependent economic systems where inefficiencies can easily arise from allocations contrived through independent bilateral negotiations. We meet this challenge with the 'smart market': a coordination center applies optimization algorithms (linear and nonlinear mathematical programming developed in operations research) to the private bids and offers submitted by decentralized agents to compute prices and allocations. This activity differs from classical engineering optimization in that the parameters of the program are solicited from individuals

W.W. Cooper and A.B. Whinston (eds.), New Directions in Computational Economics, 41–54.

who have an incentive to provide this information, but who may attempt to manipulate the solution depending upon the properties of the mechanism. In the field we can never know the true willingness to pay or accept (WTP or WTA) of the various agents but only what they have revealed to the coordination center. The resulting allocation and price set (dual variables to agent's defined constraints) is always the solution to a surrogate problem which we can only hope is close to that of the actual underlying surplus maximization problem. But in the laboratory we have control over the WTP and WTA: for example we can tell a potential buyer that any time he buys a unit of some fictitious commodity being exchanged he can resell it to the house for a fixed price. Thus, we know the exact solution to the underlying surplus maximization problem and can measure deviations of actual outcomes from this ideal.

The design objective in 'smart market' engineering is to combine the coordination advantages of central dispatch with the information advantages of decentralized ownership. This includes defining institutional rule variations which might overcome agent incentives to manipulate outcomes. The conventional wisdom and some experimental results (McCabe *et al.* 1990) indicate that one should expect more efficient allocations in economic network systems when coordination of multiple multi-party transactions is not left up to a bilateral telephone market, but executed by a central computer. It is quite natural for socialist regimes to gravitate toward this notion of a centrally controlled 'smart market'; while in capitalist regimes both regulated and private sector firms which already engage in minimal cost engineering need not stretch the concept very far to understand the potential welfare benefits to society at large – though some may not relish the thought – of a centrally coordinated competitive system.

The experimental research program in 'smart market' engineering has been motivated by the need to allocate airport runway rights, and energy in natural gas pipeline networks, and electric power networks (McCabe *et al.* 1991). New potential applications are being developed for telecommunication networks, scheduling environments, assignment and transportation problems, and auctioning of spectrum, land use, and time slot rights. Actual applications have been made in land use by New Zealand and proposed by a large utility for firm pipeline rights. Yet, considering the proliferation of potential field applications and the new willingness to consider alternative forms of institutional design to govern these network systems, there exists a dearth of corresponding economic theory: certainly theory lags experimental output which itself is still thin.

In this paper we would like to present the laboratory development of a market institution for trading natural gas in a pipeline network. This institution has evolved over the past 5 years through thousands of hours of subject participation, professional analysis and continuous reprogramming. One thing is painfully obvious in this process: it is not a trivial matter to engineer the most efficient market possible, yet the cost of doing so in the laboratory is infinitesimal compared to the potential cost of an inefficient or failed field implementation.

2. COMPOSITE GOODS

In July of 1987 the Federal Energy Regulatory Commission (FERC) provided us with a mandate to develop an auction system which might be viable for the trading of natural gas in a deregulated scenario. Drawing on our previous experience with our development of an airport time slot auction (Rassenti *et al.* 1982), we suspected that any successful candidates would have to coordinate multilateral sell-transport-buy deals as well as set prices. We set out to test this hypothesis in the simplest network environment possible: one production node and one consumption node with direct transportation between. In these initial experiments the commodity being exchanged was a nameless good to our experimental subjects, but in our analysis (McCabe *et al.* 1990) we labelled it a 'composite good' since the buyer must contract with more than one agent to receive a unit of the delivered good.

A typical value and cost environment for this experiment is given in Table I. There are 12 decision makers: six buyers at the consumption node, three transporters capable of making deliveries along parallel pipeline links, and 6 sellers at the production node (three independents and one owned by each of the transporters). Table I lists each seller's and transporter's private supply schedule (the costs of engaging in trade), and each buyer's private demand schedule (the redemption values for units purchased during a trading period). These experimenter induced supply and demand schedules, which are unobservable in the economy, serve to motivate experimental subjects as agents are motivated in the economy. These schedules are known only to their individual owners (and the experimenter) and are unknown to all others including the computing center in a 'smart market'. The computer operates only on information reported to it by the agents.

We devised two institutional scenarios for examining economic activity in this simple network. The first, Gas Bargain, was a two-part market which separated the negotiation of gas contracts from the securing of transportation. In the first part the buyers and sellers are paired according to size and preference. Each pair negotiates the price and quantity of a natural gas contract in a timed period. In the second part a uniform price for transportation is determined in a sealed offer market in which the three transporters make sealed offers to carry the fixed demand for transportation.

TABLE I

Demand and supply schedules for a two node experimental environment

Decision-maker	Unit cost or value	Units capacity	Unit cost or value	Units capacity	Competitive profits	Equilibrium units
Wellhead Producer						
1	110	2	195	3	170	5
2*	145	2	215	3	100	2
3	110	2	215	3	170	2
4*	145	2	185	3	130	5
5	110	2	210	3	170	2
6*	145	2	175	3	160	5
Pipelines						
1	30	8	50	3	200	8
2	30	8	60	3	200	8
3	45	8	65	3	50	5
Buyers						
1	330	2	240	3	160	2
2	300	3	250	2	150	4
3	320	2	230	3	140	2
4	290	3	260	2	140	5
5	310	3	220	2	180	3
6	280	3	270	2	130	5
			Total Surplus		2250	

*Owed by pipelines 1 through 3, respectively.
Competitive equilibrium: wellhead price, $P_W = 195$; pipeline price, $P_P = 55$; delivery price, $P_D = 250$; quantity, $Q = 21$. All values and costs are in tokens which convert to cash at 200 tokens per dollar.

The second institution, Gas Auction Net was a linear program based 'smart market'. Sellers submit location specific offers to produce units at their input point; transporters submit offers to transport units on specific links; and buyers submit bids to buy delivered units at their outake points. Each of these schedules is a step function – each step stating a price per unit and a quantity. The unit prices to buy and sell define the coefficients of the objective function and the quantities define the flow constraints of a linear programming (LP) problem that maximizes system surplus (revealed aggregate gains from exchange) for all parties. Once all of the price quantity messages are sub-

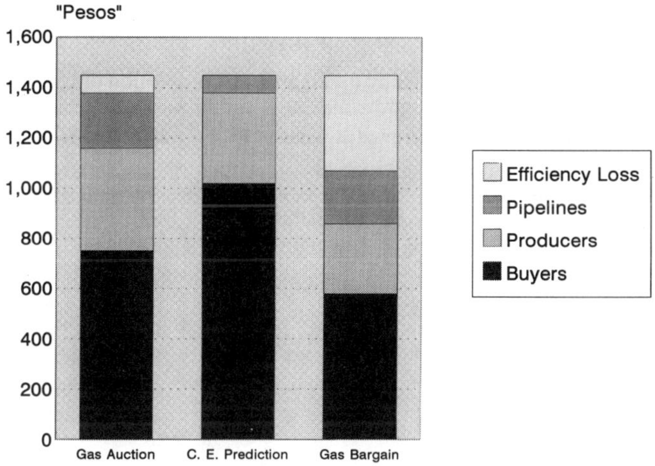

Fig. 1. Comparison of profit shares: environment (E1).

mitted to the coordinating center, the LP is solved to determine the optimal non-discriminating price at every node in the network and the flows on each link. All buyers at the same node pay the same price, all sellers (producers) at the same node receive the same price and all transporters (pipelines) receive like node-to-node price differentials.

The results of an efficiency comparison between the Bargain and Auction (smart) markets are summarized in Figure 1. In this design (Design I) Gas Auction is Pareto superior to Gas Bargain since buyers and producers are made better off while pipelines maintain their profits. The relative rent-seeking power of pipelines is therefore reduced in the Gas Auction Net experiments. Since the environment of Design I was very favorable to pipeline market power, we created a more neutral induced supply and demand environment (Design II, related in Table I) which we tested only with Gas Auction Net. The results are summarized in Table II. The more neutral environment dramatically reduced the proportion of c.e. shares the line owners earned. This comparison shows how the results can be sensitive to the supply and demand environment. Armed with some evidence that a 'smart market' was the way to go, and that there was no inherent market power attributable to being any particular type of player in a network economy we proceeded to examine some more complicated network scenarios.

3. COMPLEX GAS NETWORKS

Figure 2 describes a nine-node network for auction experiments. This configuration with two different associated sets of induced values and costs were the

TABLE II

Estimation of efficiency and shares as a proportion of c.e. values

Efficiency measure	Experiment	Design I		Experiment	Design II	
		Y_t	n		Y_t	n
	3e	0.928	24	8e	0.903	30
Total	6e	0.943	30	9e	0.940	30
	7ee	0.960	30	10ee	0.933	30
	3e	0.776	24	8e	0.847	30
Buyers	6e	0.652	30	9e	0.951	30
	7ee	0.727	30	10ee	1.02	30
	3e	1.01	24	8e	1.00	30
Producers	6e	1.01	30	9e	0.988	30
	7ee	1.02	30	10ee	0.963	30
	3e	2.24	24	8e	0.613	30
Line owners	6e	4.19	30	9e	0.889	30
	7ee	3.52	30	10ee	0.781	30
Production	3e	0.0106	24	8e	1.16	30
Owned by	6e	0.0040	30	9e	0.91	30
Lines	7ee	0.0030	30	10ee	0.86	30

All efficiencies, $Y_t = \bar{E}_t$ (observed)/E_t (c.e.), normalized as a fraction of their respective c.e. surpluses. An exception is for production by pipelines in Design I with zero c.e. surplus which is measured as a fraction of the maximal total surplus.

FERC approved designs used for the set of experiments reported in McCabe *et al.* 1989. In a U.S. deregulated scenario an exchange institution for the natural gas industry would have to deal with perhaps 40,000 producers, 2,000 line owners and 5,000 wholesale buyers. This layout was intended to capture many more of the essential elements of a complicated network scenario (e.g. bottleneck pipelines, the junction J) than our initial experimentation.

A series of 12 experiments, 6 with one design and 6 with an alternative design, were executed using the 'smart market' Gas Auction Net described in the previous section. Contemporaneously Charles Plott (1988) executed a series of experiments using the same designs but a different institutional arrangement. He reasoned that given the superb performance of the continuous double auction throughout the experimental economics literature, we ought to give it a shot in this environment. So he constructed an institution in which 19 simultaneous double auctions would be run concurrently (1 for each node and 1 for each link) for a given period of time. In such a system it

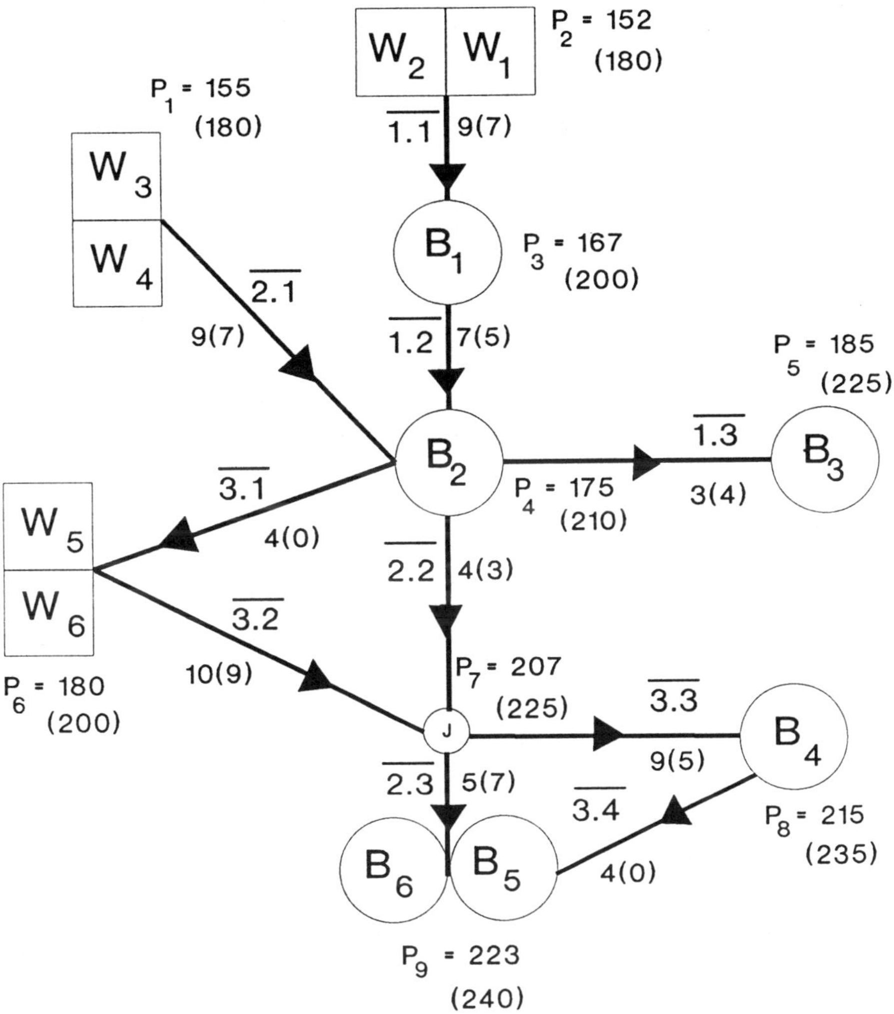

Fig. 2. Nine-node network design for auction experiments. The circles are wholesale buyers of natural gas, the boxes are wellhead producers. Pipelines connect wellheads with buyers. For example, pipeline owner 2 has three pipeline legs: 2.1, connecting producers W3 and W4 to buyer B2, and 2.2 and 2.3, carrying gas through junction *J* to B5 and B6. The symbols $P_1 = 155$, $P_2 = 152$, and so on are (nonunique) c.e. prices at each node corresponding to maximum possible surplus. The corresponding gas flows are shown in parentheses on each pipeline leg: 9 units on leg 2.1, 4 units on 3.1, and so forth. The prices and flows in parentheses are from an alternative design.

becomes necessary for agents to participate in multiple markets to get transactions completed. Once again the results indicated that the 'smart market' was Pareto superior , while its overall efficiency dominated the double auction market by 90% to 74%. Even when secondary markets were instituted to fix initial double auction misallocations, efficiency was elevated to only about 85% due to the coordination difficulties subjects were unable to overcome.

Though the average efficiencies observed in the Gas Auction Net were encouraging, we became concerned with other issues. The environment chosen for these experiments was static: the cost and value parameters did not vary from period to period. We observed extreme inter-period price stability, but some unexpected downward blips in efficiency (quantity exchanged) even toward the final periods of the experiments. These blips had also been present in the composite goods experiments. Gas Auction Net prices, but not efficiencies, were quite resistant to manipulating efforts on the part of participating agents except in parts of the networks involving monopoly pipelines.

Our next phase of experimentation, funded by the Energy Information Association, tried to address these issues simultaneously (Rassenti *et al.* 1994). We converted the Gas Auction Net from a black box sealed offer-bid institution to one with real time feedback in a timed period. Thus after initial bids and offers were collected, the participating subjects were informed of the tentative allocation and a three-minute clock was started. During the next three minutes they could improve their bids and offers as frequently as they wished until the final allocation was determined. We thought this feedback would eliminate downward efficiency blips in later periods. It achieved hardly any improvement in this regard. However we are confident that a real time feedback mechanism will track c.e. movements in a dynamically adjusting cost/value environment much more competently than a one shot sealed offer-bid.

With regard to the pipeline monopoly problem we instituted the concept of cotenancy in the Gas Auction Net. The physical requirement that only one capital facility is adequate does not imply that the market for services need be organized as a monopoly. Thus monopoly generators, pipelines or distribution centers could be required to be jointly owned by at least two or three cotenants who share costs but submit independent offers or bids.[1] We compared the performance of Gas Auction Net with and without cotenants on pipeline segments 1.1, 1.2, 1.3, 2.1 and 3.2 (which showed the most evidence of monopoly power in the price data without cotenants). With the addition

---

[1] Since our research was initiated, wellhead gas has been completely deregulated, a negotiated spot contract (30 day) market has developed, and today over one-half of all gas is being traded spot, the rest under long term contracts. Pipelines continue to be regulated on a cost-of-service basis for primary holders of transportation rights, but such rights can be freely brokered to third parties. This transportation secondary market is now large and highly competitive. There are over 1400 such 'cotenant' rights holders on the 21 trunk pipeline systems. Node prices and node price differences now move as martingales over time. Thus, the optimization problem is being solved by the arbitrage operations of thousands of agents in a labor intensive telephone market (see DeVany and Walls 1992).

of cotenants, overall efficiency increases while buyer prices decreased and producer prices increased.

4. UNIFORM PRICE DOUBLE AUCTIONS AND COMPOSITE GOOD REVISITED

Until this point the mechanism remained plagued by the sudden downward blips in efficiency. We resolved to discover their cause and hopefully rectify the problem through appropriate institutional adjustments. Reviewing the data collected in all the Gas Auction Net experiments led us to the following observation: subjects settle into a behavioral equilibrium in which the marginal value (cost) units near the c.e. are almost completely revealed but their inframarginal units (most profitable) are greatly under revealed. Figure 3 shows a typical late period in a composite good experiment.

The nearly flat supply and demand realizations, with many tied bid and offers, illustrate the mechanism by which each interest group protects itself from unfavorable pricing initiatives from their opposites. It is interesting to note that in this environment there exist many competitive/Nash equilibria. They consist of selecting some price in the equilibrium tunnel, and having at least one more bid and offer tied at that price than the largest number of units traded by an individual. Such equilibria seem to be natural attractors in uniform price markets. Under such conditions it is easy to see that if you are an agent who is trading many units by virtue of a bid (offer) at the market price in the current period, then adjusting your bid (offer) by the smallest increment in your own favor, while everyone else repeats his previous action, would result in your being cut out of the final allocation while the market price would not be affected.

One might imagine that the feedback mechanism, relative to the black box sealed offer/bid procedure, should help alleviate that problem, but it induces its own problems. Since agents have a chance to improve their bids and offers they greatly underreveal or withhold completely in the initial stages of the auction. Initial trades might occur at a substantial distance from equilibrium prices, and, as volume increases, there is a question of whether the institution can overcome the price inertia which sets in. There is always a tendency for some subjects to withhold to the dying seconds of the auction. A final flurry of bids and offers can occur without the benefit of feedback and potential responses.

In order to more closely examine the nature of uniform price rules in auctions, we decided to conduct a series of experiments uncomplicated by the composite good problem of gas networks. In McCabe *et al.* (1992) we use a simple one node buyer/seller environment to examine many variants of the uniform price double auction (UPDA). The double auction part of the name derives from the fact that we only consider real time feedback mechanisms

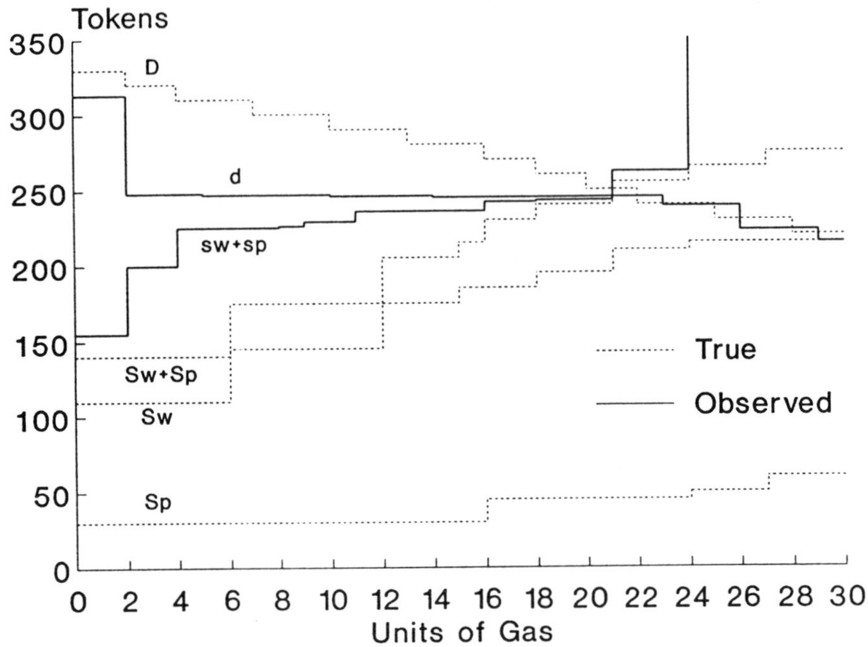

Fig. 3. Comparison of observed and true demand and supply. D, shown dotted, is the true WTP demand schedule; Sw is the true WTA of wellhead suppliers; Sp is the true WTA supply of pipeline transportation. The c.e. supply of delivered gas is $Sw + Sp$. The true c.e. price of pipeline transportation, 55 tokens, is the c.e. delivered price, 250 tokens, minus the c.e. wellhead price, 195 tokens. Actual bids (reported WTP), for one auction period, are shown as the solid step function, d. The vertical sum of actual wellhead offers plus pipeline transportation offers (reported WTA for delivered gas) is the solid step function, $sw + sp$. The near-horizontal supply and demand schedules, near the true c.e. (unknown to all subjects), is typical after the first few periods. Subjects approximate c.e. outcomes without revealing their true WTP or WTA.

which provide some form of continuous bid/ask spread to the participating agents. They are as close to the continuous double auction (NYSE) as one can contrive without having discriminatory prices.

In fact UPDA is a two-sided call market: a market in which all trades are executed at a specific point in time at a specific price. Though we arrived at examining UPDA through our desire to fine tune Gas Auction Net, in today's world of finance it is important in its own right. Within a year after we had commenced our UPDA research Wunsch Systems (now known as the Arizona Stock Exchange) quite independently introduced a variant of UPDA as the basis for a call market securities exchange which would compete with the NYSE and others. The NYSE itself began as a call market, but as volume increased and manual accounting became impossible it was forced to change to a system where specialists managed the continuous trading of various securities. With the advent of the computer age the call market, with its attractive uniform pricing feature, may again become the institution of choice.

We have examined UPDA with variations on what information is provided subjects, how the bid-ask spread is determined, when new bids and offers are sorted into the existing list, and how the auction ends. There are cross treatments effects, and it is not trivially apparent how to generalize some of these rules to Gas Auction Net, but from this research we have so far distilled the following initial round of changes:

1. Do not report the current market price only the indicated volume. The volume as it builds serves as encouragement to get an accepted trade, while the price serves as a congesting focus which is especially hazardous to efficiency if it is off the mark.
2. Report the bid/offer spread on the basis of rejected bids and offers only. This rule provides dynamic equivalence to the continuous double auction and good behavioral consequences in helping to overcome intraperiod price inertia.
3. Allow the agents a special 'I accept' key which they can press to immediately accept the current terms of the opposing side of the bid/offer spread. Again providing continuous double auction equivalence and helping to avoid higher transactions costs, especially during end game congestion.

We reran the composite good auction with these changes. We also allowed subjects the freedom to submit more bids and offers than they had steps, and to bid above value or below cost (though there seems to be no viable strategic reason to do so) in an effort to impose less rational control over the subjects as there might be in the field.

Table III below summarizes the results of these new composite good experiments. They used the cost/value environment given in Table I and are directly comparable to the Design II experiments of Table II. However, only the first 15 periods of the experienced (e) runs and 17 periods of the super-experienced (ee) runs are included, since in two hours our new subjects had to read more complicated instructions, and execute periods which lasted several minutes longer.

The results suggest that the modified institution performs more efficiently, and with less inter-period variance in outcomes. This is especially noticeable in the first five periods where subjects are as yet unfamiliar with the cost-value environment; this suggests better ability to track in non-stationary environments. Yet even in the later periods of the experiments there is a significant difference: 3 or 4% of the dollar volume traded daily in the gas industry represents large sums in a $40 billion industry.

TABLE III

Trading efficiencies under alternative institutional rules for environment given in Table I

		Original Institution			Modified Institution		
		n	μ	σ	n	ν	σ
Periods	e	10	0.722	0.165	20	0.888	0.059
1–5	ee	5	0.785	0.169	10	0.923	0.040
	all	15	0.743	0.165	30	0.900	0.055
6–15	e	20	0.907	0.075	40	0.941	0.054
(6–17)	ee	12	0.926	0.071	24	0.966	0.033
	all	32	0.914	0.073	64	0.950	0.048

n = number of observations; ν = mean efficiency; σ = standard deviation of efficiency; e = once experienced subjects; ee = twice experienced.

Amongst twice experienced subjects in the modified institution there was only one downward blip to below 90% efficiency. It occurred when one low cost seller held out for a higher price by a few tokens. He didn't trade and neither did some high valued buyer bidding at the margin. In the next period the price increased by 2 tokens and everyone traded. The following period the price was down again but the seller refused to take another hit to reinforce his previous effort. The anatomy of blips is becoming clearer. Under the circumstances of the behavioral equilibrium being jointly enforced, they most often represent unsuccessful attempts to manipulate price. The modified institution seems to reinforce the notion of the futility of such behavior. Occasionally, there are also blips due to failed attempts to make a last minute trade. That is why the 'I accept' key is so important. Any timed auction invites end game strategizing. We sometimes observed periods where 50% of the trades would be executed in the last 3 seconds of the period. There do exist other technologies to reduce end game strategizing. The period end could be uncertain (any time between time x and time y); or there could be an increasing premium paid for bids and offers submitted closer to the period end (as in the Arizona Stock Exchange). Neither of these alternatives has yet been tested in the laboratory.

5. CONCLUSION AND FUTURE RESEARCH

Through five years of market engineering research we have come to the realization that institutional design problems are complex and sensitive and can consume much time and capital. There is very little theory to guide this research, yet very much at stake. Squeezing an average percentage point of efficiency per trading period out of a national or international energy, transportation or communications market could generate hundreds of millions of dollars of surplus, compared to which the cost of a comprehensive market engineering program would be insignificant. The benefits of developing 'smart market' technology should also spill over into the internal organization of firms. There are hundreds of applications where 'smart markets' with agents expressing their willingness to pay or accept could take hold: for example, the entire domain of scheduling problems.

With respect to gas networks we intend to pursue several veins of research. We intend to examine environments with dynamically changing costs and values to fine-tune the tracking prowess of Gas Auction Net. Following this we would like to examine environments where long term contracting and/or an inter-period market for the exchange of rights in the network interact with the single period spot market. Included in this research would be the potential for capital investment in facility expansion. A wonderful by-product of the 'smart market' is the clear message it delivers (via uniform prices) as to the value of capital investment.

We are also not yet convinced that the UPDA call market provides the clearly best institutional basis for a centrally controlled network economy, though we feel it may be the most saleable because of precedent. At the Economic Science Laboratory we have recently investigated several other institutions and one of them, Double Dutch (McCabe *et al.* 1992), out performs UPDA in the one node buy/sell environment. In it the price initiative is removed from participating agents. Opposing price clocks count toward each other while agents simply indicate their willingness to trade at quoted clock prices. Importing this institution to a network economy would require some complicated computer coordination (the clocks don't always all run at the same time) but provide a very simple message space for the agents to master.

Finally, as 'smart market' applications are made in more complex environments, nonlinearities will require the use of heuristics for timely allocations (e.g. computer scheduling, communications routing, electric power dispatching). The market engineering process will then include the selection of an appropriate heuristic for an institutional context. The most efficient heuristics (in the computational sense) will not necessarily foster dynamic behavioral responses which will lead to the most efficient 'smart market' allocations. We are beginning research in this area.

ACKNOWLEDGEMENTS

We are grateful for research support from the National Science Foundation, grant # IRI–8921141 entitled, 'Experiments in Computer Coordinated Decentralized Resource Allocation Systems'. from the Information, Robotics and Intelligent Systems Division.

BIBLIOGRAPHY

DeVany, A. and W. D. Walls, 1992, 'When barriers to markets fall: Pipeline deregulation, spot markets, and the topology of the natural gas markets', The University of California Transportation Center, Working Paper No. 123, Berkeley, California.

McCabe, K., S. Rassenti and V. Smith, 1989, 'Designing "smart" computer assisted markets: An experimental auction for gas networks', *Journal of Political Economy* 5, 259–283.

McCabe, K., S. Rassenti and V. Smith, 1990, 'Auction design for composite goods', *Journal of Economic Behavior and Organization* 14, 127–149.

McCabe, K., S. Rassenti and V. Smith, 1991, 'Smart computer-assisted markets', *Science* 254, 534–538.

McCabe, K., S. Rassenti and V. Smith, 1992, 'Designing call auction institutions: Is double Dutch the best', *Economic Journal* 102, 9–23.

McCabe, K., S. Rassenti and V. Smith, 1992, 'Designing a uniform price double auction", in Friedman, Geanakoplos, Lane and Rust (Eds.), *The Double Auction Market: Institutions, Theories and Laboratory Evidence, Proceedings of the Santa Fe Institute*, Addison-Wesley.

Plott, C., 1988, 'Research on pricing in a gas transportation network', Technical Report 88–2, Washington: FERC, Office of Economic Policy.

Rassenti, S., S. Reynolds and V. Smith, 1994, 'Cotenancy and competition in an experimental auction market for natural gas pipeline networks', *Economic Theory*, forthcoming.

Rassenti, S., V. Smith and R. Bulfin, 1982, 'A combinatorial auction mechanism for airport time slot allocation', *Bell Journal of Economics* 13, 402–417.

PART TWO

Modeling Computational Economic Systems

HANS M. AMMAN AND DAVID A. KENDRICK

Nonconvexities in Stochastic Control Models: An Analysis

ABSTRACT. Though nonconvexities in the cost-to-go function of adaptive control problems were first found more than ten years ago with numerical models, it is only recently that they have been confirmed by Mizrach with analytical methods. He used MacRae's simple single-state and single-control model and confirmed the earlier numerical result that the source of the nonconvexity was the probing component of the cost-to-go. Mizrach's results have been extended in this paper in two ways. First the probing function has been characterized and the resulting character has been found to support the use of algorithms which exploit this character to find the global optimum even in the face of the local optima caused by the nonconvexities. Secondly, a new source of nonconvexities has been found in the cautionary component of the cost-to-go. This paper contains the derivations for these results.

Nonconvexities in numerical solutions to active learning stochastic control problems which were reported by Kendrick (1978) and Norman *et al.* (1979) have recently been confirmed in the theoretical analysis of Mizrach (1991). This and a companion paper seeks to characterize the main component functions and add intuition to Mizrach's results. This paper provides the detailed derivations which underlie the results in the companion paper which is Amman and Kendrick (1992).

The test bed for the results cited above has been MacRae's (1972) single-state single-control two period stochastic control model. That model is:

Find (u_0, u_1) to minimize

$$J = E\left\{\frac{1}{2}\, w_2 x_2^2 + \frac{1}{2}\sum_{k=0}^{1}(w_k x_k^2 + \lambda_k u_k^2)\right\} \tag{0-1}$$

subject to

$$x_{k+1} = a x_k + b u_k + c + \varepsilon_k \quad \text{for} \quad k = 0, 1, \tag{0-2}$$

$$x_0 = 0. \tag{0-3}$$

W.W. Cooper and A.B. Whinston (eds.), New Directions in Computational Economics, 57–94.

The parameter values used by MacRae are

$$a = 0.7 \quad b = -0.5 \quad c = 3.5 \quad \sigma_e^2 = q = 0.2$$
$$w_k = 1, \forall k \quad \lambda_k = 1, \forall k \quad \sigma_b^2 = 0.5 \quad \sigma_a^2 = \sigma_c^2 = 0.$$

Also the desired paths in Equation (0-1) are implicitly set to zero so

$$\tilde{x}_k = 0 \quad \tilde{u}_k = 0 \quad \forall k.$$

This problem has a very simple structure that enables one to see whether or not nonconvexities occur in such a simple problem and then to track down the source of those nonconvexities. So the strategy used by Mizrach and followed here is to derive all of the stochastic control results for the MacRae model by specializing the derivations in Kendrick (1981) to the particular case of a single-state, single-control problem with no measurement error. The MacRae problem has the additional advantage that it has been solved using the dual control algorithm of Tse and Bar-Shalom (1973) as described in detail in Chapter 11 of Kendrick (1981).

In the Tse and Bar-Shalom algorithm the total approximate cost-to-go is separated into three components – deterministic, cautionary and probing. At period k of an N period model with $N - k$ periods to go the total cost-to-go can be written as

$$J_{N-k} = J_{D,N-k} + J_{C,N-k} + J_{P,N-k}, \tag{0-4}$$

where the D, C, and P subscripts represent the three components.

When Kendrick and Norman first encountered the nonconvexity in the MacRae problem the cause was traced to the probing term. This paper continues in that tradition. The deterministic and cautionary terms are convex. The probing term is nonconvex. So when the three terms are summed the result may be a convex function.

Also the work in 1978–1979 found the nonconvexity in a version of the MacRae problem which had ten periods rather than two and which treated all three parameters a, b and c as uncertain. Consequently, at that time it was not known whether or not the nonconvexity would appear in problems with as few as two time periods and with a single unknown parameters. Mizrach (1991) advanced our understanding by showing that the nonconvexity could arise in a two-period version of the MacRae problem with only the b parameter unknown.

In summary, the nonconvexity in stochastic control problems arises from nonconvexity in the probing component of the cost-to-go and can occur in problems with as few as two time periods and one uncertain parameter. Here we will follow Mizrach's lead by analyzing the probing term to see which components of that term cause the nonconvexity. We do this by developing the probing term from the parameters of the MacRae problem in such a way as to provide additional insight as to the cause of the nonconvexities.

The first four sections of this paper are concerned with deriving and characterizing the probing term. The probing term has two components, a covariance matrix and a $\mathcal{R}$ term. The expression for the covariance matrix is derived in Section 1. The $\mathcal{R}$ term is dependent on the nominal paths, therefore Section 2 contains the derivation of the nominal states and control. This material is then used in Section 3 to derive the $\mathcal{R}$ term. The results from the first three sections are then brought together in Section 4 to provide a mathematical and numerical characterization of the probing term. This is followed in Sections 5 and 6 with derivation of the cautionary and deterministic terms. Then the total cost-to-go is assembled in Section 7.

1. THE PROBING TERM: COVARIANCE MATRIX

In the Tse and Bar-Shalom (1973) framework the original state vector, x, of the model is augmented with a vector of the unknown parameters, θ (like a, b and c), to create a new state vector

$$z = \begin{bmatrix} x \\ \theta \end{bmatrix}. \tag{1-1}$$

Corresponding to this state vector there is a covariance matrix

$$\Sigma = \begin{bmatrix} \Sigma^{xx} & \Sigma^{x\theta} \\ \Sigma^{\theta x} & \Sigma^{\theta\theta} \end{bmatrix}, \tag{1-2}$$

where Σ^{xx} models the uncertainty associated with the original state variables and $\Sigma^{\theta\theta}$ models the uncertainty in the subset of the parameters which are treated as uncertain.

Also, the Tse and Bar-Shalom framework make a distinction between the following covariance matrices

$$\Sigma_{k/k} \quad \Sigma_{k+1/k} \quad \Sigma_{k+1/k+1}.$$

$\Sigma_{k/k}$ is the uncertainty associated with the system at time k when it has been measured and estimated at time k. $\Sigma_{k+1/k}$ is the uncertainty projected for period $k+1$ when the system has been measured at period k. And $\Sigma_{k+1/k+1}$ is the uncertainty in period $k+1$ after the system is measured in period $k+1$.

For the MacRae problem $\Sigma^{xx}_{k/k}$, $\Sigma^{x\theta}_{k/k}$ and $\Sigma^{\theta x}_{k/k}$ for all k will all be equal to zero because measurement error is not present in that model. Therefore the probing term from Equation (10-51) of Kendrick (1981) can be written in the form

$$J_{P,N-k} = \frac{1}{2}\, tr \sum_{j=k+1}^{N-1} (\mathcal{R}_j \Sigma^{\theta\theta}_{j/j}), \tag{1-3}$$

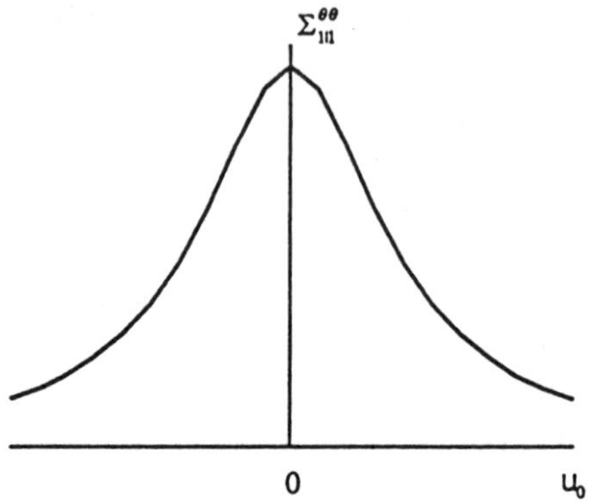

Fig. 1. Parameter uncertainty.

where $\mathcal{R}_j$ is the $\mathcal{R}$ term which will be defined later and $\Sigma_{j/j}^{\theta\theta}$ is the covariance matrix for the unknown parameters.

We want to evaluate the cost-to-go at period zero with N periods to go so $k = 0$. Also the problem has two periods so $N = 2$. Finally, the only uncertain parameter in the case at hand is b so $\Sigma_{j/j}^{\theta\theta}$ and $\mathcal{R}_j$ are one dimensional and the trace operator can be dropped. We considered the notational change of replacing $\Sigma_{j/j}^{\theta\theta}$ with σ_b^2 and $\mathcal{R}_j$ with r_t at this point in the exposition since these two elements are scalars rather than matrices. Also, in the following we will discuss these elements as function of the initial period control. However, the adoption of the scalar notation style makes the relationship to the previous work more difficult. Therefore, we simply ask the reader to keep in mind that $\Sigma_{j/j}^{\theta\theta}$ and $\mathcal{R}_j$ are scalars in the following.

Then Equation (1-3) can be rewritten as

$$J_{P,N-k} = \frac{1}{2}\,\mathcal{R}_1\Sigma_{1/1}^{\theta\theta}. \tag{1-4}$$

The first problem then is to find the functional form of the covariance term $\Sigma_{1/1}^{\theta\theta}$ and the $\mathcal{R}$ term $\mathcal{R}_1$ and see how their interaction can produce a nonconvex function. We will show that there is a functional relationship between u_0 and $\Sigma_{1/1}^{\theta\theta}$ like that presented above in Figure 1. Thus increases or decreases in the control variable u_0 from zero result in decreases in the variance of the parameter b.

Next consider the $\mathcal{R}$ term which is plotted against the control variable in period zero in Figure 2. The $\mathcal{R}$ term $\mathcal{R}_1$ is a quadratic function of the form shown.

The product of these two terms can produce a nonconvexity. A plot of the product $\mathcal{R}_1\Sigma_{1/1}^{\theta\theta}$ has the form as in Figure 3. So the nonconvexity in the probing term results from the interaction of the $\mathcal{R}_1$ and $\Sigma_{1/1}^{\theta\theta}$ terms.

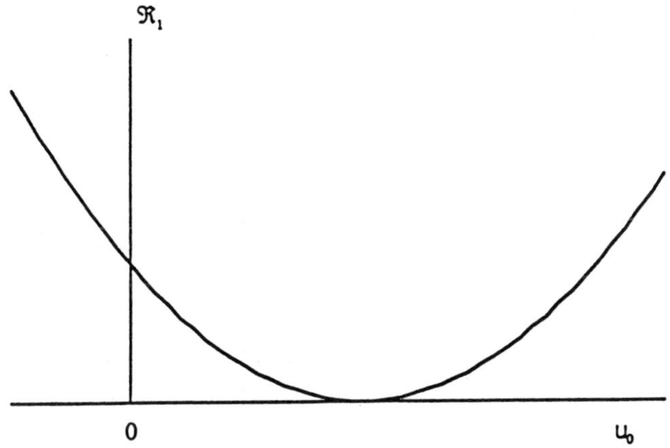

Fig. 2. $\mathcal{R}$ term.

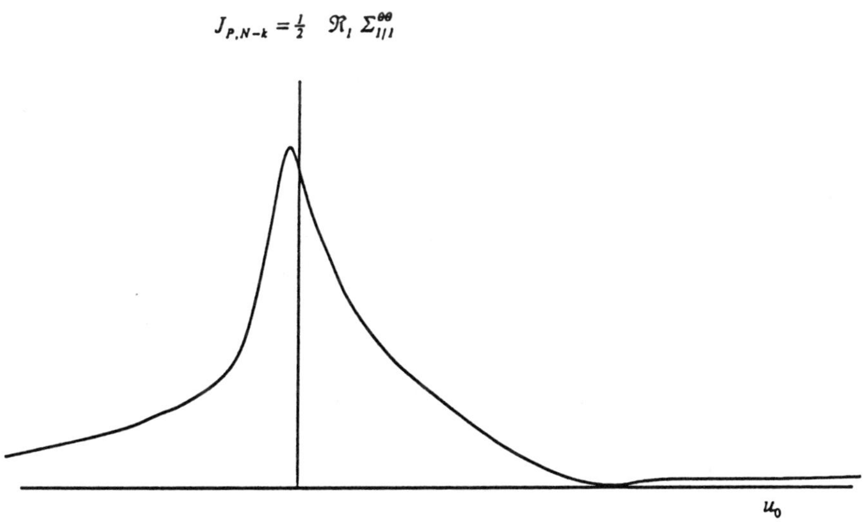

Fig. 3. The probing term.

We will show in more detail below that the covariance function in Figure 1 is of the form

$$\Sigma_{1/1}^{\theta\theta} = \frac{1}{h(u_0)}\,, \tag{1-5}$$

where h is a quadratic function of u_0. Also we will show that the $\mathcal{R}$ term is a function of the form

$$\mathcal{R}_1 = g(u_0), \tag{1-6}$$

where g is a quadratic function of u_0. Thus the probing cost term is of the form

$$J_{P,N-k} = \frac{1}{2}\mathcal{R}_l\Sigma_{1/1}^{\theta\theta} = \frac{1}{2}\frac{g(u_0)}{h(u_0)}\,. \tag{1-7}$$

So the $J_{P,N-k}(u_0)$ function is a ratio of two quadratic functions and this function can be nonconvex.

The following provides the mathematical development to show that the $h(u_0)$ and $g(u_0)$ are each quadratic forms.

Consider first the $h(u_0)$ function and begin by using Equation (11-33) in Kendrick (1981) with $H = 1$ because there is no measurement error in the MacRae model

$$\Sigma_{1/1}^{\theta\theta} = \Sigma_{1/0}^{\theta\theta} - \Sigma_{1/0}^{\theta x}S_1^{-1}\Sigma_{1/0}^{x\theta}\,. \tag{1-8}$$

Hereafter all equation references of the form (K10-xx) or (K11-xx) refer to Chapters 10 and 11 respectively of Kendrick (1981).

The term $\Sigma_{1/0}^{\theta\theta}$ is defined in Equation (K11-17) as

$$\Sigma_{1/0}^{\theta\theta} = D\Sigma_{0/0}^{\theta\theta}D' + G_0. \tag{1-9}$$

However, since the parameters are not time varying in the MacRae model we have $D = 1$ and $G_0 = 0$. Also the only uncertain parameter is b and its initial variance is σ_b^2. Then Equation (1-9) can be rewritten as

$$\Sigma_{1/0}^{\theta\theta} = \sigma_b^2. \tag{1-10}$$

Next consider the $\Sigma_{1/0}^{\theta x}$ element in Equation (1-8). From Equation (K11-16) it is

$$\Sigma_{1/0}^{\theta x} = D\Sigma_{0/0}^{\theta x}A' + D\Sigma_{0/0}^{\theta\theta}f_{\theta 0}^{x\prime} \tag{1-11}$$

and from Equation (K11-14)

$$f_{\theta 0}^{x} = \tilde{x}_{0/0}a_\theta + u_0^{\mathcal{T}}b_\theta + c_\theta. \tag{1-12}$$

In the case at hand since b is the only unknown parameter $b_\theta = 1$ and a_θ and c_θ are both zero. Therefore

$$f_{\theta 0}^{x} = u_0^{\mathcal{T}}. \tag{1-13}$$

Note that $u_0^{\mathcal{T}}$ here means the trial value of the control for period 0. To simplify the notation from here forward we will use simply u_0 instead of $u_0^{\mathcal{T}}$.

Using Equation (1-13) and $\Sigma_{0/0}^{\theta\theta} = \sigma_b^2$ in Equation (1-11) along with $D = 1$ and $\Sigma_{0/0}^{\theta x} = 0$ yields

$$\Sigma_{1/0}^{\theta x} = \sigma_b^2 u_0. \tag{1-14}$$

Now we have all the terms in Equation (1-8) except S_1. This term is defined below Equation (K11-31) using $H_1 = 1$ as

$$S_1 = \Sigma_{1/0}^{xx} + R_1. \tag{1-15}$$

The term $\Sigma_{1/0}^{xx}$ in turn is defined in Equation (K11-13). Using that expression with $\Sigma_{0/0}^{xx} = 0$ and $\Sigma_{0/0}^{\theta x} = 0$, since there is no measurement error, yields

$$\Sigma_{1/0}^{xx} = f_{\theta 0}^{x} \Sigma_{0/0}^{\theta\theta} f_{\theta 0}^{x'} + Q_0. \tag{1-16}$$

Since the covariance of the additive noise term Q_0 is a scalar in this case and is not time varying let

$$q = Q_0. \tag{1-17}$$

Then the use of Equations (1-13) and (1-17) in (1-16) yields

$$\Sigma_{1/0}^{xx} = \sigma_b^2 u_0^2 + q. \tag{1-18}$$

Then we can use Equation (1-18) in (1-15) along with the fact that the measurement error covariance R_1 is zero to obtain

$$S_1 = \sigma_b^2 u_0^2 + q. \tag{1-19}$$

Now we have all the elements required in Equation (1-8) to define $\Sigma_{1/1}^{\theta\theta}$, i.e., we can substitute Equations (1-10), (1-14), and (1-19) into (1-8) to obtain

$$\Sigma_{1/1}^{\theta\theta} = \sigma_b^2 - \frac{(\sigma_b^2 u_0)^2}{\sigma_b^2 u_0^2 + q}, \tag{1-20}$$

or

$$\Sigma_{1/1}^{\theta\theta} = \frac{\sigma_b^2[\sigma_b^2 u_0^2 + q] - (\sigma_b^2 u_0)^2}{\sigma_b^2 u_0^2 + q}, \tag{1-21}$$

$$\Sigma_{1/1}^{\theta\theta} = \frac{1}{\left(\frac{1}{\sigma_b^2 q}\right)(\sigma_b^2 u_0^2 + q)}. \tag{1-22}$$

Thus the inverse of the covariance function referred to in Equation (1-5) is

$$h(u) = \left(\frac{1}{\sigma_b^2 q}\right)(\sigma_b^2 u_0^2 + q) \tag{1-23}$$

which is, as promised, a quadratic function in the control variable for the zero time period.

2. NOMINAL STATES AND CONTROLS

We cannot proceed directly to the derivation of the $\mathcal{R}$ function $g(u)$. Rather it is necessary first to derive the paths for the nominal state and control variables.

Begin with the computation of $\tilde{K}$ and $\tilde{p}$ since these will be needed to compute the feedback rule. The feedback rule will be needed in turn to compute the nominal paths of states and controls. Follow Equation (K11-7) to obtain

$$\tilde{K}_2 = W_2 = w_2, \tag{2-1}$$

since W_2 is the scalar w_2 in the problem at hand

$$\tilde{p}_2 = -W_2'\tilde{x}_2 = -w_2\tilde{x}_2, \tag{2-2}$$

where $\tilde{x}_2$ is the desired path.

Next repeat these calculations for period one using the Riccati equation for period one in Equation (K11-7)

$$\tilde{K}_1 = A'[I - \tilde{K}_2 B\mu_1 B']\tilde{K}_2 A + W_1 \tag{2-3}$$

with

$$\mu_1 = [\Lambda_1 + B'\tilde{K}_2 B]^{-1}$$

for the problem at hand which is all scalars this becomes

$$\tilde{k}_1 = a[1 - \tilde{k}_2 b^2 \mu_1]\tilde{k}_2 a + w_1, \tag{2-4}$$

where

$$\mu_1 = [\lambda_1 + \tilde{k}_2 b^2]^{-1}. \tag{2-5}$$

Substitute Equation (2-5) into (2-4) to obtain

$$\tilde{k}_1 = a\left[1 - \frac{\tilde{k}_2 b^2}{\lambda_1 + \tilde{k}_2 b^2}\right]\tilde{k}_2 a + w_1, \tag{2-6}$$

or

$$\tilde{k}_1 = a^2\left[\frac{\lambda_1 + \tilde{k}_2 b^2 - \tilde{k}_2 b^2}{\lambda_1 + \tilde{k}_2 b^2}\right]\tilde{k}_2 + w_1, \tag{2-7}$$

or

$$\tilde{k}_1 = a^2\left[\frac{\lambda_1}{\lambda_1 + \tilde{k}_2 b^2}\right]\tilde{k}_2 + w_1. \tag{2-8}$$

Then substitute Equation (2-1) into (2-8) to obtain

$$\tilde{k}_1 = a^2 \left[\frac{\lambda_1}{\lambda_1 + w_2 b^2} \right] w_2 + w_1. \tag{2-9}$$

Next compute $\tilde{p}_1$ using Equation (K11-8) in the text

$$\tilde{p}_1 = -A\tilde{K}_2 B\mu_1 \left[B'(\tilde{K}_2 c + \tilde{p}_2) - \Lambda_1 \tilde{u}_1 \right] + A'[\tilde{K}_2 c + \tilde{p}_2]. \tag{2-10}$$

Convert this to scalars and substitute Equations (2-1) and (2-2) into (2-10) to obtain

$$\tilde{p}_1 = -aw_2 b\mu_1 \left[b(w_2 c - w_x \tilde{x}_2) - \lambda_1 \tilde{u}_1 \right] + a(w_2 c - w_2 \tilde{x}_2). \tag{2-11}$$

Substitute Equation (2-5) into (2-11) and collect terms to obtain

$$\tilde{p}_1 = -\frac{aw_2 b}{(\lambda_1 + w_2 b)} \left[bw_2(c - \tilde{x}_2) - \lambda_1 \tilde{u}_1 \right] + aw_2(c - \tilde{x}_2). \tag{2-12}$$

Now that $\tilde{K}$'s and $\tilde{p}$'s are computed the next task is to calculate the projected state for period one, i.e. $\hat{x}_{1/0}$. To do this use Equation (K11-10) from the text.

$$\hat{x}_{1/0} = A\hat{x}_{0/0} + B(\theta_{0/0})u_0^T + c + tr[a_\theta \Sigma_{k/k}^{\theta x}]/ \tag{2-13}$$

Since b is the only uncertain parameter in the model at hand $a_\theta = 0$ and the last term will drop out. Also the initial condition is $\hat{x}_{0/0} = x_0$. Then converting to scalars Equation (2-13) becomes

$$\hat{x}_{1/0} = ax_0 + bu_0^T + c. \tag{2-14}$$

Now the nominal optimal control for period one can be calculated using Equation (K11-18)

$$u_{01} = -\mu_1 \left[B(\tilde{K}_2 A\hat{x}_{1/0} + \tilde{K}_2 c + \tilde{p}_2) - \Lambda_1 \tilde{u}_1 \right]. \tag{2-15}$$

Substitution of Equations (2-1), (2-2), (2-5) and (2-14) into (2-15) and conversion to scalars yields

$$\begin{aligned} u_{01} &= -\left(\frac{1}{\lambda_1 + w_2 b^2} \right) \\ &\times \left[b\left\{ w_2 a(ax_0 + bu_0^T + c) + w_2 c - w_2 \tilde{x}_2 \right\} - \lambda_1 \tilde{u}_1 \right], \end{aligned} \tag{2-16}$$

or

$$\begin{aligned} u_{01} &= -\left(\frac{1}{\lambda_1 + w_2 b^2} \right) \\ &\times \left[b\left\{ w_2 a(ax_0 + bu_0^T + c) + w_2(c - \tilde{x}_2) \right\} - \lambda_1 \tilde{u}_1 \right]. \end{aligned} \tag{2-17}$$

Then the control value in Equation (2-17) can be used to compute the state variable for period 2 using Equation (K11-19) in the text

$$x_{02} = A\hat{x}_{1/0} + B(\theta_{0/1})u_{01} + c. \tag{2-18}$$

Substitution of Equations (2-14) and (2-17) into (2-18) and conversion to scalars yields

$$\begin{aligned} x_{02} &= a(ax_0 + bu_0^{\mathcal{T}} + c) - \frac{b}{(\lambda_1 + w_2 b^2)} \\ &\times \left[b\left\{w_2 a(ax_0 + bu_0^{\mathcal{T}} + c) + w_2(c - \tilde{x}_2)\right\} - \lambda_1 \tilde{u}_1\right] + c. \end{aligned} \tag{2-19}$$

Expressions (2-14), (2-17) and (2-19) provide the nominal paths for the states and controls however, we need to simplify them so that they are functions of $u_0^{\mathcal{T}}$ only. Begin with (2-14). In this case the projected state $\hat{x}_{1/0}$ is the nominal path so we have

$$x_{01} = ax_0 + bu_0^{\mathcal{T}} + c. \tag{2-20}$$

Consider next u_{01} by rewriting Equation (2-17) using the definition of μ_1 in (2-5). This yields

$$\begin{aligned} u_{01} &= -\mu_1 \left[b\left\{w_2 a(ax_0 + bu_0^{\mathcal{T}} + c) + w_2(c - \tilde{x}_2)\right\} - \lambda_1 \tilde{u}_1\right] \\ &= -\mu_1 \left[b\left\{a^2 w_2 x_0 + abw_2 u_0^{\mathcal{T}} + acw_2 + w_2(c - \tilde{x}_2)\right\} - \lambda_1 \tilde{u}_1\right] \\ &= -\mu_1 \left[a^2 bw_2 x_0 + ab^2 w_2 u_0^{\mathcal{T}} + abcw_2 \right. \\ &\quad \left. + bw_2(c - \tilde{x}_2) - \lambda_1 \tilde{u}_1\right], \end{aligned} \tag{2-21}$$

or

$$u_{01} = \alpha u_0^{\mathcal{T}} + \beta \tag{2-22}$$

where

$$\begin{aligned} \alpha &= -\mu_1 ab^2 w_2, \\ \beta &= -\mu_1 \left[a^2 bw_2 x_0 + abcw_2 + bw_2(c - \tilde{x}_2) - \lambda_1 \tilde{u}_1\right], \end{aligned}$$

with

$$\mu_1 = \frac{1}{\lambda_1 + b^2 w_2}.$$

Now use Equation (2-18) in a scalar form to get

$$x_{02} = ax_{01} + bu_{01} + c \tag{2-23}$$

and substitute Equations (2-20) and (2-22) into (2-23) to obtain

$$\begin{aligned} x_{02} &= a(ax_0 + bu_0^{\tau} + c) + b(\alpha u_0^{\tau} + \beta) + c \\ &= a^2 x_0 + abu_0^{\tau} + ac + b\alpha u_0^{\tau} + b\beta + c, \end{aligned} \tag{2-24}$$

or

$$x_{02} = a^2 x_0 + (ab + b\alpha)u_0^{\tau} + ac + c + b\beta, \tag{2-25}$$

or

$$x_{02} = \rho u_p^{\tau} + \eta, \tag{2-26}$$

where

$$\begin{aligned} \rho &= ab + b\alpha = b(a + \alpha), \\ \eta &= a^2 x_0 + ac + c + b\beta = a(ax_0 + c) + c + b\beta. \end{aligned}$$

For the particular numerical values of the MacRae problem with penalty weights for both state and controls of one, and desired paths equal to zero and initial state equal to zero we have

$$\begin{aligned} w_2 &= 1, \quad \lambda_1 = 1, \quad \tilde{x}_2 = 0 \\ \tilde{u}_1 &= 0, \quad x_0 = 0. \end{aligned}$$

In this case the u_{01} from Equation (2-22) reduces to

$$u_{01} = \alpha u_0^{\tau} + \beta, \tag{2-27}$$

where

$$\alpha = -\frac{ab^2}{1 + b^2}, \tag{2-28}$$

$$\beta = -\frac{1}{1 + b^2}[abc + bc] = -\frac{1}{1 + b^2}(ac + c) = -\frac{(1 + a)bc}{1 + b^2}. \tag{2-29}$$

Also the state x_{02} becomes using Equation (2-26)

$$x_{02} = \rho u_0^{\tau} + \eta, \tag{2-30}$$

where

$$\rho = b(a + \alpha),$$

or

$$\rho = b\left(a - \frac{ab^2}{1 + b^2}\right),$$

or

$$\rho = b\left(\frac{a + ab^2 - ab^2}{1 + b^2}\right) = \frac{ab}{1 + b^2}, \tag{2-31}$$

and

$$\eta = a(ax_0 + c) + c + b\beta, \tag{2-32}$$

$$\eta = ac + c + b\beta,$$

since

$$x_0 = 0, \quad \tilde{x}_2 = 0, \quad \tilde{u}_1 = 0, \quad w_2 = 1, \quad \lambda_1 = 1.$$

Also using the lines below Equation (2-22) we obtain

$$\begin{aligned}
\eta &= c(a+1) - b\mu_1\left[a^2bw_2x_0 + abcw_2 + bw_2(c - \tilde{x}_2) - \lambda_1\tilde{u}_1\right] \\
&= c(a+1) - b\mu_1[abc + bc] = c(a+1) - \frac{ab^2c + b^2c}{a + b^2} \\
&= \frac{c(a+1)(1+b^2) - ab^2c - b^2c}{1 + b^2} \\
&= \frac{ca + c + ab^2c + b^2c - ab^2c - b^2c}{1 + b^2},
\end{aligned}$$

or

$$\eta = \frac{1}{1 + b^2}(ac + c). \tag{2-33}$$

In summary then the parameters are

$$\begin{aligned}
\alpha &= -\left(\frac{ab^2}{1 + b^2}\right), \quad \beta = -\left(\frac{b}{1 + b^2}\right)(ac + c), \\
\rho &= \left(\frac{ab}{1 + b^2}\right), \quad \eta = \left(\frac{1}{1 + b^2}\right)(ac + c).
\end{aligned} \tag{2-34}$$

3. DERIVATION OF THE $\mathcal{R}$ TERM

The next step is derive the

$$\mathcal{R}_1 = g(u)$$

function from Equation (1-6) above. The expression for $\mathcal{R}_1$ and therefore $g(u)$ is obtained from Equation (K11-34) in the text as

$$\begin{aligned} g(u) &= \left\{[D'K_2^{\theta x} + f_{\theta 1}^{x'} K_2^{xx}]B + p_2^x b_\theta\right\} \mu_1 \\ &\times \left\{B'[K_2^{xx} f_{\theta 1}^x + K_2^{x\theta} D] + p_2^x b_\theta\right\}. \end{aligned} \tag{3-1}$$

For the MacRae model $D = 1$ and $b_\theta = 1$. Using these two and converting to scalars converts Equation (3-1) to

$$g(u) = \left\{[k_2^{\theta x} + f_{\theta 1}^x k_2^{xx}]b + p_2^x\right\} \mu_1 \left\{b[k_2^{xx} f_{\theta 1}^x + k_2^{x\theta}] + p_2^x\right\}. \tag{3-2}$$

Next derive $k_2^{\theta x}$. From Equation (K11-20)

$$k_2^{\theta x} = 0. \tag{3-3}$$

Also from the lines above Equation (K11-20) recall that

$$K_k^{xx} = \tilde{K}_j. \tag{3-4}$$

So from Equation (K11-7)

$$K_2^{xx} = w_2. \tag{3-5}$$

Also from Equation (K11-22)

$$p_2^x = \tilde{K}_2 x_{02} + \tilde{p}_2 \tag{3-6}$$

and from Equation (K11-7)

$$\tilde{p}_2 = -W_2' \tilde{x}_2, \tag{3-7}$$

or for the case at hand

$$\tilde{p}_2 = -w_2 \tilde{x}_2. \tag{3-8}$$

Also from Equation (K11-7)

$$\tilde{K}_2 = w_2. \tag{3-9}$$

Then substitution of Equations (3-8) and (3-9) into (3-6) yields

$$p_2^x = w_2 x_{02} - w_2 \tilde{x}_2, \tag{3-10}$$

or

$$p_2^x = w_2(x_{02} - \tilde{x}_2). \tag{3-11}$$

Then substitution of Equations (3-3), (3-5) and (3-11) into (3-2) yields

$$g(u) = \left\{ f_{\theta 1}^{x'} w_2 b + w_2(x_{02} - \tilde{x}_2) \right\} \mu_1 \times \left\{ b w_2 f_{\theta 1}^{x} + w_2(x_{02} - \tilde{x}_2) \right\}. \tag{3-12}$$

Then from Equation (K11-23) along with $a_\theta = c_\theta = 0$ and $b_\theta = 1$ we have

$$f_{\theta 1}^{x} = u_{01}. \tag{3-13}$$

And from the line below Equation (K11-23)

$$\mu_1 = (\lambda_1 + b^2 w_2)^{-1}. \tag{3-14}$$

So substitution of Equations (3-13) and (3-14) into (3-12) yields

$$g(u) = \{ w_2 b u_{01} + w_2(x_{02} - \tilde{x}_2) \} \left(\frac{1}{\lambda_1 + b^2 w_2} \right) \times \{ b w_2 u_{01} + w_2(x_{02} - \tilde{x}_2) \}, \tag{3-15}$$

$$g(u) = \left(\frac{w_2^2}{\lambda_1 + b^2 w_2} \right) (b u_{01} + x_{02} - \tilde{x}_2)^2. \tag{3-16}$$

Also the nominal path variables u_{01} and x_{02} are functions of the search value of the control variable in period zero, $u_0^{\mathcal{T}}$. From Equations (2-22) and (2-26) we have

$$u_{01} = \alpha u_0^{\mathcal{T}} + \beta \tag{3-17}$$

and

$$x_{02} = \rho u_0^{\mathcal{T}} + \eta. \tag{3-18}$$

Substitution of Equations (3-17) and (3-18) into (3-16) yields

$$g(u) = \left(\frac{w_2^2}{\lambda_1 + b^2 w_2} \right) \times \left[b(\alpha u_0^{\mathcal{T}} + \beta) + \rho u_0^{\mathcal{T}} + \eta - \tilde{x}_2 \right]^2. \tag{3-19}$$

In the following u_0 is used instead of $u_0^{\mathcal{T}}$ for simplicity. Consider only the bracket term from Equation (3-19) and substitute in the parameter values from the original model using Equation (2-34).

$$\begin{aligned} y &= b(\alpha u_0 + \beta) + \rho u_0 + \eta - \tilde{x}_2 \\ &= (b\alpha + \rho) u_0 + b\beta + \eta - \tilde{x}_2 \end{aligned}$$

$$= \left[-b\left(\frac{ab^2}{1+b^2}\right) + \frac{ab}{1+b^2}\right] u_0$$

$$- b\frac{b}{(1+b^2)}(ac+c) + \left(\frac{1}{1+b^2}\right)(ac+c) - \tilde{x}_2$$

$$= \left(\frac{-ab^3+ab}{1+b^2}\right) u_0 + \left(\frac{1}{1+b^2}\right)(ac+c)(1-b^2) - \tilde{x}_2$$

$$= \left(\frac{ab(1-b^2)}{1+b^2}\right) u_0 + \frac{(1-b^2)}{1+b^2}(ac+c) - \tilde{x}_2, \tag{3-20}$$

$$y = \frac{1-b^2}{1+b^2}(abu_0 + ac + c) - \tilde{x}_2. \tag{3-21}$$

Substitution of Equation (3-21) back into (3-19) yields the $g(u)$ function in terms of the parameters from the original model, i.e.

$$f(u) = \left(\frac{w_2^2}{\lambda_1 + b^2 w_2}\right)\left[\frac{(1-b^2)}{(1+b^2)}(abu_0 + ac + c) - \tilde{x})2\right]^2. \tag{3-22}$$

Then the function $g(u)$ can be written as

$$g(u) = \phi_1(\phi_2 u_0 + \phi_3)^2, \tag{3-23}$$

where

$$\phi_1 = \frac{w_2^2}{\lambda_1 + b^2 w_2}, \quad \phi_2 = \frac{(1-b^2)}{1+b^2)}\, ab,$$

$$\phi_3 = \frac{(1-b^2)}{(1+b^2)}(ac+c) - \tilde{x}_2. \tag{3-24}$$

Now we have derived both the $g(u)$ and $h(u)$ functions, i.e. Equations (1-23) and (3-23). These can be substituted into Equation (1-7) to obtain the cost-to-go for period $k = 0$, i.e.

$$J_{PN} = \frac{1}{2}\,\mathcal{R}_1 \Sigma_{1/1}^{\theta\theta} = \frac{1}{2}\,\frac{g(u)}{h(u)}. \tag{3-25}$$

Also σ is used instead of σ_b for the sake of simplicity in notation.

$$J_{PN} = \left(\frac{\sigma^2 q}{2}\right)\frac{\phi_1(\phi_2 u_0 + \phi_3)^2}{(\sigma^2 u_0^2 + q)}. \tag{3-26}$$

Thus the probing term is the ratio of two quadratic functions in u_0.

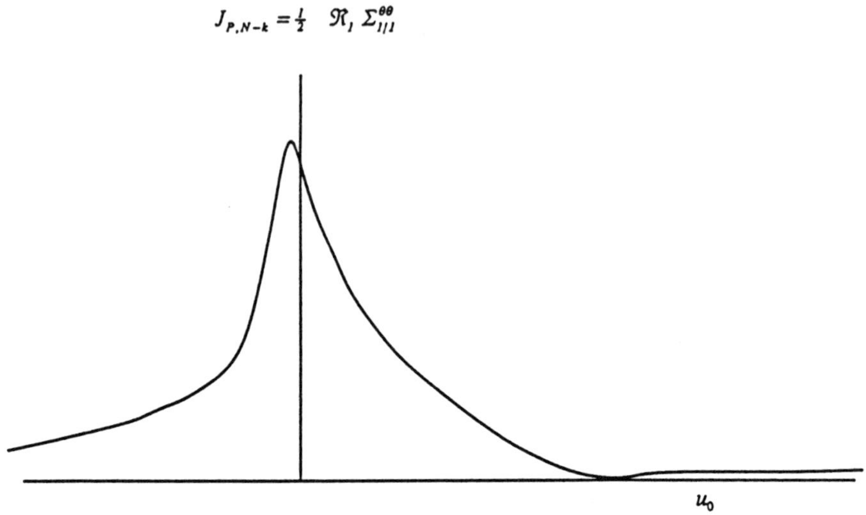

Fig. 4. The probing function.

4. CHARACTERIZATION OF PROBING FUNCTION

In the following we will show that the probing function has the general form shown in Figure 4. The function is positive at all values of u_0. The first derivative of the function has two roots which correspond to the maximum and minimum shown. At the minimum the value of the function is zero. The limits of the function as u_0 approaches plus or minus infinity are strictly positive and identical.

To see that the function is positive at all values of u_0 observe from Equation (3-26) that in

$$J_{PN} = \left(\frac{\sigma^2 q \phi_1}{2}\right) \frac{(\phi_2 u_0 + \phi_3)^2}{\sigma^2 u_0^2 + q}, \tag{4-1}$$

the variances of the coefficients, σ^2, and of the additive error term, q, are both positive. Also from Equation (3-24)

$$\phi_1 = \frac{w_2^2}{\lambda_1 + b^2 w_2} \tag{4-2}$$

is also positive since the penalty weights λ_1 and w_2 are both positive.

Also the function $(\phi_2 u_0 + \phi_3)^2$ and $\sigma^2 u_0^2 + q$ are both positive so J_{PN} is positive for all values of u_0.

Next consider the roots of the probing term. To simplify the notation a little define

$$\psi = \frac{\phi^2 q \phi_1}{2}, \tag{4-3}$$

so that Equations (4-1) becomes

$$J_{PN} = \frac{\psi(\phi_2 u_0 + \phi_3)^2}{\sigma^2 u_0^2 + q}. \tag{4-4}$$

Then the first derivative is

$$\begin{aligned}\frac{\partial J_{PN}}{\partial u_0} &= \psi(\phi_2 u_0 + \phi_3)^2(-1)(\sigma^2 u_0^2 + q)^{-2}(2\sigma^2 u_0) \\ &\quad + \psi(\sigma^2 u_0^2 + q)^{-1}(2)(\phi_2 u_0 + \phi_3)(\phi_2) \\ &= \frac{2\psi(\phi_2^2 u_0 + \phi_2\phi_3)}{\sigma^2 u_0^2 + q} - \frac{2\psi\sigma^2 u_0(\phi_2 u_0 + \phi_3)^2}{\sigma^2 u_0^2 + q)^2}\end{aligned} \tag{4-5}$$

$$\frac{\partial J_{PN}}{\partial u_0} = \frac{2\psi[(\phi_2^2 u_0 + \phi_2\phi_3)(\sigma^2 u_0^2 + q) - \sigma^2 u_0(\phi_2 u_0 + \phi_3)^2]}{(\sigma^2 u_0^2 + q)^2}. \tag{4-6}$$

Since both ψ and $(\sigma_2 u_0^2 + q)^2$ are strictly positive in the MacRae case, we only need to focus on the condition under which the bracketed term would be zero in order to find the roots of the first derivative of the probing term.

Expansion of the term in brackets yields

$$\begin{aligned}(\phi_2^2 u_0 &+ \phi_2\phi_3)\sigma^2 u_0^2 + (\phi_2^2 u_0 + \phi_2\phi_3)q \\ &- \sigma^2 u_0(\phi_2^2 u_0^2 + 2\phi_2\phi_3 u_0 + \phi_3^2) \\ &= \phi_2^2\sigma^2 u_0^3 + \phi_2\phi_3\sigma^2 u_0^2 + \phi_2^2 q u_0 + \phi_2\phi_3 q \\ &- \sigma^2\phi_2^2 u_0^3 - 2\sigma^2\phi_2\phi_3 u_0^2 - \sigma^2\phi_3^2 u_0 \\ &= -\phi_2\phi_3\sigma^2 u_0^2 + (\phi_2^2 q - \sigma^2\phi_3^2)u_0 + \phi_2\phi_3 q.\end{aligned} \tag{4-7}$$

This expression is a quadratic of the form

$$\tilde{a}u_0^2 + \tilde{b}u_0 + \tilde{c} \tag{4-8}$$

with

$$\tilde{a} = -\phi_2\phi_3\sigma^2, \quad \tilde{b} = \phi_2^2 q - \sigma^2\phi_3^2, \tag{4-9}$$

$$\tilde{c} = \phi_2\phi_3 q. \tag{4-9}$$

Therefore the roots of the quadratic Equation (4-7) are

$$r = \frac{-\tilde{b} \pm \sqrt{\tilde{b}^2 - 4\tilde{a}\tilde{c}}}{2\tilde{a}}. \tag{4-10}$$

Then substitution of Equation (4-9) into (4-10) yields

$$r = \frac{1}{-2\phi_2\phi_3\sigma^2}\Big[-(\phi_2^2 q - \sigma^2\phi_3^2) \pm \sqrt{(\phi_2^2 q - \sigma^2\phi_3^2)^2 - 4(-\phi_2\phi_3\sigma^2)(\phi_2\phi_3 q)}\Big]$$

$$= -\frac{1}{2\phi_2\phi_3\sigma^2}\Big[-\phi_2^2 q + \sigma^2\phi_3^2 \pm \sqrt{\phi_2^4 q^2 - 2\phi_2^2 q\sigma^2\phi_3^2 + (\sigma^2)^2\phi_3^4 + 4\phi_2^2\phi_3^2\sigma^2 q}\Big]$$

$$= -\frac{1}{2\phi_2\phi_3\sigma^2}\Big[-\phi_2^2 q + \sigma^2\phi_3^2 \pm \sqrt{(\phi_2^2 q + \sigma^2\phi_3^2)^2}\Big]. \tag{4-11}$$

$$r = -\frac{1}{2\phi_2\phi_3\sigma^2}\left[-\phi_2^2 q + \sigma^2\phi_3^2 \pm (\phi_2^2 q + \sigma^2\phi_3^2)\right]. \tag{4-12}$$

Therefore the first root is

$$r_1 = -\frac{1}{2\phi_2\phi_3\sigma^2}[2\sigma^2\phi_3^2], \tag{4-13}$$

or

$$r_1 = -\frac{\phi_3}{\phi_2}, \tag{4-14}$$

and the second root is

$$r_2 = -\frac{1}{2\phi_2\phi_3\sigma^2}(-2\phi_2^2 q), \tag{4-15}$$

or

$$r_2 = \frac{\phi_2 q}{\phi_3\sigma^2}. \tag{4-16}$$

In order to evaluate these roots it is useful to write them in terms of the parameters of the original model. Before doing so rewrite ϕ_3 from Equation (3-24) as

$$\phi_3 = \frac{1-b^2}{1+b^2}(ac+c) - \tilde{x}_2, \tag{4-17}$$

$$\phi_3 = \frac{(1-b^2)(ac+c) - (1+b^2)\tilde{x}_2}{(1+b^2)}. \tag{4-18}$$

Then substitution of Equations (3-24) and (4-18) into (4-14) yields

$$r_1 = -\frac{(1-b^2)(ac+c) - (1+b^2)\tilde{x}_2}{(1-b^2)ab}, \tag{4-19}$$

$$r_1 = -\frac{c(a+1)}{ab} + \frac{(1+b^2)}{(1-b^2)}\frac{\tilde{x}_2}{ab}. \tag{4-20}$$

Also the second root is obtained by substituting Equations (3-24) and (4-18) into (4-16) to obtain

$$r_2 = \frac{(1-b^2)(ab)}{(1-b^2)(ac+c) - (1+b^2)\tilde{x}_2}\left(\frac{q}{\sigma^2}\right), \tag{4-21}$$

$$r_2 = \frac{(1-b^2)(ab)q}{[(1-b^2)(a+1)c - (1_b^2)\tilde{x}_2]\,\sigma^2}. \tag{4-22}$$

For the MacRae problem

$$\begin{aligned} w_2 &= \lambda_1 = 1, \quad \tilde{x}_2 = 0, \quad a = 0.7, \\ b &= -0.5, \quad c = 3.5, \quad q = 0.2, \quad \sigma^2 = 0.5. \end{aligned} \tag{4-23}$$

For this case the roots become

$$r_1 = -\frac{c(a+1)}{ab} = -\frac{(3.5)(1.7)}{(0.7)(-0.5)} = \frac{5.95}{0.35} = 17.0, \tag{4-24}$$

and

$$\begin{aligned} r_2 &= \frac{(1-b^2)(ab)(q)}{[(1-b^2)(a+1)c - (1+b^2)\tilde{x}_2]\,\sigma^2} \\ &= \frac{(1-0.25)(0.7)(-0.5)(0.2)}{[(1-0.25)(1.7)(3.5)](0.5)} = \frac{-(0.75)(0.7)(0.1)}{[(0.75)(5.95)](0.5)} \\ &= -\frac{0.0525}{2.231} = -0.0235. \end{aligned} \tag{4-25}$$

So in summary the first derivative of the probing function with respect to the control in period zero has two roots, one positive and one negative. Therefore, we know that the probing components has two extreme points.

Next evaluate the function at these two extreme. First evaluate the probing function at the first root by substituting the control value u_0 from Equation (4-14) into (4-1) to obtain

$$\begin{aligned} J_{PN} &= \left(\frac{\sigma^2 q\phi_1}{2}\right)\frac{(\phi_2 u_0 + \phi_3)^2}{\sigma^2 u_0^2 + q} \\ &= \left(\frac{\sigma^2 q\phi_1}{2}\right)\left\{\phi_2\left(-\frac{\phi_3}{\phi_2}\right) + \phi_3\right\}^2\left\{\phi_2\left(-\frac{\phi_3}{\phi_2}\right)^2 + q\right\}^{-1} \\ &= \left(\frac{\sigma^2 q\phi_1}{2}\right)\{0\}\left\{\frac{\sigma^2\phi_3^2}{\phi_2^2} + q\right\}^{-1} = 0. \end{aligned} \tag{4-26}$$

So in this MacRae case the value of the probing function at the positive root of 17 is zero.

To evaluate the function at the second root substitute Equation (4-16) into (4-1) to obtain

$$
\begin{aligned}
J_{PN} &= \left(\frac{\sigma^2 q\phi_1}{2}\right)\frac{(\phi_2 u_0 + \phi_3)^2}{\sigma^2 u_0^2 + q} \\
&= \left(\frac{\sigma^2 q\phi_1}{2}\right)\left\{\phi_2\left(-\frac{\phi_2 q}{\phi_3\sigma^2}\right) + \phi_3\right\}^2 \left\{\phi_2\left(\frac{\phi_2 q}{\phi_3\sigma^2}\right)^2 + q\right\}^{-1} \\
&= \left(\frac{\sigma^2 q\phi_1}{2}\right)\left\{\frac{\phi_2^q}{\phi_3\sigma^2} + \phi_3\right\}^2 \left\{\frac{\phi_2^2 q^2}{\phi_3^2\sigma^2} + q\right\}^{-1},
\end{aligned}
\tag{4-27}
$$

$$
J_{PN} = \underset{A}{\left(\frac{\sigma^2 q\phi_1}{2}\right)} \underset{B}{\left(\frac{\phi_2^2 q + \phi_3^2\sigma^2}{\phi_3\sigma^2}\right)^2} \underset{C}{\left\{\frac{\phi_2^2 q^2 + \phi_3^2\sigma^2 q}{\phi_3^2\sigma^2}\right\}^{-1}}. \tag{4-28}
$$

If the variance of the parameter (σ^2) and of the additive error term (q) are nonzero then term A will be strictly positive provided that ϕ_1 is positive. And from Equation (4-2)

$$
\phi_1 = \frac{w_2^2}{\lambda_1 + b^2 w_2}, \tag{4-29}
$$

ϕ_1 will be positive if the penalty weights w_2 and λ_1 are positive which is the case in tracking problems. So term A is positive.

Term B is a square so it will be strictly positive provided that either of the variances are nonzero. Term C will also be positive under the same restriction. Therefore the probing function J_{PN} will be positive at the second root provided that σ^2 and q are nonzero.

To check the limit of the probing term as u_0 goes to either plus or minus infinity use Equation (3-26) to obtain

$$
\lim_{u_0 \to \pm\infty} J_{PN} = \frac{\sigma^2 q\phi_1\phi_2^2}{2\sigma^2} = \frac{q\phi_1\phi_2^2}{2}. \tag{4-30}
$$

Then substitution of Equation (3-24) into (4-30) yields

$$
\lim_{u_0 \to \pm\infty} J_{PN} = \frac{q}{2}\left(\frac{w_2^2}{\lambda_1 + b^2 w_2}\right)\left(\frac{1 - b^2}{1 + b^2}\right)^2 a^2 b^2. \tag{4-31}
$$

The right hand side of Equation (4-31) is positive so long as q is nonzero and the penalty weights w_2 and λ_1 are strictly positive which is the case in stochastic control tracking problems. Thus the probing term approaches a positive limit when u_0 approaches either plus or minus infinity.

In the case of the MacRae parameter values this limit is

$$\frac{1}{2}\frac{1}{5}\left(\frac{1}{1+\frac{1}{4}}\right)\left(\frac{1-\frac{1}{4}}{1+\frac{1}{4}}\right)^2\left(\frac{7}{10}\frac{1}{2}\right)^2$$

$$=\frac{1}{10}\left(\frac{4}{5}\right)\left(\frac{3}{4}\frac{4}{5}\right)^2\left(\frac{7}{20}\right)^2$$

$$=\frac{1}{10}\frac{4}{5}\frac{9}{25}\frac{49}{400}=0.003528.$$

So in summary the probing function is positive at all values of u_0. The function has two extreme points – a minimum where the function value is zero in the positive orthant and a maximum with a positive function value in the negative orthant. Finally, the limits of the function as u_0 approaches plus or minus infinity are strictly positive and identical.

This completes the derivation and characterization of the first of three components of the cost-to-go. Next we consider the cautionary component and then the deterministic component.

5. CAUTIONARY TERM

In this section we show that the cautionary term is a convex quadratic function of the zero period control, u_0. From Equation (K11-36) the cautionary term is

$$J_{CN}=J_{CN}^{k+1}+J_{CN}^{F} \tag{5-1}$$

where J_{CN}^{k+1} cautionary cost for period $k+1$; J_{CN}^{F} future cautionary cost. Then from Equation (K11-27) for $k=0$

$$J_{CN}^{k+1}=\frac{1}{2}\,tr(K_1^{xx}\Sigma_{1/0}^{xx})+tr(K_1^{\theta x}\Sigma_{1/0}^{x\theta}+\frac{1}{2}\,tr(K_1^{\theta\theta}\Sigma_{1/0}^{\theta\theta}). \tag{5-2}$$

Consider first the K terms in Equation (5-2), i.e. the Riccati matrices. From the lines above Equation (K11-20)

$$K_j^{xx}=\tilde{K}_j \tag{5-3}$$

and from Equation (K11-7) in this scalar case

$$K_2^{xx}=w_2 \tag{5-4}$$

and

$$K_1^{xx}=a(1-w_2b^2\mu_1)w_2a+w_1=(1-w_2b^2\mu_1)a^2w_2+w_1. \tag{5-5}$$

Next calculate the $K_1^{\theta x}$ term. Begin with Equation (K11-20)

$$K_2^{\theta x} = 0, \tag{5-6}$$

and from Equation (K11-21) with $D = 1$, $b_\theta = 1$ and $a_\theta = 0$

$$K_1^{\theta x} = f_{\theta 1}^{x} w_2 a - \left[(f_{\theta 1}^{x} w_2 b) + p_x^2 \right] \mu_1 [b w_2 a]. \tag{5-7}$$

Substitution of Equation (3-13) into (5-7) yields

$$K_1^{\theta x} = a w_2 u_{01} - [(b w_2 u_{01} + p_2^x] \, \mu_1 [a b w_2]. \tag{5-8}$$

Finally calculate the last of the Riccati matrices, $K_1^{\theta\theta}$. Begin with Equation (K11-25)

$$K_2^{\theta\theta} = 0, \tag{5-9}$$

and then use Equation (3-13), $D = 1$ and $b_\theta = 1$ in the line after Equation (K11-25) to obtain

$$K_1^{\theta\theta} = w_2 u_{01}^2 - [u_{01} w_2 b + p_2^x] \mu_1 [b w_2 u_{01} + p_2^x], \tag{5-10}$$

$$K_1^{\theta\theta} = w_2 u_{01}^2 - \mu_1 (b w_2 u_{01} + p_2^x)^2. \tag{5-11}$$

Next consider the covariance terms, Σ in Equation (5-2). They were derived earlier in Equations (1-10), (1-14) and (1-18) as

$$\Sigma_{1/0}^{xx} = \sigma^2 u_0^2 + q, \quad \Sigma_{1/0}^{\theta x} = \sigma^2 u_0, \quad \Sigma_{1/0}^{\theta\theta} = \sigma^2. \tag{5-12}$$

Substitutions of Equations (5-5), (5-8), (5-11) and (5-12) into (5-2) for the scalar case yields

$$\begin{aligned} J_{CN}^{k+1} &= \frac{1}{2} \left[(1 - w_2 b^2 \mu_1) a^2 w_2 + w_1 \right] (\sigma^2 u_0^2 + q) \\ &\quad + \left[a w_2 u_{01} - (b w_2 u_{01} + p_2^x) \mu_1 (a b w_2) \right] \sigma^2 u_0 \\ &\quad + \frac{1}{2} \left[w_2 u_{01}^2 - \mu_1 (b w_2 u_{01} + p_2^x)^2 \right] \sigma^2, \end{aligned} \tag{5-13}$$

$$\begin{aligned} J_{CN}^{k+1} &= \frac{1}{2} [a^2 w_2 + w_1 - \mu_1 a^2 b^2 w_2^2] (\sigma^2 u_0^2 + q) \\ &\quad + \left[a w_2 u_{01} - \mu_1 (a b w_2)(b w_2 u_{01} + p_2^x) \right] \sigma^2 u_0 \\ &\quad + \frac{1}{2} \left[w_2 u_{01}^2 - \mu_1 (b w_2 u_{01} + p_2^x)^2 \right] \sigma^2, \end{aligned} \tag{5-14}$$

or

$$\begin{aligned}
J_{CN}^{k+1} &= \frac{\sigma^2 u_0^2}{2}\left[a^2 w_2 + w_1 - \mu_1 (abw_2)^2\right] \\
&\quad + \frac{2\sigma^2 u_0}{2}\left[aw_2 u_{01} - \mu_1 (abw_2)(bw_2 u_{01} + p_2^x)\right] + \frac{\sigma^2}{2} \\
&\times \left[w_2 u_{01}^2 - \mu_1 (bw_2 u_{01} + p_2^x)^2\right] \\
&\quad + \frac{q}{2}\left[a^2 w_2 + w_1 - \mu_1 (abw_2)^2\right] \\
&= \frac{\sigma^2 w_2}{2}[a^2 u_0^2 + 2au_{01}u_0 + u_{01}^2] - \frac{\sigma^2 \mu_1}{2} \\
&\times \left[(abw_2)^2 u_0^2 + 2(abw_2)(bw_2 u_{01} + p_2^x)u_0 + (bw_2 u_{01} + p_2^x)^2\right] \\
&\quad + \frac{q}{2}[a^2 w_2 + w_1 - \mu_1 a^2 b^2 w_2^2] + \left(\frac{\sigma^2 w_1}{2}\right) u_0^2 .
\end{aligned}$$

$$\begin{aligned}
J_{CN}^{k+1} &= \frac{\sigma^2 w_2}{2}(au_0 + u_{01}) - \frac{\sigma^2 \mu_1}{2}(abw_2 u_0 + bw_2 u_{01} + p_2^x)^2 \\
&\quad + \frac{q}{2}\left[a^2 w_2 + w_1 - \mu_1 (abw_2)^2\right] + \left(\frac{\sigma^2 w_1}{2}\right) u_0^2 . \qquad (5\text{-}15)
\end{aligned}$$

Since from Equation (2-22)

$$u_{01} = \alpha u_0 + \beta$$

one can see by inspection of Equation (5-15) that J_{CN}^{k+1} is a quadratic function of u_0.

Next consider the future cautionary cost. From Equation (K11-29) this is

$$J_{CN}^{F} = \frac{1}{2}\, trK_2^{xx} Q_1 + trK_2^{\theta\theta} G_1 = \frac{1}{2}\, w_2 q \qquad (5\text{-}16)$$

since $K_2^{\theta\theta} = 0$. Therefore from Equations (5-1), (5-15) and (5-16) the total cautionary cost is

$$\begin{aligned}
J_{CN} &= \frac{\sigma^2 w_2}{2}(au_0 + u_{01})^2 - \frac{\sigma^2 \mu_1}{2}(abw_2 u_0 + bw_2 u_{01} + p_2^x)^2 \\
&\quad + \frac{q}{2}\left[a^2 w_2 + w_2 + w_1 - \mu_1 (abw_2)^2\right] + \left(\frac{\sigma^2 w_1}{2}\right) u_0^2, \qquad (5\text{-}17)
\end{aligned}$$

where from Equation (3-14)

$$\mu_1 = \frac{1}{\lambda_1 + b^2 w_2} .$$

Since from Equation (3-11)

$$p_2^x = w_2(x_{02} - \tilde{x}_2), \tag{5-18}$$

and from Equation (2-30)

$$x_{02} = \rho u_0 + \eta. \tag{5-19}$$

Substitution of Equation (5-19) in (5-18) yields p_2^x as a linear function of u_0.

$$p_2^x = w_2(\rho u_0 + \eta - \tilde{x}_2). \tag{5-20}$$

Also from Equation (2-22)

$$u_{01} = \alpha u_0 + \beta, \tag{5-21}$$

so u_{01} is a linear function of u_0.

Next consider some of the components of the right hand side of Equation (5-17) and substitute (5-20) and (5-21) into them. Begin with a portion of the first term, i.e.

$$au_0 + u_{01} = au_0 + \alpha u_0 + \beta = (a + \alpha)u_0 + \beta. \tag{5-22}$$

$$au_0 + u_{01} = v_1 u_0 + v_2, \tag{5-23}$$

where

$$\begin{aligned} v_1 &= a + \alpha \\ v_2 &= \beta. \end{aligned}$$

Next consider a portion of the second term of the right hand side of Equation (5-17) and substitute (5-20) and (5-21) into it to obtain

$$\begin{aligned} abw_2 u_0 \; + \; & bw_2 u_{01} + p_2^x \\ &= abw_2 u_0 + bw_2(\alpha u_0 + \beta) + w_2(\rho u_0 + \eta - \tilde{x}_2) \\ &= w_2 \left\{ [(a + \alpha)b + \rho]u_0 + b\beta + \eta - \tilde{x}_2 \right\}, \qquad (5\text{-}24) \\ &= \theta_1 u_0 + \theta_2 \qquad (5\text{-}25) \end{aligned}$$

where

$$\begin{aligned} \theta_1 &= w_2 \left[(a + \alpha)b + \rho \right] \\ \theta_2 &= w_2 \left[b\beta + \eta - \tilde{x}_2 \right]. \end{aligned}$$

Note that the Greek letter theta is being used in a different manner here than earlier in the paper. At the beginning of the paper it was used as the parameter vector. Here it is being used as a pair of parameter than help to simplify the notation.

Also, to further simplify Equation (5-17) consider the third term on the right hand side and let

$$\gamma = \frac{q}{2}\left[a^2 w_2 + w_2 + w_1 - \mu_1 (abw_2)^2\right]. \tag{5-26}$$

Then substitution of Equations (5-23), (5-24) and (5-25) into (5-17) yields

$$\begin{aligned} J_{CN} &= \frac{\sigma^2 w_2}{2}(v_1 u_0 + v_2)^2 - \frac{\sigma^2 \mu_1}{2}(\theta_1 u_0 + \theta_2)^2 + \gamma + \frac{\sigma^2 w_1}{2} u_0^2 \\ &= \frac{\sigma^2}{2}\left[w_2(v_1 u_0 + v_2)^2 - \mu_1(\theta_1 u_0 + \theta_2)^2 + w_1 u_0^2\right] + \gamma \\ &= \frac{\sigma^2}{2}\left[w_2(v_1^2 u_0^2 + 2 v_1 v_2 u_0 + v_2^2)\right. \\ &\quad \left. - \mu_1(\theta_1^2 u_0^2 + 2\theta_1\theta_2 u_0 + \theta_2^2) + w_1 u_0^2\right] + \gamma \\ &= \frac{\sigma^2}{2}\left[(w_2 v_1^2 - \mu_1 \theta_1^2 + w_1) u_0^2\right. \\ &\quad \left. + 2(w_2 v_1 v_2 - \mu_1 \theta_1 \theta_2) u_0 + w_2 v_2^2 - \mu_1 \theta_2^2\right] + \gamma, \end{aligned} \tag{5-27}$$

or

$$J_{CN} = \delta_1 u_0^2 + \delta_2 u_0 + \delta_3, \tag{5-28}$$

where

$$\begin{aligned} \delta_1 &= \frac{\sigma^2}{2}[w_2 v_1^2 - \mu_1 \theta_1^2 + w_1] \\ \delta_2 &= \sigma^2[w_2 v_1 v_2 - \mu_1 \theta_1 \theta_2] \\ \delta_3 &= \frac{\sigma^2}{2}[w_2 v_2^2 - \mu_1 \theta_2^2] + \gamma. \end{aligned}$$

Equation (5-28) shows that the cautionary component is a quadratic function of the zero period control, u_0. To show that the cautionary function is convex for the case at hand we need to show that $\delta_1 > 0$.

In order to evaluate δ_1 it is useful first to develop some of the component terms. Begin with v_1. From the line below Equation (5-23)

$$v_1 = a + \alpha, \tag{5-29}$$

and from (2-22)

$$\alpha = -\mu_1 a b^2 w_2. \tag{5-30}$$

Substitution of Equation (5-30) into (5-29) yields

$$v_1 = a - \mu_1 a b^2 w_2 = a(1 - \mu_1 b^2 w_2), \tag{5-31}$$

where from Equation (3-14)

$$\mu_1 = \frac{1}{\lambda_1 + b^2 w_2}. \tag{5-32}$$

The next term in the expression for δ_1 to develop is θ_1. From the line below Equation (5-25)

$$\theta_1 = w_2[(a + \alpha)b + \rho] \tag{5-33}$$

and from the line below Equation (2-26)

$$\rho = (a + \alpha)b. \tag{5-34}$$

Substitution of Equation (5-34) into (5-33) yields

$$\theta_1 = w_2[2(a + \alpha)b]. \tag{5-35}$$

Then substitution of Equation (5-30) into (5-35) yields

$$\theta_1 = w_2\left[2(a - \mu_1 a b^2 w_2)b\right] = w_2\left[(2a(1 - \mu_1 b^2 w_2)b\right]. \tag{5-36}$$

This expression can be simplified by substituting Equation (5-31) into it to obtain

$$\theta_1 = w_2[2v_1 b] = 2w_2 b v_1. \tag{5-37}$$

Now we are in a position to simplify the definition δ_1 by substituting Equation (5-37) into the line below (5-28) to obtain

$$\begin{aligned}
\delta_1 &= \frac{\sigma^2}{2}\left[w_2 v_1^2 - \mu_1(2w_2 b v_1)^2 + w_1\right] \\
&= \frac{\sigma^2}{2}[w_2 v_1^2 - 4\mu_1 w_2^2 b^2 v_1^2 + w_1] \\
&= \frac{\sigma^2}{2}\left[(w_2 - 4\mu_1 w_2^2 b^2)v_1^2 + w_1\right] \\
&= \frac{\sigma^2}{2}\left[w_2(1 - 4\mu_1 w_2 b^2)v_1^2 + w_1\right].
\end{aligned} \tag{5-38}$$

Substitution of Equation (5-32) into (5-38) yields

$$\begin{aligned}
\delta_1 &= \frac{\sigma^2}{2}\left[w_2\left(1 - \frac{4b^2 w_2}{\lambda_1 + b^2 w_2}\right)v_1^2 + w_1\right] \\
&= \frac{\sigma^2}{2}\left[w_2\left(\frac{\lambda_1 + b^2 w_2 - 4b^2 w_2}{\lambda_1 + b^2 w_2}\right)v_1^2 + w_1\right],
\end{aligned} \tag{5-39}$$

or

$$\delta_1 = \frac{\sigma^2}{2}\left[w_2\left(\frac{\lambda_1 - 3b^2 w_2}{\lambda_1 + b^2 w_2}\right)v_1^2 + w_1\right]. \tag{5-40}$$

Since v_1^2, σ^2, w_2, w_1 and λ_1 are positive, a sufficient condition for δ_1 to be positive is that

$$\lambda_1 > 3b^2 w_2. \tag{5-41}$$

This condition is met in the case at hand since

$$\begin{aligned} 1 &> (3)(-0.5)^2(1) \\ 1 &> 0.75. \end{aligned} \tag{5-42}$$

Also, a necessary condition for δ_1 to be positive from Equation (5-40) is

$$w_2\left(\frac{\lambda_1 - 3b^2 w_2}{\lambda_1 + b^2 w_2}\right)v_1^2 + w_1 > 0. \tag{5-43}$$

Causal inspection of the cautionary term elements in Equations (5-2) and (5-16) might lead one to believe that it is a convex function. However, if one can find a set of parameter values for which the inequality above is not true then there will exist some cases in which the cautionary term is not convex but rather concave.

For example, consider a case in which the weights in the penalty function are equal to one as in the MacRae case, i.e.

$$w_2 = w_1 = \lambda_1 = 1. \tag{5-44}$$

Also, one can drop the inequality and simplify Equation (5-43) by substituting out the v_1 term using (5-31), i.e.

$$v_1 = a(1 - \mu_1 b^2 w_2). \tag{5-45}$$

And this expression in turn can be simplified by using Equations (5-32)

$$\mu_1 = \frac{1}{\lambda_1 + b^2 w_2}. \tag{5-46}$$

Using the values of Equation (5-44) in (5-46) converts it to

$$\mu_1 = \frac{1}{1 + b^2}. \tag{5-47}$$

Substitution of Equations (5-44) and (5-47) into (5-45) then yields

$$v_1 = a\left(1 - \frac{b^2}{1 + b^2}\right) = a\left(\frac{1 + b^2 - b^2}{1 + b^2}\right) = \frac{a}{1 + b^2}. \tag{5-48}$$

Substitution of Equations (5-44) and (5-48) into (5-43) and dropping the inequality yields

$$\begin{aligned} w_2\left(\frac{\lambda_1 - 3b^2 w_2}{\lambda_1 + b^2 w_2}\right) v_1^2 + w_1 &= \left(\frac{1-3b^2}{1+b^2}\right)\frac{a^2}{(1+b^2)^2} + 1 \\ &= \frac{a^2(1-3b^2)}{(1+b^2)^3} + 1 = \frac{a^2(1-3b^2) + (1+b^2)^3}{(1+b^2)^3}. \end{aligned} \tag{5-49}$$

The last expression will be negative or positive depending on the sign of

$$\zeta = a^2(1-3b^2) + (1+b^2)^3. \tag{5-50}$$

Examine the value of this function when $a = 5$ and $b = 2$. In this case

$$\begin{aligned} \zeta &= 25(1-12) + (5)^3 = 25(-11) + 125 \\ &= -275 + 125 = -150. \end{aligned} \tag{5-51}$$

So this provides a case in which δ_1 is negative and the cautionary cost term is concave. Since the deterministic term is convex as will be discussed in the next section, the addition of a convex deterministic term to a concave cautionary term could produce a nonconvex cost-to-go even if the probing term was convex. Therefore, there are at least two possible sources of nonconvexities in the cost-to-go, namely (1) the initial variance of the b parameter and (2) a set of parameter values which are such that the cautionary term is concave.

6. DETERMINISTIC TERM

Like the cautionary term the deterministic term has two components

$$J_{DN} = J_{DN}^{Nk} + J_{DN}^{F}, \tag{6-1}$$

where J_{DN}^{Nk} = the deterministic cost for period k and period N; J_{DN}^{F} = the deterministic cost for future periods other than k and N.

From Equation (K11-26) for $k = 0$ and with $F = 0$ in this tracking model

$$J_{DN}^{Nk} = \frac{1}{2}(u_0 - \tilde{u}_0)'\Lambda_0(u_0 - \tilde{u}_0) + \frac{1}{2}(x_{02} - \tilde{x}_2)'W_2(x_{02} - \tilde{x}_2), \tag{6-2}$$

or in scalar form

$$J_{DN}^{Nk} = \frac{\lambda_0}{2}(u_0 - \tilde{u}_0)^2 + \frac{w_2}{2}(x_{02} - \tilde{x}_2)^2. \tag{6-3}$$

Then substitution of Equation (2-26) into (6-3) yields

$$J_{DN}^{Nk} = \frac{\lambda_0}{2}(u_0 - \tilde{u}_0)^2 + \frac{w_2}{2}(\rho u_0 + \eta - \tilde{x}_2)^2. \tag{6-4}$$

Next we consider the deterministic cost for future periods other than k and N by using Equation (K11-28) for $k = 0$

$$\begin{aligned} J_{DN}^F &= \frac{1}{2}(x_{01} - \tilde{x}_1)' W_1 (x_{01} - \tilde{x}_1) \\ &\quad + \frac{1}{2}(u_{01} - \tilde{u}_1)' \Lambda_1 (u_{01} - \tilde{u}_1), \end{aligned} \tag{6-5}$$

or in the scalar case

$$J_{DN}^F = \frac{w_1}{2}(x_{01} - \tilde{x}_1)^2 + \frac{\lambda_1}{2}(u_{01} - \tilde{u}_1)^2. \tag{6-6}$$

Then substitution of Equations (2-20) and (2-22) into (6-6) yields

$$J_{DN}^F = \frac{w_1}{2}(ax_0 + bu_0 + c - \tilde{x}_1)^2 + \frac{\lambda_1}{2}(\alpha u_0 + \beta - \tilde{u}_1)^2. \tag{6-7}$$

The total deterministic cost is then obtained by substituting Equations (6-4) and (6-7) into (6-1)

$$\begin{aligned} J_{DN} &= \frac{\lambda_0}{2}(u_0 - \tilde{u}_0)^2 + \frac{w_2}{2}(\rho u_0 + \eta - \tilde{x}_2)^2 \\ &\quad + \frac{w_1}{2}(ax_0 + bu_0 + c - \tilde{x}_1)^2 + \frac{\lambda_1}{2}(\alpha u_0 + \beta - \tilde{u}_1)^2. \end{aligned} \tag{6-8}$$

So the deterministic cost is a quadratic function of the initial control value u_0, i.e.

$$J_{DN} = \psi_1 u_0^2 + \psi_2 u_0 + \psi_3. \tag{6-9}$$

7. TOTAL COST-TO-GO

From Equation (K11-38) the total cost-to-go for period $k = 0$ is

$$J_N = J_{DN} + J_{CN} + J_{PN}. \tag{7-1}$$

Substitution of Equations (3-26), (5-28) and (6-9) into (7-1) yields

$$\begin{aligned} J_N &= (\psi_1 + \delta_1)u_0^2 + (\psi_2 + \delta_2)u_0 + (\psi_3 + \delta_3) \\ &\quad + \left(\frac{\sigma^2 q}{2}\right) \frac{\phi_1(\phi_2 u_0 + \phi_3)^2}{(\sigma^2 u_0^2 + q)}. \end{aligned} \tag{7-2}$$

The derivative of this function is a complex function of u_0, and the function has several extreme points.

Since analytical methods do not provide much insight into the character of the total cost-to-go function (7-2) we have used numerical methods to analyze the function.

As the analysis above suggests there are at least two circumstances under which nonconvexities can occur in this simple adaptive control problem. Both are affected by the value of σ^2. In our experience if σ^2 is sufficiently small nonconvexities do not occur. That is, if the initial parameter uncertainty is small enough one need not be concerned with local optima. However, as the initial parameter uncertainty increases two potential sources of nonconvexities can arise. The first source of nonconvexities is in the probing term and the second source is in the cautionary term. We will discuss these in turn giving numerical examples of each one.

7.1. Nonconvexities from the Probing Term

This source appears to be fundamental to adaptive control and occurs as σ^2 gets large in the MacRae problem even with the base set of parameter values for a, b and c. Moreover, it occurs even for relatively small values of σ^2. For example the nonconvexity appears when σ^2 is increased from the MacRae values of 0.5 to magnitudes as small as 2. The reason it occurs is that when the initial parameter uncertainty is large there is a premium attached to choosing large positive or negative values of the control variable in order to decrease the variance of the uncertain parameter. This source of nonconvexities is discussed by Mizrach (1991, pp. 534–538).

Consider first a case where the MacRae parameter values are used for all the parameters except the covariance of the b parameter σ^2. For this term we use the value of $\sigma^2 = 4$ rather than 0.5 in order to illustrate a case where the nonconvexity is sharply defined.

For this case the deterministic term is as shown in Figure 5. It has the expected quadratic and convex shape. Consider next the cautionary term which is shown in Figure 6. It is also quadratic and is convex in this as in most cases.

Thirdly consider the probing term which is shown in Figure 7. It has the shape which was discussed earlier with a peak near $u_0 = 0$. Accordingly the maximum lies at $u_0 = -0.235$, the minimum at $u_0 = 17.0$ and the asymptotic value is 0.003528 as derived in Equations (4-7), (4-8) and (4-13). Unlike Figures 5 and 6, Figure 7 is not drawn to scale in order to emphasize its shape.

When the three components are added the resulting total cost-to-go with $\sigma^2 = 4$ is as shown in Figure 8.

The nonconvexity results in their being two local minima for the function, one for a positive and one for a negative value of u_0. The two minima are at

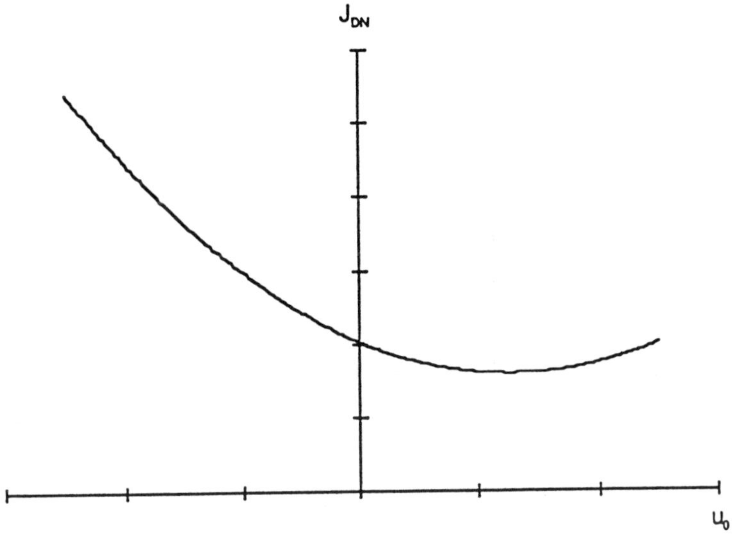

Fig. 5. Deterministic term.

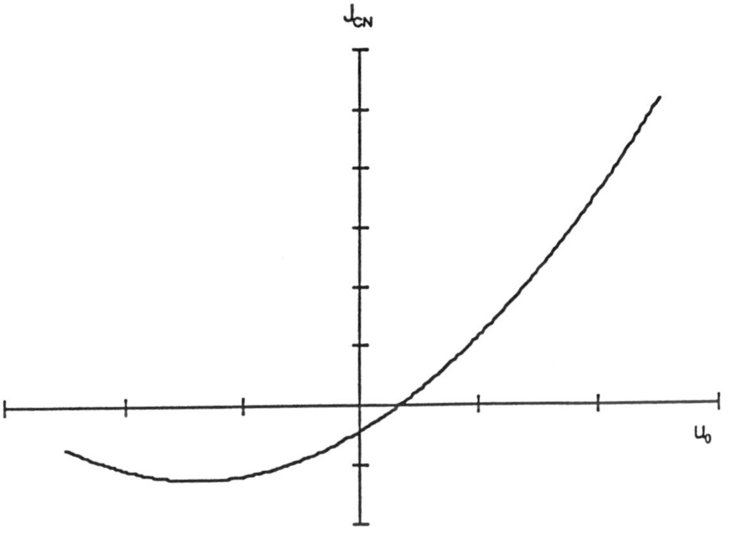

Fig. 6. Cautionary term.

$u_0 = -1.58$ with a value of $J_N = 5.795$ and at $u_0 = 0.51$ with a value of $J_N = 19.521$.

Since the shape of the total cost-to-go function is altered substantially as σ^2 is increased we have plotted this function with various values of σ^2 in Figure 9. When σ^2 is small the function is convex but as σ^2 gets progressively larger the nonconvexity appears and two local optima occur.

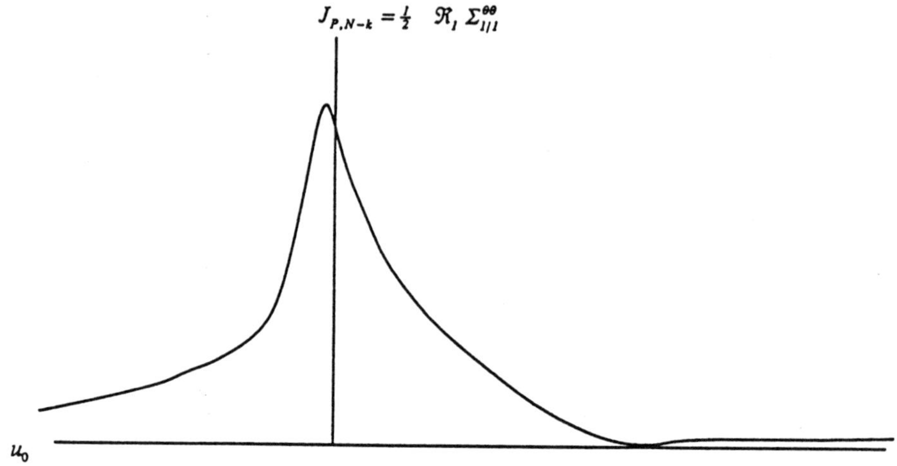

Fig. 7. Probing term.

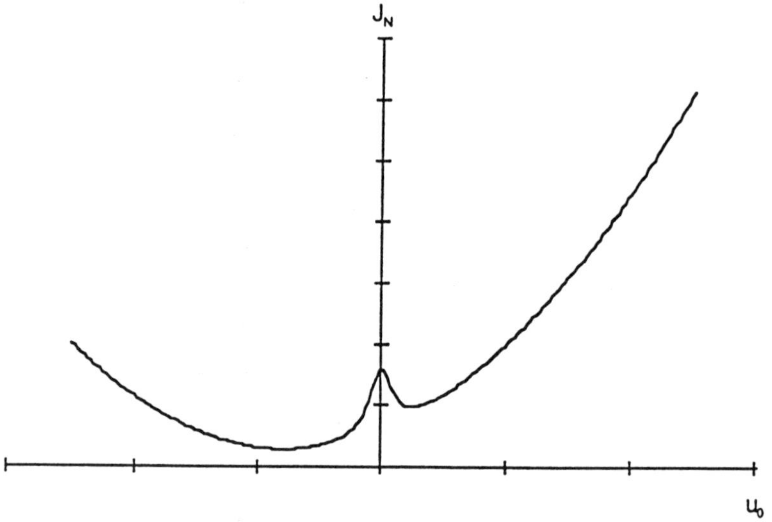

Fig. 8. Total cost-to-go for period zero.

7.2. Nonconvexities from the Cautionary Term

The second potential source of nonconvexities in the MacRae problem is the cautionary term. This nonconvexity occurs when the cautionary term switches from convex to concave. This happens in the MacRae problem when the parameters a and b have certain combinations of values as shown in Equation (5-50). In a slightly more general way, when the penalty weights are not equal to one as they are in the MacRae problem, the shape of the

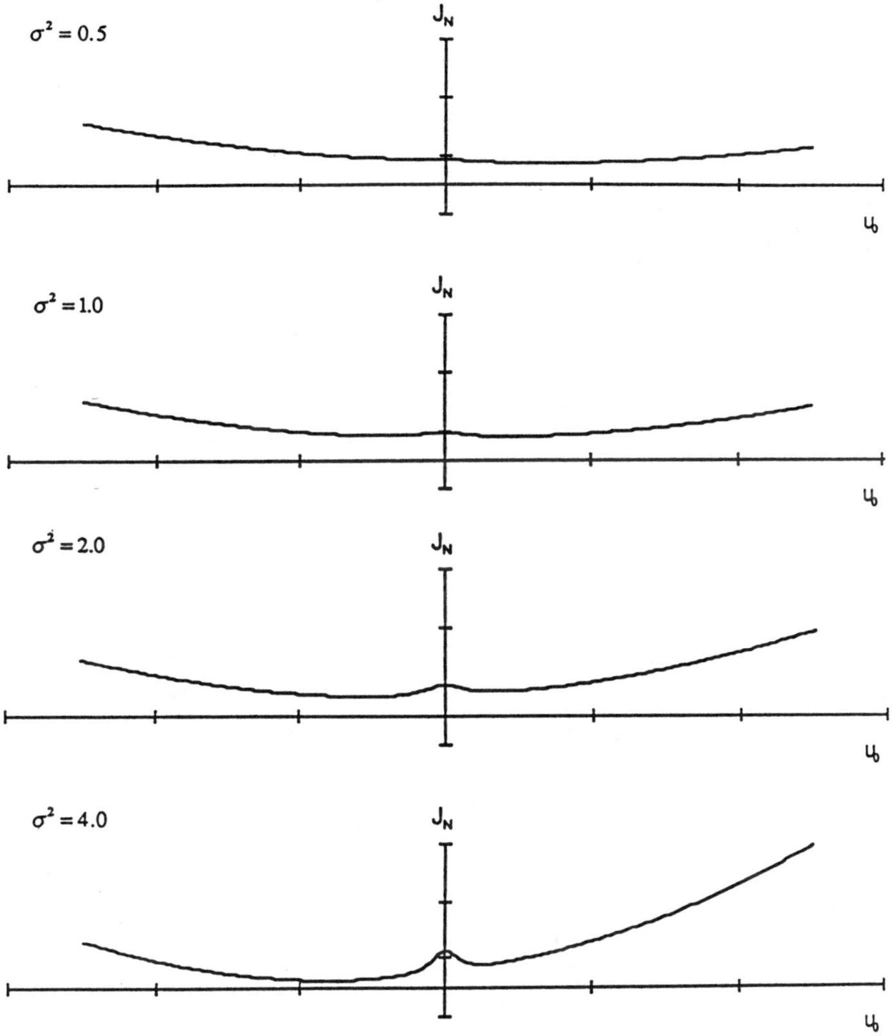

Fig. 9. Effects of parameter variance on cost-to-go function.

cautionary term depends on values for a, b, w_1, w_2 and λ_1 as shown in Equations (5-42) and (5-49).

However, even if the cautionary term is concave the cost-to-go function will usually be convex because the deterministic term is always convex and is frequently larger in magnitude than the cautionary term. A crucial determinant of the magnitude of the cautionary term is the parameter variance, σ^2. In our experience it is only when this variance gets large that a concave cautionary function can overcome the convex deterministic function to produce a concave cost-to-go function.

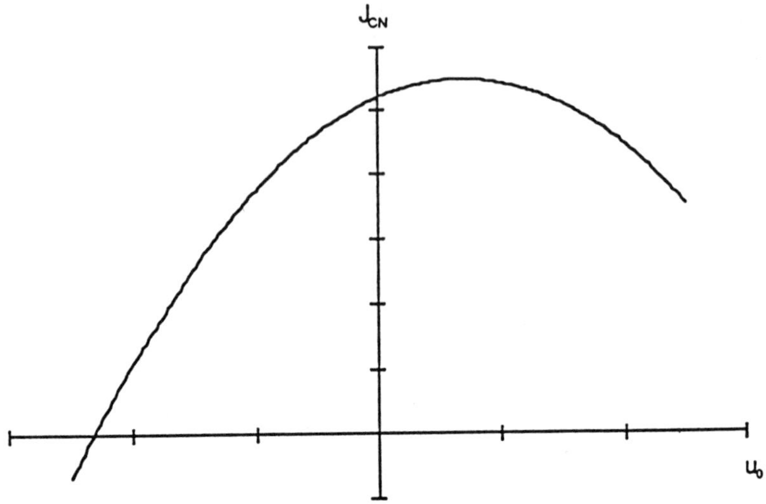

Fig. 10. Cautionary cost: a concave case.

We found a concave cautionary function when we changed the MacRae values of $a = 0.7$ and $b = -0.5$ to values of $a = 5$ and $b = 2$. This resulted in a concave cost-to-go function only after σ^2 was increased from the MacRae level of 0.5 to a level beyond 20. We are hopeful that these kinds of parameter values and variances will prove to be unusual in applied adaptive control problems so that this source of nonconvexity will be uncommon.

As was discussed in Section 5 certain parameter values will result in the cautionary term being concave rather than convex. An example of this sort is shown in Figure 10. Since both the deterministic term and the cautionary term are quadratic functions the sum of these two components of the cost-to-go will also be a quadratic function.

The potential impact of a concave cautionary function on the total cost-to-go is illustrated in Figure 11.

When the cautionary function is not only concave but also large enough to overcome the convex shape of the deterministic term as occurs in Figure 11 the total cost-to-go is concave except for the effect of the probing term. The probing term adds a spike to the function. Thus as is shown at the bottom of Figure 11 the total cost-to-go is like a hill with a spike on top. Since we are minimizing the optimal solution will occur at large values of u_0, either plus or minus and will occur at an upper or lower bound of u_0 if they exist.

However, there is another danger this case illustrates. If one used a gradient method to solve this problem and began with a small positive value of u_0, the algorithm could find the local optimum which is just to the right of zero. This of course is one of the most costly solutions rather than the least costly solutions. While the danger of such an occurrence is real and makes clear

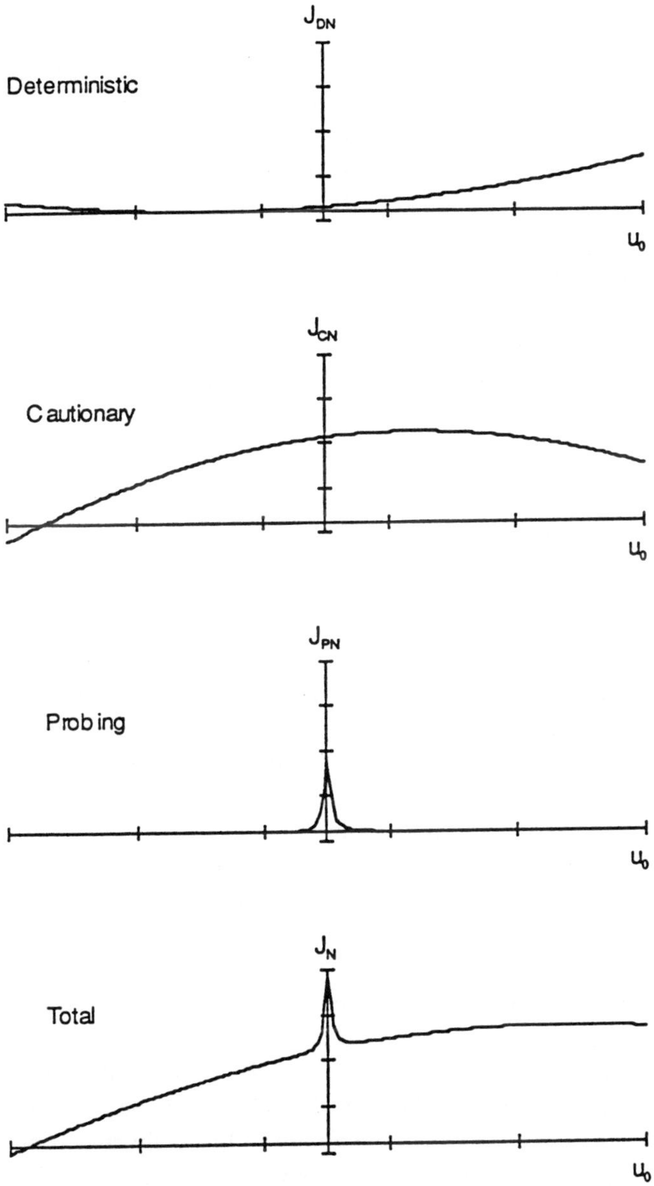

Fig. 11. A concave cautionary cost and its effect on total cost.

that one should be cautious in using gradient methods to solve dual control problems, we are hopeful that this kind of case will occur only infrequently in applied problems.

8. SUMMARY AND CONCLUSIONS

There is increasing evidence that nonconvexities may be a fundamental part of active learning stochastic control problems. While the Tse and Bar-Shalom method is only one of a number of different ways to solve this class of problems, the sources of the nonconvexity in this approach appears to be so central to the problem that nonconvexities are likely to be found in other solution methods.

When the nonconvexities were first encountered it was uncertain whether they were fundamental or due to numerical problems. Moreover, the numerical results were for ten period, three parameter versions of the MacRae problem so it was not known whether the nonconvexities would appear in simpler models.

As discussed earlier Mizrach (1991) has recently used analytical and numerical methods to show that the nonconvexities can occur even in problems with a single unknown parameter and only two time periods. He confirmed the earlier finding that the nonconvexities arose from the probing term. We have carried this result forward by characterizing the probing function in detail and showing the exact source of the nonconvexities from that term. We have shown here that the probing term is a ratio of two quadratic functions. Also, the probing term is a positive function with a single maxima and a single minima and at the minimum the function value is zero. If the maximum of the probing function is large enough relative to the deterministic and cautionary terms the resulting total cost-to-go function will be nonconvex.

The source of the nonconvexity from the probing term is the initial variance of the unknown parameter σ^2. In numerical experiments we can cause the nonconvexity to appear or disappear simply by changing the value of σ^2.

The presence of nonconvexities can cause models to become numerically difficult or impossible to solve. However, the character of the nonconvexities from the probing term will, we believe, give rise to some efficient numerical procedures. For example, in the one parameter problem studied here it appears that the total cost-to-go is not rippled with many local minima but rather has only two local minima. Search algorithms can be developed to exploit this fact. Also, since the probing function has only two roots one can easily compute those roots and then concentrate the search on the total cost-to-go in those neighborhoods.

The nonconvexities which arise from the cautionary term are of a different character. They require certain combinations of parameter values before they appear and large values of σ^2 before they make the cost-to-go functions nonconvex. When they occur they can result in a cost-to-go function with a shape that makes numerical optimization difficult.

The cautionary term is normally convex but when the conditions described above occur it can become concave and of sufficient magnitude to cause the total cost-to-go function to become concave so that the minimizing values of the control variable will be a upper or lower bound of that variable. Worse, the function can have a spike on the top of the concave hill. This spike comes from the probing term and can produce a local optima which could indicate to a gradient method that an optimal solution was obtained when in fact a very poor solution was obtained.

In spite of the potential difficulties, we can conclude on a hopeful note. First, it may well be that the initial covariance for most economic models will be sufficiently small that nonconvexities do not arise. Even when they do occur, if learning is fairly rapid the covariance will be reduced enough by the second or third time period that the usual convex shape of the cost-to-go function is restored. When nonconvexities do occur it seems that most of the time they will be from the probing term. In the MacRae problem this results in a characteristic shape for the cost-to-go function which can be exploited by optimization algorithms. We are hopeful that this kind of result will hold as more complex examples are studied. Moreover, computational speeds are increasing to the point that even when full grid search methods are required by the nonconvexities one can use them on models of some size. Also, the grid search for active learning problems does not have to be performed in the space of the parameters which could be very large but in the space of the control variables which will be limited to a small number of controls in many economic models.

In summary this work points the finger to the covariance of the parameter, σ^2, as the main source of the nonconvexity. If σ^2 is relatively large one must be on guard for nonconvexities. Since this is most likely to occur in period zero one must be particularly alert for problems in that time period. Also, in our experience, a rapid decline in σ^2 from one period to another is an indication that nonconvexities might occur. This phenomenon of a rapid declining σ^2 is most likely to occur in the first time step when one begins with a σ^2 which is an input to the control model. In the second period σ^2 is re-estimated by the algorithm, incorporating most of the learning effects, which makes nonconvexities less likely to occur. So there is reason in stochastic control codes not to guess high initial values for the variance of the parameters but rather to use a value which has been estimated from the model.

ACKNOWLEDGEMENT

We would like to thank Audie Dobbs for help in typing this paper.

BIBLIOGRAPHY

Amman, H. M. and D. A. Kendrick, 1992, 'Non-convexities in stochastic control models', Center for Economic Research, University of Texas, Austin, Texas, Paper No. 92-1.

Kendrick, D. A., 1978, 'Non-convexities from probing an adaptive control problem', *Journal of Economic Letters* 1, 347–351.

Kendrick, D. A., 1981, *Stochastic Control for Economic Models*, New York: McGraw–Hill.

MacRae, E. C., 1972, 'Linear decision with experimentation', *Annals of Economic and Social Measurement* 1, 437–448.

Mizrach, B., 1991, 'Non-convexities in a stochastic control problem with learning', *Journal of Economic Dynamics and Control* 15, 515–538.

Norman, A., M. Norman, and C. Palash, 1979, 'Multiple relative maxima in optimal macroeconomic policy: An illustration', *Southern Economic Journal* 46, 274–279.

Tse, E. and Y. Bar-Shalom, 1973, 'An actively adaptive control for linear systems with random parameters', *IEEE Transactions on Automatic Control* AC-17, 38–52.

ANNA NAGURNEY, STEN THORE AND JIE PAN

The Modeling and Computation of Generalized Goal Programming Problems

ABSTRACT. In this paper we show how the theory of variational inequalities can be applied to the formulation, qualitative analysis, and computation of generalized goal programming problems. The theoretical framework is developed in the context of a new competitive economic model in the presence of negative economic externalities. The model allows the decision maker to impose supply goals at production locations and transportation goals between supply and demand locations, along with associated penalties for failure to comply. This work may be viewed as a contribution to the development of mathematical methodologies for policy modeling.

1. INTRODUCTION

Goal programming is a mathematical formulation which in an optimization framework has found wide application in both operations research and management science (see the original paper by Charnes *et al.* (1955), the subsequent treatment in Charnes and Cooper (1961), the survey paper of Charnes and Cooper (1977), and the references therein). In this paper we focus our attention on competitive economic markets with negative economic externalities and show how the generalization of goal programming through the use of variational inequality theory can address the formulation, qualitative analysis, and computation of economic equilibrium patterns in the presence of target goals.

Societal concern with national energy policy, water and air pollution, global warming, the transportation of hazardous materials, and urban congestion is bringing the study of negative externalities to the fore. The development of methodologies for the analysis of negative economic externalities is, hence, a topic which merits increasing attention.

In particular, we consider a competitive market economy involving 1) the supply of some commodity (such as a natural resouce, energy, or agricultural produce) at several locations; 2) the subsequent shipment of these supplies to several consumer locations; and 3) the final deliveries at these locations to cover consumer demand. The shipment between a pair of supply and demand

W.W. Cooper and A.B. Whinston (eds.), New Directions in Computational Economics, 95–120.

locations is charged a unit transaction cost which is assumed to include the transportation cost.

The economic system is then subjected to goal programming in the following manner. A decision maker is concerned with the possible oversupply at the supply locations, as well as the possible overshipment between the pairs of supply and demand locations, resulting in the depletion of natural resources, environmental damage, or other negative externalities. The decision maker formulates target supply goals and target transportation goals, with assessed unit penalties for failure to comply. The penalties may be different for oversupply and overshipment, and for undersupply and undershipment.

In this paper we utilize the theory of variational inequalities to formulate, analyze, and solve such a market model. We also interpret the penalties associated with over/undersupplies and with over/undershipments in terms of taxes/subsidies. In the absence of targets and associated penalties, the model reduces to the spatial market model studied in Nagurney (1987a).

The development of mathematical frameworks to investigate the effects of policy interventions in competitive markets has been recently addressed by several authors. For example, Greenberg and Murphy (1985) developed an optimization formulation of competitive markets in the case of price regulations on the production side. Thore (1986) considered the presence of price floors and ceilings in the context of the classical spatial price equilibrium problem (cf. Samuelson 1952) and Takayama and Judge (1971)) and gave an optimization formulation of the resulting disequilibrium. Faxen and Thore (1990), on the other hand, considered the presence of sticky wages in the context of labor markets respresented by a network model. For a survey of the use of mathematical programming approaches to the study of economic disequilibrium, we refer the reader to Thompson and Thore (1990).

More recently, Nagurney and Zhao (1990, 1991) showed that disequilibrium spatial markets, in which the economic state no longer possesses an optimization formulation, can be studied as variational inequality problems, and proposed alternative variational inequality decomposition algorithms for the computation of the disequilibrium patterns. In this paper, in contrast, we introduce policy interventions on both the transportation links and on the production side but in the form of goal targets, rather than in the form of price floors and ceilings. In the case of symmetry assumptions on the governing economic functions – which we do not restrict our model to – the equilibrium conditions are actually the Kuhn-Tucker conditions of an appropriately constructed optimization problem. Such equivalences have been established in the context of traffic network equilibrium problems by Beckmann *et al.* (1956) and in spatial price equilibrium problems by Samuelson (1952) and Takayama and Judge (1971).

This paper is organized as follows. In Section 2 we develop the new general model, state the equilibrium conditions, and give the variational inequality formulation of the problem. We then discuss two special cases of the model, in which goal targets are placed only on the supplies, and only on the commodity shipments. In Section 3 we provide the qualitative theory for the model, in particular, the existence and uniqueness results for the solution pattern. In Section 4 we introduce an algorithm for the computation of the equilibrium, which we then apply in Section 5 on several numerical examples. In Section 6 we summarize and conclude.

2. THE MODEL

In this section we develop the competitive economic market model in the presence of target supply and transportation goals. That is, we consider goals imposed on the producers, in that certain production levels are to be met, and goals imposed on the level of commodity shipments between locations. Deviations from the supply targets in terms of overproduction or underproduction are penalized, as are deviations from the transportation targets in terms of overshipment and undershipment.

The notation that we utilize is defined as follows. Let $i = 1, \ldots, m$ denote the supply location index and $j = 1, \ldots, n$ denote the demand location index. Let $s = [s_i]$ denote the column vector of supplies, $d = [d_j]$ the column vector of demands, and $Q = [Q_{ij}]$ the matrix of nonnegative commodity shipments from the supply locations to the demand locations. The column vector of supply goals is denoted by $s^\# = [s_i^\#]$, whereas, the column vectors of nonnegative oversupply and undersupply are denoted, respectively, by $\Delta^+ = [\Delta_i^+]$, $\Delta^- = [\Delta_i^-]$. Finally, the matrix of commodity transportation targets is denoted by $Q^\# = [Q_{ij}^\#]$, with the column vectors of nonnegative overshipments and undershipment denoted, respectively, by $\delta^+ = [\delta_{ij}^+]$, and $\delta^- = [\delta_{ij}^-]$.

The feasibility conditions are:

$$s_i = \sum_{j=1}^{n} Q_{ij}, \quad i = 1, \ldots, m, \tag{1}$$

and

$$d_j = \sum_{i=1}^{m} Q_{ij}, \quad j = 1, \ldots, n, \tag{2}$$

where

$$s_i - \Delta_i^+ + \Delta_i^- = s_i^\#, \quad i = 1, \ldots, m, \tag{3}$$

and

$$Q_{ij} - \delta_{ij}^{+} + \delta_{ij}^{-} = Q_{ij}^{\#}, \quad i = 1, \dots, m; \quad j = 1, \dots, n. \tag{4}$$

Equations (1) and (2) state, respectively, that the supply of a commodity at a location must be equal to the commodity shipments out of the location, and the demand for a commodity at a location must be equal to the commodity shipments into the location. Equation (3) states that the supply goal at supply market i is equal to the supply quantity at supply location i minus the possible oversupply above the goal plus the possible undersupply below the goal. Equation (4) reflects that the transportation goal between supply location i and demand location j must be equal to the commodity shipment between the pair of locations minus the possible overshipment above the goal plus the possible undershipment below the goal. Let K denote the closed convex subset of $R_{+}^{3m+3mn+n}$ consisting of $(s, Q, d, \Delta^{+}, \Delta^{-}, \delta^{+}, \delta^{-})$ such that (1), (2), (3), and (4) hold.

Let π_i denote the supply price at supply location i and ρ_j denote the demand price at demand location j. We then group the supply prices into a supply price row vector $\pi \in R^m$ and the demand prices into a demand price row vector $\rho \in R^n$. Let c_{ij} denote the unit transaction cost between supply location i and demand location j and we assume that the transaction cost includes the transportation cost. We group the transaction costs into a row vector $c \in R^{mn}$.

Let M_i denote the unit penalty to be assessed for oversupply at supply location i and let N_i denote the unit penalty to be assessed for undersupply at supply location i. We then group the oversupply penalties into a row vector $M \in R^m$ and the undersupply penalties into a row vector $N \in R^m$. Let μ_{ij} then denote the unit penalty to be assessed for overshipment between supply location i and demand location j and let η_{ij} denote the unit penalty to be assessed for undershipment between the pair of locations. We group the overshipment penalties into a row vector $\mu \in R^{mn}$ and the undershipment penalties into a row vector $\eta \in R^{mn}$.

We assume, as in general market equilibrium models (see, e.g., Florian and Los (1982), Dafermos and Nagurney (1984)) that the supply price at a supply location may depend, in general, upon the entire vector of supplies, i.e.,

$$\pi = \pi(s), \tag{5}$$

where π is a known smooth function, and the demand price at a demand location may depend upon the entire vector of demands, i.e.,

$$\rho = \rho(d), \tag{6}$$

where ρ is a known smooth function.

The transaction cost associated with shipping the commodity between a pair of supply and demand locations may, in turn, depend, in general, upon the entire vector of commodity shipments, i.e.,

$$c = c(Q), \tag{7}$$

where c is a known smooth function.

In the absence of target production goals and target transportation goals, and associated penalties of oversupply, undersupply, overshipment, and undershipment, and under the assumption of perfect competition, the well-known spatial price equilibrium conditions (cf. Samuelson (1952) and Takayama and Judge (1971)) are given by: For all pairs of markets (i, j) a pattern (s, Q, d) is in equilibrium if and only if it satisfies:

$$(\pi_i(s) + c_{ij}(Q) - \rho_j(d)) \times Q_{ij} = 0 \tag{8}$$

$$\pi_i(s) + c_{ij}(Q) - \rho_j(d) \geq 0, \quad Q_{ij} \geq 0. \tag{9}$$

Conditions (8) and (9) state that a commodity will be shipped between a pair of locations, provided that the supply price at the producing location plus the cost of transportation is equal to the demand price at the consuming location. There will be no shipment if the supply price plus the transportation cost exceeds the demand price. As was shown in Florian and Los (1982) (see also Dafermos (1982), Nagurney (1987a)), the variational inequality formulation of the spatial price equilibrium conditions (8) and (9) is given by:

Determine (s, Q, d) satisfying (1) and (2) such that

$$\begin{gathered}\pi(s) \cdot (s' - s) + c(Q) \cdot (Q' - Q) - \rho(d) \cdot (d' - d) \geq 0, \\ \text{for all} \quad (s', Q', d') \quad \text{satisfying} \quad (1), (2).\end{gathered} \tag{10}$$

In the presence of target goals, the governing equilibrium conditions now take the following form: For all pairs of markets (i, j) a pattern $(s, Q, d, \Delta^+, \Delta^-, \delta^+, \delta^-) \in K$ is in equilibrium if and only if it satisfies:

$$(\pi_i(s) + c_{ij}(Q) - \rho_j(d) + t_i + \tau_{ij}) \times Q_{ij} = 0 \tag{11}$$

$$\pi_i(s) + c_{ij}(Q) - \rho_j(d) + t_i + \tau_{ij} \geq 0, \quad Q_{ij} \geq 0, \tag{12}$$

$$t_i \begin{cases} = M_i, & \text{if} \quad s_i > s_i^{\#} \\ \in [-N_i, M_i], & \text{if} \quad s_i = s_i^{\#} \\ = -N_i, & \text{if} \quad s_i < s_i^{\#}, \end{cases} \tag{13}$$

and

$$\tau_{ij} \begin{cases} = \mu_{ij}, & \text{if} \quad Q_{ij} > Q_{ij}^{\#} \\ \in \left[-\eta_{ij}, \mu_{ij}\right], & \text{if} \quad Q_{ij} = Q_{ij}^{\#} \\ = -\eta_{ij}, & \text{if} \quad Q_{ij} < Q_{ij}^{\#}. \end{cases} \tag{14}$$

Note that (13) is equivalent to

$$(t_i - M_i)\Delta_i^+ = (t_i + N_i)\Delta_i^- = 0, \quad -N_i \le t_i \le M_i, \tag{15}$$

whereas (14) is equivalent to

$$(\tau_{ij} - \mu_{ij})\delta_{ij}^+ = (\tau_{ij} + \eta_{ij})\delta_{ij}^- = 0, \quad -\eta_{ij} \le \tau_{ij} \le \mu_{ij}. \tag{16}$$

In the special case where there are only supply target goals, that is, Equation (3), but not (4) must hold; analogously, (13) and (15), but not (14) and (16) must hold, then the above model collapses to the one developed in Thore *et al.* (1992). For that model, however, heretofore, no computational procedure was available. On the other hand, in the case where the economic markets are subject to only transportation target goals, that is, Equation (4), but not (3) must hold; analogously, (14) and (16) must hold, but not (13) and (15), then the above model collapses to a special model in which negative externalities are associated only with transporting the commodity.

We now discuss the above economic conditions in depth. The value of t_i is interpreted as an excise tax levied on supplies at supply location i if t_i is positive; the value of $-t_i$ is interpreted as a unit subsidy paid to supplies at supply location i if t_i is negative. In the case of an optimal oversupply above the supply goal, there will be an excise tax levied on the supply. The magnitude of the tax equals the unit penalty for oversupply. However, if there turns out to be an undersupply below the goal, a unit subsidy should be paid to the suppliers. The subsidy should equal the unit penalty for undersupply. Finally, if the stated supply goal can be exactly met, there may be a tax *or* a subsidy. The excise tax, t_i, if $t_i > 0$, — if there is one — will not exceed the unit penalty of oversupply; the subsidy, $-t_i$, if $t_i < 0$, will not exceed the penalty for undersupply.

Analogously, in the case of overshipment above the goal, the excise tax τ_{ij} levied on the shipments will be equal to the unit penalty for overshipment. On the other hand, if there results an undershipment below the target goal, then a unit subsidy of the same amount as the unit penalty for undershipment must be paid. Finally, if the transportation target goals can be attained precisely, then there may be a tax or a subsidy.

Note that condition (15) implies that there can be only an oversupply or an undersupply. Similarly, condition (16) implies that there can only be an overshipment or an undershipment.

We now establish that the economic conditions can be formulated as a variational inequality problem. In particular, we have the following result:

Theorem 1. A pattern of supplies, commodity shipments, demands, oversupply and undersupply levels, and overshipment and undershipment levels $(s, Q, d, \Delta^+, \Delta^-, \delta^+, \delta^-)$ in K with an attendant row vector of Lagrange multipliers (t, τ) associated with constraints (3) and (4), respectively, satisfies the economic equilibrium conditions (12), (13), (14), ((15) and (16)) in the presence of supply and transportation goals and associated penalties if and only if it satisfies the variational inequality:

$$\begin{aligned}&\pi(s)\cdot(s'-s)+c(Q)\cdot(Q'-Q)-\rho(d)\cdot(d'-d)\\&\quad+M\cdot(\Delta^{+'}-\Delta^+)+N\cdot(\Delta^{-'}-\Delta^-)\\&\quad+\mu\cdot(\delta^{+'}-\delta^+)+\eta\cdot(\delta^{-'}-\delta^-)\geq 0\\&\quad\text{for all}\quad(s',Q',d',\Delta^{+'},\Delta^{-'},\delta^{+'},\delta^{-'})\in K.\end{aligned}\tag{17}$$

Proof: We first establish the "if" part of Theorem 1, that is, we prove that any solution $(s, Q, d, \Delta^+, \Delta^-)$ in K with an attendant row vector of Lagrange multipliers (t, τ) that satisfies (12), (13), and (14), must also satisfy the variational inequality (17).

From (11) we have that

$$(\pi_i(s)+c_{ij}(Q)-\rho_j(d))\cdot Q_{ij}=(-\tau_{ij}-t_i)\cdot Q_{ij}.$$

From (15) and (16) it follows that

$$\begin{aligned}\tau_{ij}\delta_{ij}^+&=\mu_{ij}\delta_{ij}^+,\quad t_i\Delta_i^+=M_i\Delta_i^+\\\tau_{ij}\delta_{ij}^-&=-\eta_{ij}\delta_{ij}^-,\quad t_i\Delta_i^-=-N_i\Delta_i^-.\end{aligned}$$

Therefore,

$$\begin{aligned}&\sum_{ij}(\pi_i(s)+c_{ij}(Q)-\rho_j(d))\cdot Q_{ij}\\&\quad+\sum_{ij}(\mu_{ij}\delta_{ij}^++\eta_{ij}\delta_{ij}^-)\\&\quad+\sum_i(M_i\Delta_i^++N_i\Delta_i^-)\\&\quad=\sum_{ij}-\tau_{ij}(Q_{ij}-\delta_{ij}^++\delta_{ij}^-)\\&\quad+\sum_i-t_i(\sum_j Q_{ij}-\Delta_i^++\Delta_i^-)\\&\quad=\sum_{ij}-\tau_{ij}Q_{ij}^{\#}+\sum_i-t_is_i^{\#}.\end{aligned}\tag{18}$$

Next, observe that

$$\begin{aligned}
&\sum_{ij}(\pi_i(s) + c_{ij}(Q) - \rho_j(d)) \cdot Q'_{ij} \\
&\quad + \sum_{ij}(\mu_{ij}\delta^{+'}_{ij} + \eta_{ij}\delta^{-'}_{ij}) \\
&\quad + \sum_{i}(M_i\Delta^{+'}_i + N_i\Delta^{-'}_i) \\
&\quad \geq \sum_{ij} -\tau_{ij}(Q'_{ij} - \delta^{+'}_{ij} + \delta^{-'}_{ij}) \\
&\quad + \sum_{i} -t_i(\sum_j Q'_{ij} - \Delta^{+'}_i + \Delta^{-'}_i) \\
&\quad = \sum_{ij} -\tau_{ij}Q^{\#}_{ij} + \sum_i -t_i s^{\#}_i
\end{aligned} \tag{19}$$

for any point $(s', Q', d', \Delta^{+'}, \Delta^{-'}, \delta^{+'}, \delta^{-'})$ in K, so that, by addition and by simplifying terms, we obtain variational inequality (17).

Turning now to the "only if" part of Theorem 1, let $(s,\ Q,\ d,\ \Delta^{+},\ \Delta^{-},\ \delta^{+},\ \delta^{-})$ solve (17). Then the same point also solves the *linear* programming problem:

$$\begin{aligned}
\text{Minimize} \quad &\sum_{ij}(\pi_i(s) + c_{ij}(Q) - \rho_j(d)) \cdot Q'_{ij} \\
&+ \sum_i M_i\Delta^{+'}_i + \sum_i N_i\Delta^{-'}_i + \mu_{ij}\delta^{+'}_{ij} + \eta_{ij}\delta^{-'}_{ij}
\end{aligned} \tag{20}$$

subject to $Q', \Delta^{+'}, \Delta^{-'}, \delta^{+'}, \delta^{-'} \geq 0$, and satisfying constraints (3) and (4).

From the Kuhn-Tucker conditions to the above problem we recover the equilibrium conditions (12), (13), and (14), where t_i is the dual variable associated with constraint (3), and τ_{ij} is the dual variable associated with constraint (4). The proof is complete.

We emphasize that in the case where the Jacobian matrices of the supply price, demand price, and transaction cost functions are symmetric, then the above equilibrium conditions can be reformulated as an optimization problem, as was observed by Beckmann *et al.* (1956) in the framework of the traffic network equilibrium conditions and by Samuelson (1952) and Takayama and Judge (1971) in the case of spatial price equilibrium conditions. Indeed, in the special "symmetric" case, the equilibrium conditions are the Kuhn-Tucker conditions of the following optimization problem:

$$\text{Minimize} \quad \sum_{i=1}^{m} \int_{0}^{\sum_{j=1}^{n} Q_{ij}} \pi_i(x)dx + \sum_{i=1}^{m}\sum_{j=1}^{n} \int_{0}^{Q_{ij}} c_{ij}(y)dy$$

$$- \sum_{j=1}^{n} \int_{0}^{\sum_{i=1}^{m} Q_{ij}} \rho_j(z)dz + \sum_{i=1}^{m}(M_i\Delta_i^+ + N_i\Delta_i^-)$$

$$+ \sum_{i=1}^{m}\sum_{j=1}^{n}(\mu_{ij}\delta_{ij}^+ + \eta_{ij}\delta_{ij}^-) \tag{21}$$

subject to the nonnegativity assumptions on the variables and constraints (3) and (4).

The above model, hence, in the symmetric case is a goal programming problem. However, as the above results demonstrate, goaling is not limited to optimization problems, but can be generalized via the theory of variational inequalities to handle competitive economic markets subject to target goals, as well.

The theory of variational inequalities has already been used to study a plethora of equilibrium problems in operations research and economics, including traffic network equilibrium problems (see, e.g., Dafermos 1980, 1982; Florian and Spiess 1982), oligopolistic market equilibrium problems (Gabay and Moulin 1980; Dafermos and Nagurney 1987; Qiu 1991; Flam and Ben-Israel 1990), human migration problems (Nagurney 1989; Nagurney *et al.* 1992), and general economic equilibrium problems (Dafermos 1990; Zhao and Dafermos 1991). The above model demonstrates a novel use of variational inequality theory in the formulation and study of policy interventions.

3. QUALITATIVE PROPERTIES OF EXISTENCE AND UNIQUENESS

In this section we present the qualitative results for the general market model in the presence of supply and transportation target goals developed in Section 2. We first provide our existence result and then the uniqueness result. In particular, we establish that, under certain monotonicity conditions on the supply price, demand price, and transaction cost functions (cf. Nagurney 1987b), and nontrivial penalties, existence and uniqueness of the equilibrium pattern are guaranteed. Hence, we have the following

Theorem 2. Assume that the supply price and the demand price functions

$\pi(s)$ and $-\rho(d)$ are monotone and that the transaction cost function $c(Q)$ is strongly monotone. Assume also that $M_i^2 + N_i^2 \neq 0$, for all i, and that $\mu_{ij}^2 + \eta_{ij}^2 \neq 0$ for all i, j. Then there exists a solution to variational inequality (17).

Proof: Let $\bar{\delta}_{ij}^+ = \bar{\delta}_{ij}^- = 0$, $\bar{\Delta}_i^+ - \bar{\Delta}_i^- = \sum_j Q_{ij}^\# - s_i^\#$ and $\bar{Q}_{ij} = Q_{ij}^\#$ for all i and j. Then

$$\begin{aligned}
&\sum_{ij}(\pi_i(s) + c_{ij}(Q) - \rho_j(d)) \cdot (Q_{ij} - \bar{Q}_{ij}) \\
&\quad + \sum_i (M_i(\Delta_i^+ - \bar{\Delta}_i^+) + N_i(\Delta_i^- - \bar{\Delta}_i^-)) \\
&\quad + \sum_{ij} (\mu_{ij}(\delta_{ij}^+ - \bar{\delta}_{ij}^+) + \eta_{ij}(\delta_{ij}^- - \bar{\delta}_{ij}^-)) \\
&\quad = \sum_{ij}(\pi_i(s) + c_{ij}(Q) - \rho_j(d)) \cdot (Q_{ij} - Q_{ij}^\#) \\
&\quad + \sum_i M_i(\Delta_i^+ - \bar{\Delta}_i^+) + N_i(\Delta_i^- - \bar{\Delta}_i^-) \\
&\quad + \sum_{ij} \mu_{ij}\Delta_{ij}^+ + \nu_{ij}\Delta_{ij}^-.
\end{aligned} \tag{22}$$

Since

$$\begin{aligned}
\|(\Delta^+, \Delta^-, \delta^+, \delta^-, Q)\|^2 &= \sum_i \Delta_i^{+^2} + \sum_i \Delta_i^{-^2} \\
&\quad + \sum_{ij} \delta_{ij}^{+^2} + \sum_{ij} \delta_{ij}^{-^2} + \sum_{ij} Q_{ij}^2,
\end{aligned}$$

if $\sum_{ij} Q_{ij}^2$ is bounded, while $\sum_i(\Delta_i^{+^2} + \Delta_i^{-^2})$+$\sum_{ij}(\delta_{ij}^{+^2}$+$\delta_{ij}^{-^2})$ is sufficiently large, by the assumption that $M_i \geq 0, N_i \geq 0$ and $M_i^2 + N_i^2 \neq 0$, for all i, and $\mu_{ij} \geq 0$, $\eta_{ij} \geq 0$ and $\mu_{ij}^2 + \eta_{ij}^2 \neq 0$, for all i, j, we have that

$$\begin{aligned}
&\sum_{ij}(\pi_i(s) + c_{ij}(Q) - \rho_j(d)) \cdot (Q_{ij} - Q_{ij}^\#) \\
&\quad + \sum_i (M_i(\Delta_i^+ - \bar{\Delta}_i^+) + N_i(\Delta_i^- - \bar{\Delta}_i^-)) \\
&\quad + \sum_{ij} (\mu_{ij}\delta_{ij}^+ + \eta_{ij}\delta_{ij}^-) \geq 0.
\end{aligned} \tag{23}$$

On the other hand, if $\sum_{ij} Q_{ij}^2$ is not bounded, and is taken to be sufficiently large, then by the monotonicity assumption, and an application of Schwarz's inequality we conclude that

$$\sum_{ij}(\pi_i(s) + c_{ij}(Q) - \rho_j(d)) \cdot (Q_{ij} - Q^{\#}_{ij})$$

$$= \sum_{ij}((\pi_i(s) + c_{ij}(Q) - \rho_j(d)) - (\pi_i(\sum_j Q^{\#}_{ij})$$

$$+ c_{ij}(Q^{\#}) - \rho_j(\sum_i Q^{\#}_{ij}))) \cdot (Q_{ij} - Q^{\#}_{ij})$$

$$+ \sum_{ij}(\pi_i(\sum_j Q^{\#}_{ij}) + c_{ij}(Q^{\#}) - \rho_j(\sum_i Q^{\#}_{ij})) \cdot (Q_{ij} - Q^{\#}_{ij})$$

$$\geq \alpha \sum_{ij}(Q_{ij} - Q^{\#}_{ij})^2 - (\sum_{ij}(\pi_i(\sum_j Q^{\#}_{ij})$$

$$+ c_{ij}(Q^{\#}) - \rho_j(\sum_i Q^{\#}_{ij}))^2)^{\frac{1}{2}} \cdot (\sum_{ij}(Q_{ij} - Q^{\#}_{ij})^2)^{\frac{1}{2}} > 0, \tag{24}$$

where α is a positive parameter used in the definition of strong monotonicity.

Therefore, the variational inequality satisfies the coercivity condition of a theorem of More (1974), from which existence of a solution to the variational inequality then follows.

Theorem 3. Under the same conditions as imposed in Theorem 2, uniqueness of the solution pattern is also guaranteed.

Proof: Suppose that $(\Delta^+, \Delta^-, \delta^+, \delta^-, Q)$ and $(\bar{\Delta}^+, \bar{\Delta}^-, \bar{\delta}^+, \bar{\delta}^-, \bar{Q})$ are two distinct solutions of the variational inequality (17). Then

$$\sum_{ij}(\pi_i(s) + c_{ij}(Q) - \rho_j(d)) \cdot (\bar{Q}_{ij} - Q_{ij})$$

$$+ \sum_i M_i(\bar{\Delta}^+_i - \Delta^+_i) + \sum_i N_i(\bar{\Delta}^-_i - \Delta_i)$$

$$+ \sum_{ij} \mu_{ij}(\bar{\delta}^+_{ij} - \delta^+_{ij}) + \sum_{ij} \eta_{ij}(\bar{\delta}^-_{ij} - \delta_{ij}) \geq 0 \tag{25}$$

and

$$\sum_{ij}(\pi_i(\bar{s}) + c_{ij}(\bar{Q}) - \rho_j(\bar{d})) \cdot (Q_{ij} - \bar{Q}_{ij})$$

$$+ \sum_i M_i(\Delta^+_i - \bar{\Delta}^+_i) + \sum_i N_i(\Delta^-_i - \bar{\Delta}^-_i)$$

$$+ \sum_{ij} \mu_{ij}(\delta^+_{ij} - \bar{\delta}^+_{ij}) + \sum_{ij} \eta_{ij}(\delta^-_{ij} - \bar{\delta}^-_{ij}) \geq 0. \tag{26}$$

Adding then (25) and (26), we obtain

$$\sum_{ij}(\pi_i(\bar{s}) + c_{ij}(\bar{Q}) - \rho_j(\bar{d}) - (\pi_i(s) + c_{ij}(Q) - \rho_j(d)))$$
$$\cdot (Q_{ij} - \bar{Q}_{ij}) \geq 0. \tag{27}$$

But, under the strong monotonicity assumption on $c(Q)$ and monotonicity of $\pi(s), -\rho(d)$, we must have that

$$\sum_{ij}(\pi_i(\bar{s}) + c_{ij}(\bar{Q}) - \rho_j(\bar{d}) - (\pi_i(s) + c_{ij}(Q) - \rho_j(d))$$
$$\cdot (Q_{ij} - \bar{Q}_{ij}) \leq -\alpha \sum_{ij} (Q_{ij} - \bar{Q}_{ij})^2$$

Hence, we conclude that $Q_{ij} = \bar{Q}_{ij}$, for all i and j.

Therefore, from (25) and (26) we have that

$$\sum_i M_i(\bar{\Delta}_i^+ - \Delta_i^+) + \sum_i N_i(\bar{\Delta}_i^- - \Delta_i^-)$$
$$+ \sum_{ij} \mu_{ij}(\bar{\delta}_{ij}^+ - \delta_{ij}^+) + \sum_{ij} \eta_{ij}(\bar{\delta}_{ij}^- - \delta_{ij}^-) \geq 0 \tag{28}$$

$$\sum_i M_i(\Delta_i^+ - \bar{\Delta}_i^+) + \sum_i N_i(\Delta_i^- - \bar{\Delta}_i^-)$$
$$+ \sum_{ij} \mu_{ij}(\delta_{ij}^+ - \bar{\delta}_{ij}^+) + \sum_{ij} \eta_{ij}(\delta_{ij}^- - \bar{\delta}_{ij}^-) \geq 0. \tag{29}$$

Also, we have that

$$\bar{\delta}_{ij}^+ - \bar{\delta}_{ij}^- = \bar{Q}_{ij} - Q_{ij}^{\#} = Q_{ij} - Q_{ij}^{\#} = \delta_{ij}^+ - \delta_{ij}^-.$$

Hence,

$$\bar{\delta}_{ij}^+ - \delta_{ij}^+ = \bar{\delta}_{ij}^- - \delta_{ij}^-. \tag{30}$$

From (28) and (25), for fixed (i,j), we set in (17) $Q'_{kl} = Q_{kl}$, $\delta_{kl}^{+'} = \delta_{kl}^+$, $\delta_{kl}^{-'} = \delta_{kl}$ for all $(k,l) \neq (i,j)$, and $Q'_{ij} = \bar{Q}_{ij} = Q_{ij}$, $\delta_{ij}^{+'} = \bar{\delta}_{ij}^+$, $\delta_{ij}^{-'} = \bar{\delta}_{ij}^-$. We then have that

$$s'_i = \sum_j Q'_{ij} = \sum_j Q_{ij} = s_i.$$

Consequently, $\Delta_k^{+'} = \Delta_k^+$, $\Delta_k^{-'} = -\Delta_k^-$ for all k is feasible.

By using now (30), it follows that

$$(\mu_{ij} + \eta_{ij}) \cdot (\bar{\delta}^+_{ij} - \delta^+_{ij}) \geq 0.$$

Similarly, from (29) and (26), for fixed (i, j), we set in (17), $Q'_{kl} = \bar{Q}_{kl}$, $\delta^{+'}_{kl} = \bar{\delta}^+_{kl}$, $\delta^{-'}_{kl} = \delta_{kl}$ for all $(k, l) \neq (i, j)$, and $Q'_{ij} = Q_{ij} = \bar{Q}_{ij}$, $\delta^{+'}_{ij} = \delta^+_{ij}$, and $\delta^{-'}_{ij} = \delta^-_{ij}$. We then have that

$$s'_i = \sum_j Q'_{ij} = \sum_j \bar{Q}_{ij} = \bar{s}_i.$$

Consequently, $\Delta^{+'}_k = \bar{\Delta}^+_k$, $\Delta^{-'}_k = \bar{\Delta}^-_k$, for all k is feasible.

By applying now (30), it follows that

$$(\mu_{ij} + \eta_{ij}) \cdot (\delta^+_{ij} - \bar{\delta}^+_{ij}) \geq 0.$$

Hence, $\delta^+_{ij} = \bar{\delta}^+_{ij}$ for all i, j. It thus follows that $\delta^-_{ij} = \bar{\delta}^-_{ij}$.

Then (28) and (29) reduce to

$$\sum_i M_i(\bar{\Delta}^+_i - \Delta^+_i) + \sum_i N_i(\bar{\Delta}_i - \Delta^-_i) \geq 0$$

$$\sum_i M_i(\Delta^+_i - \Delta^+_i) + \sum_i N_i(\Delta^-_i - \bar{\Delta}^-_i) \geq 0.$$

By the same arguments as above, we have that $\Delta^+_i = \bar{\Delta}_i$, $\Delta^-_i = \bar{\Delta}^-_i$ for all i.

The proof is complete.

4. THE COMPUTATIONAL PROCEDURE

In this section we propose an algorithm for the computation of the equilibrium production, consumption, trade, oversupply/undersupply, and overshipment/undershipment pattern for the market model introduced in Section 2. The algorithm converges under the assumption that the supply price π and demand price ρ functions are monotone and that the transaction cost function c is strongly monotone. As shown in Section 3, under such conditions the equilibrium pattern exists, and is unique. We then specialize the algorithm to two cases, the first case being the model in which goal targets are imposed only on the supplies, and the second, the model in which the goal targets are imposed only on the commodity shipments.

The algorithm is a version of the method of multipliers (cf. Gabay 1983), which in the goal programming framework has as an advantage its splitting feature. In particular, it resolves the variational inequality problem (17) into a series of two simpler variational inequality subproblems, with only nonnegativity constraints. The first subproblem takes the form of the variational inequality governing the well-known spatial price equilibrium problem, for which numerous efficient algorithms exist (see, e.g., Nagurney 1987b; Nagurney and Zhao 1990, and the references therein). The second variational inequality subproblem is a very simple linear problem in the $(\Delta^+, \Delta^-, \delta^+, \delta^-)$ variables only and is, in fact, separable, respectively, into the (Δ^+, Δ^-) and (δ^+, δ^-) variables. This subproblem, in turn, can be solved via a Gauss-Seidel decomposition method described in Nagurney (1987a).

We now state the algorithm.

The Variational Inequality Algorithm. Given a sequence of parameters $0 < r_1 \leq r_2 \leq r_3 \leq \ldots$,

Step 0: Set the iteration count $t = 0$.

Initialize $({\Delta^+}^0_i, {\Delta^-}^0_i, {\delta^+_{ij}}^0, {\delta^-_{ij}}^0)$, and λ^0_i, λ^0_{ij}, for $i = 1, \ldots, m$; $j = 1, \ldots, n$.

Step 1: Compute $(s^{t+1}, Q^{t+1}, d^{t+1})$, where $s^{t+1}_i = \sum_j Q^{t+1}_{ij}$, $d^{t+1}_j = \sum_i Q^{t+1}_{ij}$ and satisfies:

$$\sum_{i=1}^{m} (\pi_i(s^{t+1}) + r_t(s^{t+1} - (\Delta^+_i)^t + (\Delta^-_i)^t - s^{\#}_i) - \lambda^t_i) \cdot (s'_i - s^{t+1}_i)$$

$$+ \sum_{i=1}^{m} \sum_{j=1}^{n} (c_{ij}(Q^{t+1}) + r_t(Q^{t+1}_{ij} - (\delta^+_{ij})^t + (\delta^-_{ij})^t - Q^{\#}_{ij}) - \lambda^t_{ij})$$

$$\cdot (Q'_{ij} - Q^{t+1}_{ij}) - \sum_{j=1}^{n} \rho_j(d^{t+1}) \cdot (d'_j - d^{t+1}_j) \geq 0 \quad \text{for all} \quad Q'_{ij} \geq 0,$$

$$s'_i = \sum_{j=1}^{n} Q'_{ij}, \ d'_j = \sum_{i=1}^{m} Q'_{ij}, \quad \text{for all} \quad i, j. \tag{31}$$

Step 2: Compute $((\delta^+)^{t+1}, (\delta^-)^{t+1}, (\Delta^+)^{t+1}, (\Delta^-)^{t+1})$ satisfying:

$$\sum_{i=1}^{m} (M_i + r_t(-s^{t+1}_i + (\Delta^+_i)^{t+1} - (\Delta^-_i)^{t+1} + s^{\#}_i) + \lambda^t_i)$$

$$\cdot (\Delta^{+'}_i - (\Delta^+_i)^{t+1})$$

$$+ \sum_{i=1}^{m} (N_i - r_t(-s^{t+1}_i + (\Delta^+_i)^{t+1} - (\Delta^-_i)^{t+1} + s^{\#}_i) - \lambda^t_i)$$

$$\cdot (\Delta^{-'}_i - (\Delta^-_i)^{t+1})$$

$$+\sum_{i=1}^{m}\sum_{j=1}^{n}(\mu_{ij} - r_t(Q_{ij}^{t+1} - (\delta_{ij}^{+})^{t+1} + (\delta_{ij}^{-})^{t+1} - Q_{ij}^{\#}) + \lambda_{ij}^{t})$$

$$\cdot (\delta_{ij}^{+\prime} - (\delta_{ij}^{+})^{t+1})$$

$$+\sum_{i=1}^{m}\sum_{j=1}^{n}(\eta_{ij} + r_t(Q_{ij}^{t+1} - (\delta_{ij}^{+})^{t+1} + (\delta_{ij}^{-})^{t+1} - Q_{ij}^{\#}) - \lambda_{ij}^{t})$$

$$\cdot (\delta_{ij}^{-\prime} - (\delta_{ij}^{-})^{t+1}) \geq 0$$

$$\text{for all} \quad \Delta_i^{+\prime} \geq 0, \Delta_i^{-\prime} \geq 0, \delta_{ij}^{+\prime} \geq 0, \delta_{ij}^{-\prime} \geq 0,$$

$$i = 1, \ldots, m; \quad j = 1, \ldots, n. \tag{32}$$

Let

$$\lambda_i^{t+1} = \lambda_i^t + r_t(s_i^{\#} - s_i^{t+1} + (\Delta_i^{+})^{t+1} - (\Delta_i^{-})^{t+1}).$$

Let

$$\lambda_{ij}^{t+1} = \lambda_{ij}^t + r_t(Q_{ij}^{\#} - Q_{ij}^{t+1} + (\delta_{ij}^{+})^{t+1} - (\delta_{ij}^{-})^{t+1}).$$

Step 3: If convergence has been reached within a prespecified tolerance ϵ, then stop; otherwise, set $t = t + 1$, and go to Step 1.

Notice that in Steps 1 and 2, the respective subproblems are strongly monotone, and, hence, the sequence of iterates s^{t+1}, Q^{t+1}, d^{t+1}, $(\Delta^{+})^{t+1}$, $(\Delta^{-})^{t+1}$, $(\delta^{+})^{t+1}$, $(\delta^{-})^{t+1}$ is well-defined.

Observe that the above algorithm can be adapted to compute the solutions to two distinct cases of the general model introduced in Section 2; in particular, to the model with only supply target goals, considered in Thore *et al.* (1992), and to the model with only transportation target goals. The adaptation of the above algorithm to these cases, is as follows. In the former model, i.e., the one with only supply targets, the second term of the variational inequality subproblem (31) in Step 1 reduces to the term $\sum_{ij} c_{ij}(Q^{t+1}) \cdot (Q'_{ij} - Q_{ij}^{t+1})$, and only the first two terms in the variational inequality subproblem (32) in Step 2 are retained. On the other hand, in the latter model, that is, the one with only transportation targets, then the first term in the variational inequality subproblem (31) in Step 1 above reduces to $\sum_i \pi_i(s_i^{t+1}) \cdot (s'_i - s_i^{t+1})$, whereas, the first and second terms in (32) in Step 2 above now no longer appear.

The variational inequality algorithm above can, hence, be applied to compute solutions to a variety of modeling scenarios, which we illustrate with numerical examples in the subsequent section.

This algorithm is, in fact, a specialization of an algorithm developed for a class of variational inequalities to which our generalized goal programming problem belongs. We now briefly overview this class of variational inequalities, highlight its relationship with our model, and leave further theoretical development to the Appendix. Additional theoretical results and applications can be found in Pan (1992).

Consider the following class of variational inequality problem:
Find $x \geq 0, z \geq 0$, satisfying $Bx + Az = f$ and

$$(A_1(x), x' - x) + (A_2(z), z' - z) \geq 0 \tag{33}$$

for all $x' \geq 0, \quad z' \geq 0$, satisfying $Bx' + Az' = f$.

In the Appendix, we state the assumptions of problem (33). Under those assumptions, we utilize the dual formulation of the problem and the theory of the proximal point method (cf. Rockafellar 1976a, 1976b) to develop a convergent algorithm for the problem. We refer the reader to the Appendix for details and references.

Hence, we can rewrite (17) in the above form of (33) as follows. Let

$$x = (Q_{11}, Q_{21}, \ldots, Q_{m1}, \ldots, Q_{1n}, \ldots, Q_{mn})^T$$

$$B = \begin{pmatrix} I_{mn \times mn} \\ I_{mn} \cdots I_{mn} \end{pmatrix}_{(mn+m) \times mn}$$

$$z = (\Delta_{11}^+, \ldots, \Delta_{mn}^+, \Delta_{11}^-, \ldots, \Delta_{mn}^-, \Delta_1^+, \ldots, \Delta_m^+, \Delta_1^-, \ldots, \Delta_m^-)^T$$

$$A = \begin{pmatrix} -I_{mn \times mn}, I_{mn \times mn} & 0_{mn \times 2m} \\ 0_{m \times 2mn} & -I_{mm}, I_{mm} \end{pmatrix}_{(mn+m) \times (2mn+2m)}$$

$$f = (Q_{11}^\#, \ldots, Q_{mn}^\#, s_1^\#, \ldots, s_m^\#)^T$$

and

$$A_1(x) = \{\pi_i(s) + c_{ij}(Q) - \rho_j(d) : 1 \leq i \leq m, 1 \leq j \leq n\} : \\ R^{mn} \mapsto R^{mn}$$

$$A_2(z) = \{(\mu_{ij}, \eta_{ij}, M_i, N_i) : 1 \leq i \leq m, 1 \leq j \leq n\} : \\ R^{2mn+2m} \mapsto R^{2mn+2m}.$$

Observe that $A_1(x)$ is strongly monotone with respect to x, if c is strongly monotone with respect to Q, π is monotone with respect to s, and $-\rho$ is monotone with respect to d. Also, $A_2(z)$ is monotone with respect to z. Clearly, both A_1 and A_2 are continuous. Therefore, all of the assumptions are met in this model for convergence of the algorithm.

In the next section we provide numerical results on a variety of market equilibrium examples with target supply and transportation goals.

TABLE I

Numerical results for the variational inequality algorithm for economic markets with supply targets only*

m	n	$M \in [1, 10], N = 0, s^{\#} \in [10, 50]$					
10	10	0.36(13)	7;	3;	0.02;	31.56;	10.86
20	20	2.56(14)	8;	12;	1.40;	48.90;	13.38
30	30	10.62(14)	15;	15;	1.26;	43.94;	15.72
40	40	28.41(14)	21;	19;	0.52;	39.77;	17.12
		$M \in [1, 10], N \in [1, 10], s^{\#} = 10$					
10	10	0.26(13)	2;	8;	40.0;	14.33;	7.16
20	20	2.34(14)	0;	20;	0.08;	49.64;	18.55
30	30	9.37(14)	4;	26;	0.19;	51.07;	19.44
40	40	12.77(14)	5;	35;	0.33;	35.71;	14.52
		$M \in [1, 10], N \in [1, 10], s^{\#} = 50$					
10	10	0.42(14)	10;	0;	24.97;	42.45;	32.90
20	20	3.36(14)	18;	2;	5.73;	50.00;	23.18
30	30	8.04(14)	27;	3;	2.15;	44.48;	21.72
40	40	14.12(14)	40;	0;	4.60;	45.27	25.68

* CPU time in sec. (t), # of Δ_i^-'s > 0; # of Δ_i^+'s > 0;
min. abs. dev. for supply targets; max. abs. dev. for supply targets;
ave. abs. dev. for supply targets.

5. NUMERICAL RESULTS

In this section we describe the results of our numerical experimentation for the algorithm presented in Section 4 on a variety of examples.

The problems we considered ranged in size from ten supply markets and ten demand markets through forty supply markets and forty demand markets. We first computed solutions to problems in which only supply targets were imposed and then to problems in which only transportation targets were imposed. The results of these tests are reported in Tables I and II, respectively. In Table III we report numerical results for the general model with goal targets on both the supplies and commodity shipments.

The market equilibrium problems were generated in the following manner. For each problem class, we considered three sets of problems. In the first class and the first set of problems, the supply targets, $s_i^{\#}; i = 1, \ldots, m$, were generated randomly and uniformly in the range $[10, 50]$; in the second set, the supply targets were set equal to 10 for all the supply locations, and in

TABLE II

Numerical results for the variational inequality algorithm for economic markets with transportation targets only*

m	n	$\mu \in [1, 10], \eta = 0, Q^{\#} \in [10, 50]$					
10	10	0.048(8)	100;	0;	1.50;	45.81;	26.73
20	20	0.302(8)	400;	0;	1.29;	48.38;	31.67
30	30	0.824(10)	897;	3;	7.13;	48.92;	27.50
40	40	2.60(10)	1599;	1;	1.09;	48.29;	28.23
		$\mu \in [1, 10], \eta \in [1, 10], Q^{\#} = 10$					
10	10	0.05(9)	87;	9;	0.00;	16.19;	7.79
20	20	0.38(10)	383;	6;	0.00;	10.00;	8.61
30	30	0.93(10)	884;	10;	0.00;	18.71;	9.04
40	40	3.28(10)	1592;	3;	0.00;	17.83;	9.39
		$\mu \in [1, 10], \eta \in [1, 10], Q^{\#} = 50$					
10	10	0.048(8)	100;	0;	21.70;	50.00;	47.08
20	20	0.344(8)	400;	0;	26.47;	50.00;	48.43
30	30	0.854(10)	900;	0;	18.18;	50.00;	48.95
40	40	2.89(10)	1000;	0;	20.25;	50.00	49.36

* CPU time in sec. (t), # of δ_{ij}^-'s > 0; # of δ_{ij}^+'s > 0; min. abs. dev. for transportation targets; max. abs. dev. for transportation targets; ave. abs. dev. for transportation targets.

the third set, the supply targets were set equal to 50 for all the supplies. In this class of problems there were no imposed transportation targets. We next considered problems with only transportation targets. In the first set of this class, the transportation goal targets $Q^{\#}_{ij}$; $i = 1, \ldots, m$; $j = 1, \ldots, n$, were generated randomly and uniformly in the range $[10, 50]$; in the second set, the transportation targets were set equal to 10 for all transportation links, and in the third set, the transportation targets were set equal to 50 for all links. Finally, in the last class of problems, those with both supply and transportation targets, each set was generated to lie in the union of the respective sets of the previous two classes. In all of the examples, except for those in the first set of each class, the penalty terms μ_{ij} and η_{ij} and M_i and N_i were generated randomly and uniformly in the ranges $[1, 10]$. In the first set of examples in the first class, we set all of the $N_i; i = 1, \ldots, m$, to zero; in the second class, we set all $\eta_{ij} = 0; i = 1, \ldots, m; j = 1, \ldots, n$, to zero; in the last class and the first set, we set all the N_i's and η_{ij}'s to zero. This was done in order to

TABLE III

Numerical results for the variational inequality algorithm for economic markets with both supply targets and transportation targets*

m	n	$M \in [1,10], N = 0, s^{\#} \in [10,50]$ $\mu \in [1,10], \eta = 0, Q^{\#} \in [10,50]$					
10	10	0.07(9)	7;	3;	0.00;	32.04;	10.58
			100;	0;	5.72;	48.71;	31.01
20	20	0.47(10)	9;	11;	0.00;	65.18;	16.06
			400;	0;	.16;	49.36;	31.18
30	30	2.40(10)	13;	16;	0.00;	60.32;	19.01
			899;	1;	.05;	49.34;	31.63
40	40	5.24(11)	21;	19;	0.00;	43.62;	17.95
			1599;	1;	1.22;	48.92;	28.23
		$M \in [1,10], N \in [1,10], s^{\#} = 10$ $\mu \in [1,10], \eta \in [1,10]$ $Q^{\#} = 10$					
10	10	0.07(10)	2;	8;	0.00;	15.95;	7.99
			98;	1;	0.00;	10.00;	8.27
20	20	0.57(11)	2;	18;	0.00;	64.46;	20.70
			385;	12;	0.00;	14.27;	8.77
30	30	3.25(11)	8;	20;	0.00;	62.19;	23.05
			884;	6;	0.00;	12.41;	9.08
40	40	5.90(11)	10;	30;	0.00;	57.04;	17.69
			1592;	3;	0.00;	17.08;	9.39
		$M \in [1,10], N \in [1,10], s^{\#} = 50$ $\mu \in [1,10], \eta \in [1,10], Q^{\#} = 50$					
10	10	0.07(9)	10;	0;	0.00;	41.89;	31.79
			100;	0;	30.52;	50.00;	48.17
20	20	0.48(10)	17;	2;	0.00;	44.55;	23.48
			400;	0;	19.12;	50.00;	48.46
30	30	3.02(11)	22;	6;	0.00;	50.00	25.98
			900;	0;	20.97;	50.00;	49.02
40	40	5.09(10)	37;	3;	0.00;	50.00	26.70
			1000;	0;	20.72;	50.00;	49.36

* CPU time in sec. (t), # of Δ_i^-'s > 0; # of Δ_i^+'s > 0; min. abs. dev. for supply targets; max. abs. dev. for supply targets; ave. abs. dev. for supply targets.
# of δ_{ij}^-'s > 0; # of δ_{ij}^+'s > 0; min. abs. dev. for transportation targets; max. abs. dev. for transportation targets; ave. abs. dev. for transportation targets.

model negative economic externalities resulting from overproduction at the supply locations or/and overshipment along the transportation links.

The supply price functions, $\pi(s)$, were linear, of the form

$$\pi_i(s) = \sum_{l=1}^{m} r_{il} s_l + t_l. \tag{34}$$

The demand price functions $\rho(d)$, were also linear, of the form

$$\rho_j(d) = -\sum_{k=1}^{n} m_{jk} d_k + q_j, \tag{35}$$

and the transaction cost functions, $c(Q)$, were linear, that is,

$$c_{ij}(Q) = \sum_{k=1}^{m}\sum_{l=1}^{n} g_{ijkl} Q_{kl} + h_{ij}. \tag{36}$$

The Jacobians of the supply price, demand price, and transaction cost functions were asymmetric.

The above functions were generated randomly and uniformly in the ranges as follows: $r_{ii} \in [3, 10]$, $t_i \in [10, 25]$; $m_{jj} \in [1, 5]$, $q_j \in [150, 650]$; $g_{ijij} \in [1, 15]$, $h_{ij} \in [10, 25]$; with the cross-terms r_{il}, m_{jk}, and g_{ijkl}, generated so that the Jacobians were strictly diagonal dominant, thereby, guaranteeing existence and uniqueness of the equilibrium pattern.

The same function ranges had been used in the market examples solved in Nagurney and Zhao (1990, 1991). The number of cross-terms in each of the examples was, furthermore, set equal to five.

The termination criterion used was that the equilibrium conditions for each variational inequality subproblem (cf. Equations (31) and (32)) held within a tolerance of 0.5, and that $|Q_{ij}^{t+1} - Q_{ij}^{t}| \leq 0.005$, $|(\delta_{ij}^{-})^{t+1} - (\delta_{ij}^{-})^{t}| \leq 0.005$, and $(\delta_{ij}^{+})^{t+1} - (\delta_{ij}^{+})^{t}| \leq 0.005$, for all i, j, $|(\Delta_i^{+})^{t+1} - (\Delta_i^{+})^{t}| \leq 0.005$, for all i, and $|(\Delta_i^{-})^{t+1} - (\Delta_i^{-})^{t}| \leq 0.005$, for all i. The parameters r_t were set as follows: $r_0 = 1$, $r_t = r_0 \times 2^t$.

We used a Gauss-Seidel algorithm described in Nagurney (1987b) for the computation of the solution to subproblem (31) in which we, however, embedded the exact demand market equilibration algorithm developed in Dafermos and Nagurney (1989), to fully exploit the underlying network structure of the spatial price equilibrium problem. (see, also, Eydeland and Nagurney 1989). To solve the subproblem (32) we also applied a Gauss-Seidel algorithm, solving the subproblem term by term.

The algorithm was coded in FORTRAN and the system used for all of the numerical work was the IBM 3090-600J at the Cornell National Supercomputer Facility.

In all of the tables we report for each set of examples the following data: the CPU time (without input, output times), the number of iterations t, the number of supply markets / transportation links with $\Delta_i^- > 0$ / $\delta_{ij}^- > 0$, the number of supply markets / transportation links with $\Delta_i^+ > 0/\delta_{ij}^+ > 0$, the minimum absolute deviation $|s_i - s_i^\#|$ or/and $|Q_{ij} - Q_{ij}^\#|$, the maximum absolute deviation $|s_i - s_i^\#|$ or/and $|Q_{ij} - Q_{ij}^\#|$, and the average absolute deviation

$$\frac{\sum_{i=1}^m |s_i - s_i^\#|}{m}$$

or/and

$$\frac{\sum_{i=1}^m \sum_{j=1}^n |Q_{ij} - Q_{ij}^\#|}{mn}.$$

As can be seen from Table I, the algorithm converged for all of the examples. In the first set of examples, with $s_i^\# \in [10, 50]$, in any given example, there were some markets with $\Delta_i^+ > 0$, and other markets with $\Delta_i^- > 0$. This is to be contrasted with the second set, in which $s_i^\# = 10$, that is, the fixed target was set rather low, in which case there were many more markets $\Delta_i^+ > 0$. On the other hand, in the third set of examples, the opposite situation occurred, as expected, since the $s_i^\#$'s were set at 50, resulting in many of the markets underproducing as reflected in the fact that many more markets had $\Delta_i^- > 0$.

As can be seen from Table II, the algorithm converged for all of the examples, requiring, at most, only several seconds of CPU time. In the first set of examples, with $Q_{ij}^\# \in [10, 50]$, in any given example and with all $\eta_{ij} = 0$, the number of transportation links with $\delta_{ij}^+ > 0$ was negligible. This is to be contrasted with the second set, in which $Q_{ij}^\# = 10$, and the η_{ij}'s were generated to lie in the range $[1, 10]$; that is, the fixed target was set rather low, in which case there were many more markets with $\delta_{ij}^+ > 0$. On the other hand, in the third set of examples, since the $Q_{ij}^\#$'s were set at 50, all of the transportation links had undershipments as reflected in the fact that all of the δ_{ij}^-'s were greater than zero.

Finally, in Table III we report the results of the variational inequality algorithm for the general model with both supply targets and transportation targets. Note that the algorithm required only seconds of CPU time for convergence for all twelve examples.

6. SUMMARY AND CONCLUSIONS

In this paper we developed a new competitive economic market model with target goals associated with over/underproduction at the supply markets and target goals associated with over/undershipment of the commodity between supply and demand locations. We then utilized the model to show how some of the ideas set forth in classical goal programming can be synthesized with variational inequality problems. The model captures mathematically certain negative economic externalities and opens the door for the development of other models, as well. Further, it contains as a special case a model introduced earlier but for which, heretofore, no computational procedure was available.

We first established that the governing equilibrium conditions can be formulated as a variational inequality problem. We then proved that under certain monotonicity conditions the equilibrium problem is guaranteed to have a solution and the solution is unique.

We subsequently proposed an algorithm, developed for a class of variational inequalities with linear constraints, of which our model is a member of. The algorithm decomposes the variational inequality into two simpler variational inequality subproblems, the first of which has the notable feature that it is identical to the variational inequality governing the well-known spatial price equilibrium problem. The algorithm under the same conditions that guarantee existence and uniqueness of the equilibrium pattern is guaranteed to converge.

Numerical results were then presented for three classes of examples, which highlighted different modeling features. In particular, we first solved economic market problems in which only supply targets were imposed. Next we computed solutions to problems with only transportation targets. Finally, we solved examples with both supply and transportation targets, and with associated penalties for failure to comply.

This research may be viewed as a contribution to the growing literature on mathematical programming approaches to policy interventions in market models.

APPENDIX

In this appendix, we present an algorithm for a class of variational inequality problems with linear constraints. For details, we refer the reader to Pan (1992). To take full advantage of the linear structure of the constraints, we first give the dual formulation of the problem, to which the proximal point algorithm and its relaxation may then be applied.

Consider the following variational inequality problem. Given two continuous functions: $A_1 : R^n \mapsto R^n$ and $A_2 : R^m \mapsto R^m$, an $r \times n$ matrix B, an $r \times m$ matrix A, and a vector $f \in R^r$:

Find $x \geq 0, z \geq 0$ satisfying $Bx + Az = f$ and

$$(A_1(x), x' - x) + (A_2(z), z' - z) \geq 0, \quad \text{for all} \quad (x', z') \geq 0 \qquad \text{(A1)}$$

satisfying $Bx' + Az' = f$.

We now make the following assumptions regarding Equation (A1):

a) (A1) has a solution.
b) A_1 is strongly monotone (with strong monotonicity constant α) and A_2 is monotone.
c) A has full row rank r.

By using the concept of subdifferential (see, for example, Zeidler 1985), (A1) can be written as the following multivalued equation:

$$0 \in (A_1(x) + N_{K_1}(x), A_2(z) + N_{K_2}(z)) + \partial\chi_M(x, z) \tag{A2}$$

where

$$K_1 = \{x|x \geq 0\}, \quad K_2 = \{z|z \geq 0\}$$

$$M = \{(x, z)|Bx + Az = f\}.$$

Also, by definition, we have that

$$N_{K_1}(x) = \partial\chi_{K_1}(x) \begin{cases} = \{u|(u, x' - x) \leq 0, \ \forall\, x' \in K_1\}, & \text{if } x \in K_1 \\ = \emptyset, & \text{if } x \bar{\in} K_1 \end{cases}$$

$$N_{K_2}(z) = \partial\chi_{K_2}(z) \begin{cases} = \{v|(v, z' - z) \leq 0, \quad \forall\, z' \in K_2\}, & \text{if } z \in K_2 \\ = \emptyset, & \text{if } z \bar{\in} K_2 \end{cases}$$

and, noticing that since $M - (x_0, z_0)$ is a linear subspace for any $(x_0, z_0) \in M$,

$$\partial\chi_M(x, z) \begin{cases} = \partial\chi_{M-(x_0,z_0)}((x, z) - (x_0, z_0)), & \text{if} \quad (x, z) \in M \\ = \emptyset, & \text{if} \quad (x, z) \bar{\in} M \end{cases}$$

$$\partial\chi_M(x, z) \begin{cases} = (M - (x_0, z_0))^{\perp}, & \text{if} \quad (x, z) \in M \\ = \emptyset, & \text{if} \quad (x, z) \bar{\in} M. \end{cases}$$

Therefore, there exists a $u \in A_1(x) + N_{K_1}(x)$, $v \in A_2(z) + N_{K_2}(z)$ such that $(u, v) \perp M - (x_0, z_0)$ or $(u, v) \in (M - (x_0, z_0))^{\perp}$.

For any $(X, Z) \in M - (x_0, z_0)$; hence, we have that $BX + AZ = 0$, and, therefore, $yBX + yAZ = 0$, for all $y \in R^r$; that is, $(yB, yA) \in (M - (x_0, z_0))^{\perp}$, for all $y \in R^r$.

Since A has full row rank, dim$(M$-$(x_0, z_0))$=$n + m - r$ and dim $(M - (x_0, z_0))^{\perp} = r$. Thus, $(yB$,$yA)$=(u, v) for some $y \in R^r$, or $(yB$,$yA)$ $\in (A_1(x)$+$N_{K_1}(x)$,$A_2(z)$+$N_{K_2}(z))$.

Let the $m \times r$ matrix A^* be a right inverse of A, i.e., A^* satisfies $AA^* = I_{r\times r}$. Then

$$y = yAA^* \in [A_2(z) + N_{K_2}(z)]\, A^*$$

$$yB \in A_1(x) + N_{K_1}(x)$$

Hence,

$$0 \in [A_1(x) + N_{K_1}(x)] - [A_2(z) + N_{K_2}(z)]\, A^*B.$$

Therefore, if (x, z) solves (1), then (x, z) also solves the following equation

$$0 \in [A_1(x) + N_{K_1}(x)]^t - B^t(A^*)^t[A_2(z) + N_{K_2}(z)]^t \tag{A3}$$

where $Bx + Az = f$.

Equation (A3) has the following dual formulation: (x, z) solves (A3) if and only if there exists a $\lambda \in R^r$ that solves the following equation:

$$0 \in (\hat{A}_1^t)_{B^t}(\lambda) + A(A^{*t}\hat{A}_2^t)^{-1}(\lambda) - f \tag{A4}$$

where

$$\hat{A}_1 = A_1 + N_{K_1}, \quad \hat{A}_2 = A_2 + N_{K_2}$$

and

$$B^t\lambda \in \hat{A}_1^t(x), \quad Bx \in (\hat{A}_1^t)_{B^t}(\lambda).$$

By definition,

$$(\hat{A}_1^t)_{B^t}(\lambda) = \{Bx | B^t\lambda \in (\hat{A}_1(x))^t\}. \tag{A5}$$

For additional theoretical results, we refer the reader to Pan (1992).

Now we can state the proximal point algorithm and its relaxation for Equation (A4). Since A_1 is strongly monotone, hence, $A_1 + N_{K_1}$ is strongly monotone. One can then show that $(A_1 + N_{K_1})^t_{B^t}$ is maximal monotone (see Gabay 1983). Also, by continuity and monotonicity, of A_2, we know that A_2 is maximal monotone. Hence, $A_2 + N_{K_2}$ is maximal monotone (see Rockafellar 1976b). This implies that $-f + A(A^{*t}\hat{A}_2^t)^{-1}$ is maximal monotone.

The proximal point algorithm takes the following form:

$$\lambda^{n+1} = \lambda^n + r_n(f - Bx^{n+1} - Az^{n+1})$$

$$Bx^{n+1} = (\hat{A}_1^t)_{B^t}(\lambda^{n+1}), \quad \text{i.e.,} \quad B^t\lambda^{n+1} \in \hat{A}_1^t(x^{n+1})$$

$$\lambda^{n+1} \in A^{*t}\hat{A}_2^t(z^{n+1}).$$

The relaxation variant, the Douglas-Rachford (1956) method can then be written in the variational inequality form as follows:

$$(A_1^t(x^{n+1}) + B^t(r_n(Bx^{n+1} + Az^n - f) - \lambda^n), x' - x^{n+1}) \geq 0,$$
$$\text{for all } x' \geq 0$$

$$((A^*)^t A_2^t(z^n) + r_n(Bx^{n+1} + Az^n - f) - \lambda^n, y' - A^*z^n) \geq 0,$$
$$\text{for all } y' \geq 0$$

$$\lambda^{n+1} = \lambda^n + r_n(f - Bx^{n+1} - Az^n).$$

For proof of convergence of $\{x^n\}$, $\{z^n\}$, and $\{\lambda^n\}$, see Pan (1992).

ACKNOWLEDGMENTS

This research was conducted on the Cornell National Supercomputer Facility, a resource of the Center for Theory and Simulation in Science and Engineering at Cornell University, which is funded in part by the National Science Foundation, New York State, and IBM Corporation.

The first author's research was supported in part by a University Faculty Fellowship from the University of Massachusetts at Amherst, while the author was visiting the Massachusetts Institute of Technology in Cambridge. The cordiality and hospitality of the Sloan School and the Operations Research Center are warmly appreciated.

BIBLIOGRAPHY

Beckmann, M., C. B. McGuire, and C. B. Winsten, 1956, *Studies in the economics of transportation*, New Haven: Yale University Press.

Charnes, A. and W. W. Cooper, 1961, *Management models and industrial applications of linear programming*, New York: John Wiley & Sons.

Charnes, A. and W. W. Cooper, 1977, 'Goal programming and multiple objectives optimization', *European Journal of Operational Research* 1, 39–54.

Charnes, A., W. W. Cooper, and R. O. Ferguson, 1955, 'Optimal estimation of executive compensation by linear programming', *Management Science* 1, 138–151.

Dafermos, S., 1980, 'Traffic equilibrium and variational inequalities', *Transportation Science* 14, 42–54.

Dafermos, S., 1982, 'The general multimodal traffic network equilibrium problem with elastic demand', *Networks* 12, 57–72.

Dafermos, S., 1990, 'Exchange price equilibria and variational inequalities', *Mathematical Programming* 46, 391–402.

Dafermos, S. and A. Nagurney, 1984, 'Sensitivity analysis for the general spatial equilibrium problem', *Operations Research* 32, 1069–1086.

Dafermos, S. and A. Nagurney, 1987, 'Oligopolistic and competitive behavior of spatially separated markets', *Regional Science and Urban Economics* 17, 245–254.

Dafermos, S. and A. Nagurney, 1989, 'Supply and demand equilibration algorithms for a class of market equilibrium problems', *Transportation Science* 23, 118–124.

Douglas, J. and H. H. Rachford, 1956, 'On the numerical solution of the heat conduction problem in 2 and 3 space variables', *Trans. Amer. Math. Soc.* 82, 421–439.

Eydeland, A. and A. Nagurney, 1989, 'Progressive equilibration algorithms: the case of linear transaction costs', *Computer Science in Economics and Management* 2, 197–219.

Faxen, K. O. and S. Thore, 1990, 'Retraining in an interdependent system of labor markets: a network analysis', *European Journal of Operational Research* 44, 349–356.

Flam S. D. and A. Ben-Israel, 1990, 'A continuous approach to oligopolistic market equilibria', *Operations Research* 38, 1045–1051.

Florian, M. and M. Los, 1982, 'A new look at static spatial price equilibrium models', *Regional Science and Urban Economics* 12, 579–597.

Florian, M. and H. Spiess, 1982, 'The convergence of diagonalization algorithms for asymmetric network equilibrium problems', *Transportation Science* 16B, 477–483.

Gabay, D., 1983, 'Applications of the method of multipliers to variational inequalities', in M. Fortin and R. Glowinsky (Eds.), *Augmented Lagrange Methods: Applications to the Solution of Boundary-valued Problems*, Amsterdam: North Holland, pp. 299–331.

Gabay, D. and H. Moulin, 1980, 'On the uniqueness and stability of Nash equilibria in noncooperative games', in A. Bensoussan, P. S. Kleindorfer, and S. Tapiero (Eds.), *Applied Stochastic Control in Econometrics and Management Science*, Amsterdam: North Holland.

Greenberg, H. J. and F. H. Murphy, 1985, 'Computing market equilibria with price regulations using mathematical programming', *Operations Research* 33, 935–953.

More', J. J., 1974, 'Coercivity conditions in nonlinear complementarity problems', *SIAM Review* 16, 1–16.

Nagurney, A., 1987a, 'Computational comparisons of spatial price equilibrium methods', *Journal of Regional Science* 27, 55–76.

Nagurney, A., 1987b, 'Competitive equilibrium problems, variational inequalities, and regional science', *Journal of Regional Science* 27, 55–76.

Nagurney, A., 1989, 'Migration equilibrium and variational inequalities', *Economics Letters* 31, 109–112.

Nagurney, A., J. Pan, and L. Zhao, 1992, 'Human migration networks', *European Journal of Operational Research* 59, 262–274.

Nagurney, A. and L. Zhao, 1990, 'Disequilibrium and variational inequalities', *Journal of Computational and Applied Mathematics* 33, 181–198.

Nagurney, A. and L. Zhao, 1991, 'A network equilibrium formulation of market disequilibrium and variational inequalities', *Networks* 21, 109–132.

Pan, J., 1992, 'Variational inequalities in the modelling and computation of spatial economic equilibria: structural reformulations and the method of multipliers', Department of Mathematics and Statistics, University of Massachusetts, Amherst, Ph.D. Thesis.

Qiu, Y., 1991, 'Solution properties of oligopolistic network equilibria', *Networks* 71, 565–580.

Rockafellar, R. T., 1976a, 'Augmented Lagragian and applications for the proximal point algorithm in convex programming', *Mathematics of Operations Research* 1, 97–116.

Rockafellar, R. T., 1976b, 'Monotone operators and the proximal point algorithm', *SIAM Journal of Control and Optimization* 14, 877–898.

Samuelson, P. A., 1952, 'A spatial price equilibrium and linear programming', *American Economic Review* 42, 283–303.

Takayama, T. and G. G. Judge, 1971, *Spatial and Temporal Price and Allocation Models*, Amsterdam: North Holland.

Thompson, G. L. and S. Thore, 1990, 'Economic disequilibrium by mathematical programming', *Journal of Optimization Theory and its Applications*, forthcoming.

Thore, S., 1986, 'Spatial disequilibrium', *Journal of Regional Science* 26, 660–675.

Thore, S., A. Nagurney, and J. Pan, 1992, 'Generalized goal programming and variational inequalities', *Operations Research Letters* 12, 217–226.

Zeidler, E., 1985, *Nonlinear Functional Analysis and Its Applications. Vol. III: Variational Methods and Optimization*, New York: Springer-Verlag.

Zhao, L. and S. Dafermos, 1991, 'General economic equilibrium and variational inequalities', *Operations Research Letters* 10, 369–376.

R. G. THOMPSON AND ROBERT M. THRALL

Polyhedral Assurance Regions with Linked Constraints*

ABSTRACT. The duality between efficiency and zero profit maxima has long characterized the theory of perfect competition in economics. Similarly, Data Envelopment Analysis (DEA) models in ratio and convex form imply zero profit maxima under the normalizations required for the linear programming (LP) reductions. Such zero profits are implied both in the absence and in the presence of cone-ratio (CR) assurance region (AR) bounds on the multipliers. However, if the AR input-output bounds on the multipliers are linked (linked-cones – LCs), which is precluded with CRs, then the normalizations required for the LP reduction must be dispensed with; and the DEA problem must be reformulated to be meaningful. This LC reformulation, as developed here, shows efficiency and profitability are *separate* concepts; and it gives new absolute profitability and non-linear efficiency measures. Both measures are relative to the full (m + s)-dimensions of the multiplier spaces, in contrast to the (m + s - 2)-dimensions of the LP normalized multiplier spaces. For the multiple output, multiple input problem, LP computational procedures may be used to find the maximum profit solutions; for the one-output problem, a non-linear programming procedure is suggested to find the efficiency solutions. Additional research is required to find the efficiency solutions for multiple output problems.

1. INTRODUCTION

Koopmans (1953, 1951) posited a linear model of production with the set of efficient points (assumed) corresponding to a general transformation function. Several price propositions were developed with the first going from efficient points to prices having certain properties and the second going from an attainable price point to an efficient point. One of the relevant points was that none of the activities could have positive profits and, further, any positively used activity had *zero* profits.

Dorfman *et al.* (1958) used the linear model to establish relationships between competitive equilibrium and technical efficiency. As they stated, given their equilibrium premises, if firms maximize their profits competitively with respect to any set of positive prices for goods and factors, the resulting configuration of inputs and outputs will be efficient if the achieved profit is

* Working Paper No. 92

W.W. Cooper and A.B. Whinston (eds.), New Directions in Computational Economics, 121–133.

zero. Conversely, if an efficient input-output situation is given, there exist nonnegative prices and a zero profit (maximum) competitive equilibrium.[1]

More recently, Baumol *et al.*'s (1982) theory of contestable markets and industry structure has zero profit consequences. As stated by Spence (1983), "this theory is best thought of as a generalization of the theory of perfect competition ... the zero profit property is clear cut."

This development in economics was analyzed by Samuelson (1963) who highlighted the importance of *free entry*. As he so well stated, "... free entry is a condition to be looked for empirically, rather than one imposed upon the data *a priori*." With free entry, their models imply that maximum profits will be zero. All of this assumes, of course, an underlying general transformation relation between inputs and outputs.

More recently, Charnes *et al.* (1978) started from a *finite data domain* to measure productive efficiency in the spirit of Farrell (1957). They specified a fundamental input-output ratio,

$$h_j(u, v) = \sum_r u_r y_{rj} / \sum_i v_i x_{ij}, \tag{a}$$

where y_{rj} and x_{ij} are the output and input data vectors for the $j = 1, 2, \ldots, n$ decision-making units DMU_j and u_r $(r = 1, \ldots, s)$ and v_i $(i = 1, \ldots, m)$ are respectively the virtual output and input multipliers.

The ratio approach in (a) was transformed into a mathematical programming problem by specifying a set of normalizing constraints (one for each DMU_j) to require the virtual output to virtual input ratio to not exceed one for each DMU_j, $j = 1, 2, \ldots, n$.[2] That programming problem may be stated as follows for the selected DMU_o:

$$\max_{u,v} h_o(u, v) = \sum_r u_r y_{rj} / \sum_j v_i x_{ij}$$

s.t.

$$h_j(u, v) = \sum_r u_r y_{rj} / \sum_i v_i x_{ij} \leq 1, \quad j = 1, 2, \ldots, n, \tag{b}$$

Further, an additional normalizing condition $v^T x_o = 1$, where $x_o = (x_{1o}, \ldots, x_{mo})^T$ gives the DEA Multiplier Model which has as its dual the DEA Envelopment Model:

---

[1] The authors are indebted to the helpful suggestions of W. W. Cooper in response to our request for a review of an earlier draft.

[2] Note that this inequality constraint [see (b) below] effectively requires zero optimal virtual profits (and requires assumption of free entry). Also, note that positive expected profits in the presence of free entry and constant returns-to-scale do not necessarily imply unlimited firm size [see, e.g., Thompson and George 1985].

DEA Envelopment Model	DEA Multiplier Model	
(DEA LP Primal)	(DEA LP Dual)	
$\min_{\theta,\lambda} \theta$	$\max_{u,v} z = u^T y_o$	
s.t	s.t.	(c)
$Y\lambda \geq y_0$	$u \geq 0$	
$\theta x_o - X\lambda \geq 0$	$v \geq 0$	
$\lambda \geq 0$	$u^T Y - v^T X \leq 0$	
θ unrestricted in sign	$v^T x_0 = 1$	

Charnes *et al.* (1986, 1991b) not only refined the DEA efficiency measurement procedure to encompass zero data and zero virtual multipliers, but also developed efficiency classification criteria for both the input-output and the multiplier spaces. Because of the two normalizations made, the maximum dimension of the optimal normalized multiplier spaces W_j^m, $j = 1, 2, \ldots, n$ is $m + s - 2$. One major consequence of this dimensional reduction is the following immediate relationship between zero profits and DEA efficiency Z^* for DMU_o.

DEA Multiplier Theorem I

Every DEA radial (scale) efficient rated DMU_j with optimizing multipliers in W_j^m maximizes DEA virtual profits at zero; and every selected DMU_j maximizing virtual profits at zero with optimizing multipliers in W_j^m is radial (or scale) efficient. It is noted that the optimal virtual profit t_j for any DMU_j has the form

$$\begin{aligned} t_j &= \sum_{r=1}^{s} u_r y_{rj} - \sum_{i=1}^{m} v_i x_{ij} = z^* - 1 \leq 0; \\ t_j &= 0 \quad \text{if and only if} \quad z^* = 1. \end{aligned}$$

Further, development of the Assurance Region (AR) concept[3] by Thompson *et al.* (1990) provides a similar relationship between zero profits and AR-efficient *DMU*s.

DEA/AR Multiplier Theorem II

Every AR-efficient DMU_j with optimizing multipliers in W_j^m maximizes DEA/AR profits at zero; and every reference DMU_j maximizing profits at zero with optimizing multipliers in $W_j^m \cap$ AR is AR-efficient.

[3] See also the related Cone Ratio (CR) concept of Charnes *et al.* (1990).

Clearly, in the presence of (b) and/or (c) above, a fundamental touchstone between economics and DEA has been the equivalence of zero profits and efficiency. However, as will be shown below, if the input and output multipliers are linked, as commonly practiced in economics (see, e.g., Dorfman *et al.* 1958), then the normalizations involved in (b) and (c) above are no longer valid (see Thompson *et al.* 1990). Further, virtual profits are not necessarily maximized at *zero* whether or not the multipliers are bounded. Thus, the linkage of the input and output multipliers gives results standing in sharp contrast to the *zero* profit criterion.

In the developments below, we revisit some DEA fundamentals to provide a frame of reference for the linkage AR model that follows. Our objective is to pose the linkage problem and to show how some solutions may be obtained.

We note that Banker and Maindiratta (1988), building on the work of Varian (1984), have previously foregone the zero profitability criterion. However, they focused on the single-output case and assumed all positive inputs and outputs. Also, they assumed a fixed price vector for each of the n *DMUs*. These assumptions (not made here) are sufficiently restrictive that their results are both less general than and not directly comparable to ours.

2. DEA FUNDAMENTALS REVISITED

We consider a data domain D (cf. Charnes *et al.* 1991b) defined by an $(s+m)$ by n matrix

$$P = [P_1, \ldots P_n] = \begin{bmatrix} Y \\ -X \end{bmatrix}, \tag{1}$$

where $Y \geq 0$ is s by n, $X \geq 0$ is m by n, and

$$P_j = \begin{bmatrix} y_j \\ -x_j \end{bmatrix}, \quad j = 1, \ldots, n.$$

For any $(s+m)$ vector

$$w = \begin{bmatrix} u \\ v \end{bmatrix} \geq 0 \tag{2}$$

we define for $j = 1, \ldots, n$

$$f_j(w) = u^T y_j, g_j(w) = v^T x_j, h_j(w) = f_j(w)/g_j(w). \tag{3}$$

Next, for

$$W = R^+_{s+m} \tag{4}$$

consider a subset W_A called the set of *admissible multipliers*.

If dim $W_A = s + m$, we say that W_A is *full dimensional*. If $w > 0$ for every w in W_A, we say that W_A is *zero proper*.[4]

A multiplier $w = \begin{bmatrix} u \\ v \end{bmatrix}$ is called D-*improper* if either a) $f_j(w) = 0$ for all j, or b) if for some j, $h_j(w) > 0$ and $g_j(w) = 0$. Otherwise, w is called D-*proper*.

In Charnes *et al.* (1991b), the DEA Theory was developed for the choice

$$W_A = \{w \mid w \text{ is D-proper}\}. \tag{5}$$

This represented an important generalization from requiring that W_A be zero-proper. (See that paper for details.)

A subset W_A is called an *Assurance Region* (AR) if the vectors w in $W - W_A$ are deemed unreasonable as multipliers. (See Thompson *et al.* 1986, 1990) for discussion of AR.)

An AR is called *conical* if it is a cone. An important instance of a conical AR, denoted CR (for cone ratio) is defined as follows (see Charnes *et al.* 1990). Let U, V, respectively, be any convex cones in R_s^+, R_m^+ and let

$$CR = \left\{ w = \begin{bmatrix} u \\ v \end{bmatrix} \middle| u \in U, v \in V \right\}. \tag{6}$$

In most (but not all)[5] previous applications, the ARs have been CRs.

A convex polyhedral cone Z in R_k^+ can be described analytically in what may be called "sum form" as (see Charnes *et al.* 1990)

$$Z = \left\{ z \mid z = A^T \alpha, \alpha \geq 0 \right\} \tag{7}$$

where $A^T \geq 0$ is k by p, or in "intersection form" as

$$Z = \{ z \mid Cz \geq 0, z \geq 0 \} \tag{8}$$

where C is q by k.

If AR is given in sum form by (7), then it is zero proper iff $A > 0$ and it is full dimensional iff rank $A = k = s + m$. No such simple characterization is possible from the intersection specification except for a few (albeit important) special cases.

To go from sum form to intersection form or vice versa is, generally, an exponentially complex problem. However, there are some useful cases where such "double description" is practical (see Charnes *et al.* 1991a).

---

[4] Early in the development of DEA, the requirement that each component of w be $\geq \varepsilon$ where $\varepsilon > 0$ was introduced to ensure that W_A be zero proper.

[5] The W_A defined in footnote 4 is an AR which is not conical (nor a CR).

Consider a data domain D and a set W_A of D proper multipliers. For $w \in W_A$, let

$$h_o(w) = \max_j \{h_j(w) \mid g_j(w) > 0\} \tag{9}$$

and define a vector

$$e(w) = \begin{bmatrix} e_1(w) \\ \vdots \\ e_n(w) \end{bmatrix}, \tag{10}$$

where if $g_j(w) > 0$

$$e_j(w) = h_j(w)/h_o(w), \quad j = 1, \ldots, n \tag{11}$$

and otherwise $e_j(w)$ is undefined.

We call

$$e_j = \max \{e_j(w) \mid w \in W_A\} \tag{12}$$

the W_A-*efficiency* of DMU_j and say that DMU_j is *radial* (or *scale*) *efficient* if $e_j = 1$. If there exists $w > 0$ for which $e_j(w) = 1$ we call DMU_j W_A-*efficient*. Note that if W_A is zero proper, then radial W_A efficiency is equivalent to W_A efficiency.

If W_A is a polyhedral CR, then e_j can be evaluated by recourse to either of two dual linear programs (cf. Charnes *et al.* 1978, 1991b). However, if W_A is a polyhedral cone AR with input-output linkage (see Thompson *et al.* 1990), then the normalization to a linear program is no longer available for calculating e_j. We will next investigate the linkage issue.

3. LINKAGE ISSUE

Our linkage investigation is directed initially to the profitability issue and secondly to the efficiency issue. To consider W_A profitability for DMU_j, let

$$h_j^* = \max_{w \in W_A} h_j(w) \tag{13}$$

Since $h_j(\alpha w) = h_j(w)$, we can replace (13) by

$$h_j^* = \max \{h_j(w) \mid w \in W_a \text{ and } f_j(w) = 1\}. \tag{14}$$

In turn, this is equivalent to

$$h_j^* = \frac{1}{g_j^*} \tag{15}$$

where

$$g_j^* = \min\{g_j(w) \mid w \in W_A \text{ and } f_j(w) = 1\}. \tag{16}$$

If W_A is polyhedral, this is a linear program.

We give an illustrative example for the case $s = 1$, $m = 2$. Let D be defined by the data matrix

$$P = \begin{bmatrix} 1 & 1 & 1 & 1 & 1 & 1 \\ -4 & -2 & -1 & -5 & -4 & -3 \\ -1 & -2 & -4 & -1 & -4 & -1.5 \end{bmatrix}. \tag{17}$$

Then it is easy to show (using Charnes *et al.* 1991b) that

$$\begin{aligned} E &= \{DMU1, DMU2, DMU3\}, \quad E' = \{DMU6\}, \\ F &= \{DMU4\}, \quad N = \left\{DMU5\left(\text{with } \theta_5 = \frac{1}{2}\right)\right\}. \end{aligned}$$

Next, let

$$W_A = \left\{ w = \begin{bmatrix} u_1 \\ v_1 \\ v_2 \end{bmatrix} \middle| C_W \geq 0, w \geq 0 \right\} \tag{18}$$

where

$$C = \begin{bmatrix} -1 & 1 & 0 \\ 2 & -1 & 0 \\ -\frac{3}{4} & 0 & 1 \\ \frac{5}{2} & 0 & -1 \\ 0 & -\frac{1}{2} & 1 \\ 0 & \frac{3}{2} & -1 \end{bmatrix} \tag{19}$$

Figure 1 shows the intersection $\bar{W}_A$ of W_A with the plane $u_1 = 1$ (the six vertices of $\bar{W}_A$ are the columns of the matrix A^T given in (21) below.) It is easy to see that (16) now becomes

$$\min g_j(w) = g_j^* \quad \text{for} \quad w \in \bar{W}_A. \tag{20}$$

In the presence of the linked multiplier constraints, absolute unit profits are maximized by DMU_2 alone at four of the six extreme points for W_A and are jointly maximized by *DMU*s 2 and 3 at the two remaining extreme points. Virtual profits at all these points are clearly non-zero, in contrast to the zero profits for these AR-efficient *DMU*s in the absence of the linked constraints and in the presence of the two DEA normalizations.

The situation pictured in the example shows that in the one-output, two-input case, if W_A is defined as an intersection cone by a 6 by 3 matrix of form

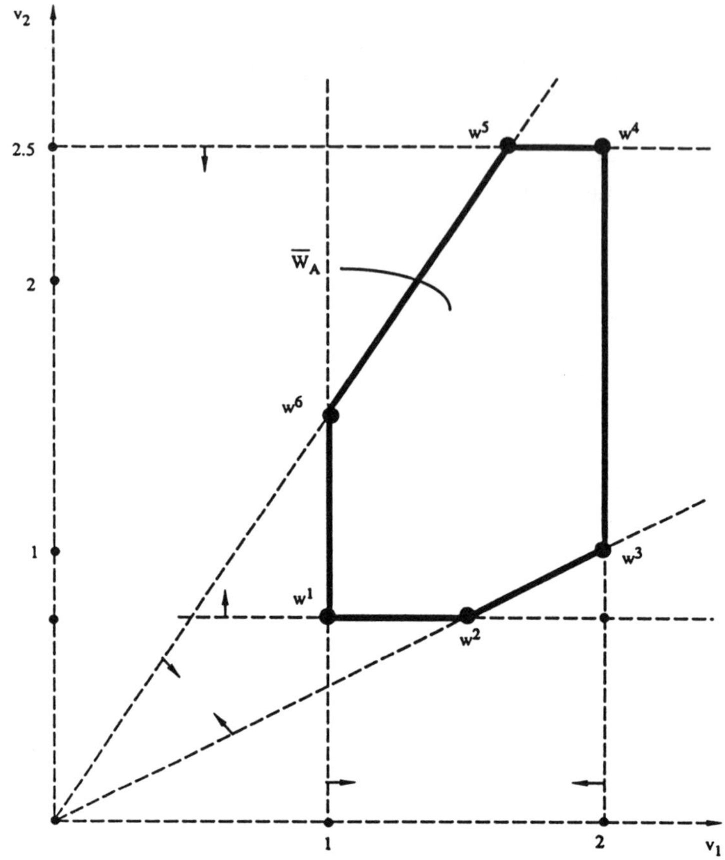

Fig. 1. $\bar{W}_A = W_A \cap (w \mid u_1 = 1)$.

TABLE I

$h_j(w^g), j = 1, \ldots, 6, g = 1, \ldots, 6.$

w^g	DMU$_j$ 1	2	3	4	5	6
w^1	0.211*	0.286°*	0.250*	0.173*	0.143*	0.242*
w^2	0.148	0.222°	0.222°	0.121	0.111	0.178
w^3	0.111	0.167°	0.167°	0.091	0.084	0.133
w^4	0.095	0.111°	0.083	0.080	0.056	0.102
w^5	0.109	0.120°	0.085	0.092	0.060	0.114
w^6	0.182	0.200°	0.142	0.154	0.100	0.190

* column max = h_j^*
° row max = $h^\circ(w^g)$

(19), then it also can be defined as a sum cone (see pp. 2025–2026 of Charnes *et al.* 1991a) having at most six extreme rays. Figure 1 displays $\bar{W}_A$ and the six vertices which define the extreme rays. Thus, for the Example,

$$W_A = \left\{ w \mid w = A^T \alpha, \alpha \geq 0 \right\}$$

where

$$A^T = \begin{bmatrix} 1 & 1 & 1 & 1 & 1 & 1 \\ 1 & 1.5 & 2 & 2 & 1.67 & 1 \\ 0.75 & 0.75 & 1 & 2.5 & 2.5 & 1.5 \end{bmatrix}. \tag{21}$$

Whenever (as with this Example) W_A has double description available, it is easy to determine the optimal output/input profitability ratio h_j^* for DMU_j.

To study W_A efficiency for DMU_j, we derive from (9), (11) and (12)

$$e_o = \max \beta h_o(w) \tag{22}$$

subject to

$$\beta h_j(w) \leq 1, \quad j = 1, \ldots, n, \tag{23}$$

and

$$w \in W_A \tag{24}$$

This is, of course, a non-linear program which we next express in an equivalent form. Let

$$E_A = \{DMU_k \in E \mid W_k \cap W_A \neq \phi\}.$$

For any $w \in W_A$ there exists $DMU_k \in E_A$ for which $h_j(w) \leq h_k(w)$, $j = 1, \ldots, n$ so that max β for this w is $1/h_k(w)$. Thus, if we set

$$e_o^k = \max\{h_o(w)/h_k(w) \mid w \in W_k \cap W_A\} \tag{25}$$

then

$$e_o = \max \left\{ e_o^k \mid DMU_k \in E_A \right\}. \tag{26}$$

Note that this approach presents two hurdles: 1) the objective function is non-linear, and 2) analytic description of W_k is, in general, an exponentially complex problem. However, in special cases one or both of these hurdles can be readily handled.

Consider the special case $s = 1$ of a single output. Then without loss of generality we may assume that every output $y_{1j} = 1$ and may also use the single degree of freedom in the choice of w from a ray $\{\alpha w^1 \mid \alpha > 0\}$ to

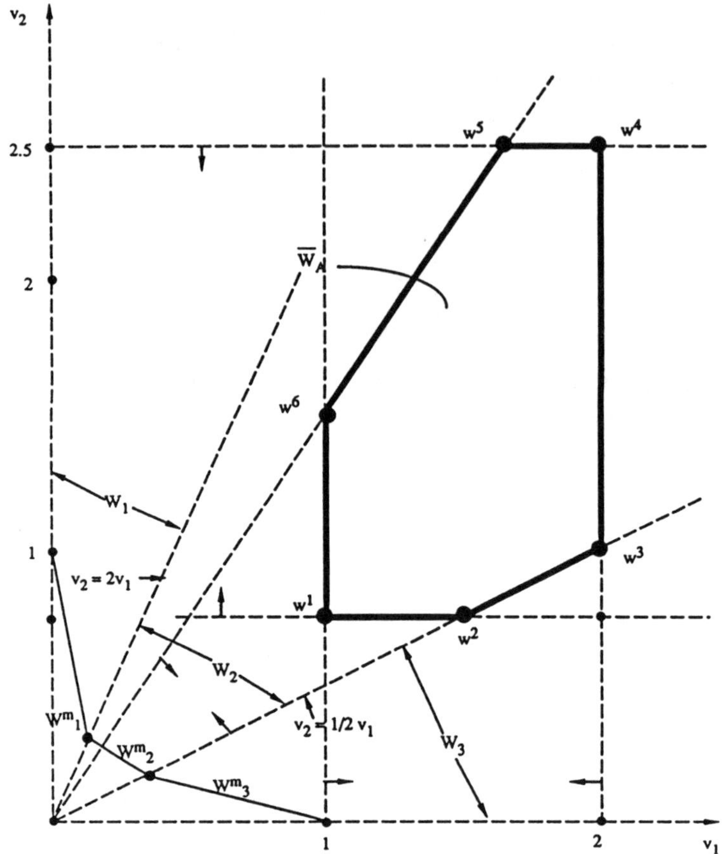

Fig. 2. The multiplier sets W_j, W_j^m and $\bar{W}_A$.

obtain $u_1 = 1$. Then $f_j(w) = 1$ for all j so that $h_j(w) = 1/g_j(w)$ and hence (22), (23), (24) are equivalent to

$$e_o = \max \beta/g_o(w) = 1/\min g_o(w)/\beta \tag{27}$$

subject to

$$\beta \leq g_j(w), \quad j = 1, \ldots, n \quad \text{and} \quad w \in \bar{W}_A. \tag{28}$$

This deals with the first hurdle. If, in addition, we assume further that there are $m = 2$ inputs then the relevant W_j are simply characterized as wedges whose spines are the positive u_1 axis. We illustrate this approach using the example with data domain *D* defined by (17) and with W_A given in intersection form by the matrix *C* of (19), and in sum form by the matrix *A* of (21).

In Figure 2 we add to Figure 1 the bounding lines for the intersections of W_1, W_2, W_3 with the plane $u_1 = 1$ and also show the normalized multiplier spaces W_j^m. We observe first that each intersection $W_j^m \cap \bar{W}_A$ is empty so that no optimal solution of the usual DEA system (c) satisfies the linked constraints defined by the matrix C. Next, we note that $W_1 \cap \bar{W}_A = \phi$, $W_2 \cap \bar{W}_A = \bar{W}_A$ and $W_3 \cap \bar{W}_A$ is the segment joining w^2 and w^3. Thus (26) reduces to

$$e_o = e_o^2 \tag{29}$$

and (25) becomes (using (27))

$$e_o = \max\left\{ \frac{g_2(w)}{g_o(w)} \middle| w \in \bar{W}_A \right\}. \tag{30}$$

Next, since $g_j(\alpha w = \alpha g_j(w)$ we may replace $\bar{W}_A$ in (30) with the following union of two intervals

$$\begin{aligned} w^I &= \left\{ w^1(\lambda) = \lambda w^1 + (1-\lambda) w^2 \right\} \\ &\cup \left\{ w^2(\mu) = \mu w^1 + (1-\mu) w^6 \right\} \end{aligned} \tag{31}$$

where $0 \leq \lambda, \mu \leq 1$.

It is easy to show that the functions

$$\frac{g_2(w^1(\lambda))}{g_o(w^1(\lambda))} \quad \text{and} \quad \frac{g_2 w^2(\mu)}{g_o w^2(\mu)}$$

have their minimum values for $\lambda = 0$ or 1 and $\mu = 0$ or 1. Hence, to calculate e_o we need only evaluate $g_2(w)/g_o(w)$ at the three vertices w^6, w^1 and w^2.

Using Table I we have

$$[e_j] = \begin{bmatrix} 0.910 \\ 1.000 \\ 1.000 \\ 0.770 \\ 0.500 \\ 0.950 \end{bmatrix} \quad \text{at} \quad \begin{bmatrix} w^6 \\ \text{all } w^g \\ w^2 \\ w^6 \\ \text{all } w^g \\ w^6 \end{bmatrix}. \tag{32}$$

In the presence of the two DEA normalizations, recall that DMU_5 was DEA-inefficient; DMU_4 was DEA-efficient, but in F; DMUs 1, 2, 3 were DEA-extreme-efficient; and DMU_6 was DEA nonextreme-efficient. Further, if the multipliers are bounded but not linked, then DMUs 2 and 3 are AR-efficient. Here, in the absence of the two DEA normalizations and in the presence of the multiplier linkage, *DMU* 2 and 3 are W_A-efficient. This result is encouraging.

More generally (still for $s = 1, m = 2$) we may expect several of the W_j to have two dimensional intersections with $\bar{W}_A$. In this case we must adjoin intersections of $\bar{W}_A$ with bounding lines of the W_j for $j \in E_A$. Again each e_o will achieve its maximum value at one of these points.

In closing this section, we note that Table I shows that w^2 is a W_A-efficient multiplier for *DMU*3 but that the profit maximizing multiplier for *DMU*3 is is w^1 and w^1 is not a W_A-efficient multiplier for *DMU*3. Thus, in general, *for a W_A-efficient DMU_j the maximum W_A-profitability need not be achieved with a W_A-efficient multiplier.*

4. SUMMARY AND CONCLUSIONS

The bounding of the multipliers in the DEA problem between inputs and outputs requires a totally new look at the issue of profitability and efficiency. Both of the normalization conditions imposed in the DEA problem, as originally posed by Charnes *et al.* (1978, 1979), must be dispensed with. This leaves only the dual-space structure following from the input-output data and linked multiplier constraints. If the linked multiplier constraint set is polyhedral, then there is a linear program for finding the maximum profit points (which are not, in general, zero); also by reversing the sign of the objective function, minimum profits can be obtained. However, efficiency determination seems more difficult because the objective function is nonlinear and an analytic description of multiplier optimizing sets is generally an exponentially complex problem. Only for the special case of a single output and two inputs have we presented a solution to the efficiency problem.

In conclusion, the long-standing zero profit assumption in economics and more recently in DEA is not tenable in DEA when the input and output multiplier constraints are linked. Solution of the resulting profit maximization and efficiency problem in the face of this linkage may require much in-depth analysis. The contribution here is offered primarily to stimulate first curiosity and then some solutions.

BIBLIOGRAPHY

Banker, R. D. and A. Maindiratta, 1988, 'Nonparametric analysis of technical and allocative efficiencies in production', *Econometrica* 56, 1315–1332.

Baumol, W. J., J. C. Panzar, and R. D. Willig, 1982, *Contestable Markets and the Theory of Industry Structure*, New York: Harcourt, Brace Jovanovich, Inc.

Charnes, A., W. W. Cooper, and E. Rhodes, 1978, 'Measuring the efficiency of decision-making units', *European Journal of Operational Research* 2, 429–444.

Charnes, A., W. W. Cooper, and E. Rhodes. 1979. 'Measuring the efficiency of decision making units', *European Journal of Operations Research* 3, 339.

Charnes, A., W. W. Cooper and R. M. Thrall, 1986, 'Classifying and characterizing efficiencies and inefficiencies in data envelopment analysis', *Operations Research Letters* 5, 105–110.

Charnes, A., W. W. Cooper, Z. M. Huang, and B. Sun, 1990, 'Polyhedral cone-ratio DEA models with an illustrative application to large commercial banks', *Journal of Econometrics* 46, 73–91.

Charnes, A., W. W. Cooper, Z. M. Huang, and D. B. Sun, 1991a, 'Relations between half-spaces and finitely generated cones', *International Journal of Systems Science* 22, 2057–2077.

Charnes, A., W. W. Cooper, and R. M. Thrall, 1991b, 'A structure for classifying and characterizing efficiencies and inefficiencies in data envelopment analysis', *Journal of Productivity Analysis* 2, 197–237.

Dorfman, R., P. A. Samuelson, and P. W. Solow, 1958, *Linear programming and economic analysis*, New York: McGraw-Hill.

Koopmans, T. C., 1951, 'Analysis of production as an efficient combination of activities', in T. C. Koopmans (Ed.), *Activity Analysis of Production and Allocation*, New York: Wiley, 33–97.

Koopmans, T. C., 1953, 'Efficient allocation of resources', *Econometrica* 19, 455–465.

Samuelson, P. A., 1963, *Foundations of Economic Analysis*, Cambridge, MA: Harvard University Press.

Seiford, L. M. and R. M. Thrall, 1990, 'Recent developments in DEA: the mathematical approach to frontier analysis', *Journal of Econometrics* 46, 7–38.

Spence, M., 1983, 'Contestable markets and the theory of industry structure: A review article', *Journal of Economic Literature* XXI, 981–990.

Thompson, R. G. and M. D. George, 1984, 'A stochastic investment model for a survival consious firm', *Annals of Operations Research* 2, 157–182.

Thompson, R. G., F. D. Singleton, Jr., R. M. Thrall, and B. A. Smith, 1986, 'Comparative site evaluations for locating high energy lab in Texas', *TIMS Interfaces* 16, 1380–1395.

Thompson, R. G., L. N. Langemeier, C. T. Lee, E. Lee, and R. M. Thrall, 1990, 'The role of multiplier bounds in efficiency analysis with application to Kansas farming', *Journal of Econometrics* 46, 93–108.

Varian, H. R., 1984, 'The nonparametric approach to production analysis', *Econometrica* 52, 579–597.

JOHN M. MULVEY*

Integrating Assets and Liabilities for Large Financial Organizations

ABSTRACT. A critical issue for large financial institutions involves the choice of methods for coordinating the firm's assets with projected liabilities. The basic problem is to preserve overall wealth while diversifying one's assets to reduce risks over a finite planning horizon. Three analytical models are proposed for the integration task, including an extension of the Markowitz portfolio model, a multi-stage stochastic program, and a multi-scenario procedure. Two of these have been implemented in large US companies. The three models are evaluated in the context of real-world applications using a novel methodology. Efficient algorithms for solving the resulting large-scale optimization models are discussed.

1. INTRODUCTION

The well-being of large, leveraged financial organizations – banks, thrifts, insurance companies, and investment houses – depends upon the careful coordination of asset management with liability controls. Many corporate failures have been caused by the mismatch of assets to liabilities, especially during volatile economic conditions. Since these organizations are so highly leveraged, net worth can quickly disappear. Unfortunately, most decision models focus on one side of the wealth equation. Typical investment strategies, for example, make recommendations about the proper mix of asset categories. But in general the liabilities are ignored in these calculations. This approach distorts the measurement of risks and rewards especially for risk averse investors and during times of volatile interest rate movements.

The issues are expressed simply enough by the key relationship: Wealth = market value of assets - NPV(liabilities). When either assets or liabilities are not priced by the marketplace, we must estimate the corresponding future cashflows and discount these to get an estimate of net present value (NPV). A planning horizon must be chosen, end effects taken into account, and estimates made for future interest rates. This procedure is common in many financial areas, for example, when determining the surplus or deficit of a

* Statistics and Operations Research, Report 92-20, July 1992, Princeton University, Princeton, NJ 08544.

W.W. Cooper and A.B. Whinston (eds.), New Directions in Computational Economics, 135–150.

pension plan the NPV of the liabilities is estimated by standard actuarial rules.

Including uncertainty complicates the NPV calculation in two ways. First, the range of possible cashflow outcomes must be estimated by statistical or other means. There are numerous approaches. We have found the concept of scenarios to be quite effective in this regard, especially when there are correlations among the various variables. (Scenarios are discussed in detail in Section 2). Second, the decision maker's attitude towards risk must be considered. There have been many efforts to quantify these attitudes ever since the landmark work of von Neumann and Morgenstern (1953).

To date, most organizations have separated the asset management decisions from the liability management issues. Different groups with very different cultures are responsible for each effort. For instance in the domain of pension planning, private firms have been able to concentrate on the asset side because the market value of their liabilities did not enter the income statement for most liability categories. This state of affairs is slowly changing as a market value analysis has been gaining ground in the actuary and the accounting professions. A prominent example is the 1987 accounting standard FASB87 which requires pension plans to use a (close to) market rate of discounting when determining a pension plan's wealth. This ruling also requires deficits (but not surpluses) to impact the income statement. In contrast, U.S. Banks use original worth for many of the asset/liability equations. (This practice is under fire from several directions and will likely be modified in the future.)

A simple example depicts the issues. Suppose that a hypothetical investor, Mr. Kim, has the following situation: an 8% $100,000 mortgage on his house with five years remaining. (To keep the calculations simple assume that there is no principal payout, the payments occur annually, and there are no tax consequences.) Mr. Kim must pay $8000 per year and the $100,000 balance at the end of the fifth year. On the asset side, we assume that Mr. Kim has assets of $150,000 which are entirely invested in a money market – currently paying 8%. Thus, Mr. Kim's current wealth is equal to $50,000 (Assets - NPV(liabilities)).

Next, the Federal Reserve decides to reduce interest rates to stimulate the economy. The short rate drops to 6% and the bank changes its money market rate accordingly to 6%. What are the consequences to Mr. Kim's wealth? The first immediate consequence is that the liability stream must be discounted at the lower rate of 6%, assuming that he does not refinance his mortgage. This drop in interest rate causes wealth to decrease to $41,575. If interest rates decrease to 4%, wealth decreases to $32,193.

To protect himself against the interest rate movements, Mr. Kim could hedge his portfolio by purchasing bonds of the proper duration so that adequate funds are available to pay out the liabilities when they are needed. The most conservative strategy, assuming that the liabilities cannot be paid out today and no refinancing, is to place $100,000 in bonds and the remainder into cash equivalents. The 100% money market mix does not provide the adequate diversification and accordingly is not the most conservative investment. This result is inconsistent with most investment models which depict cash as the safest asset category. More is said about this topic in Section 2.1.

A primary issue in investment analysis pertains to the need to indicate estimates of liability uncertainty in the computations. The risk-reward frontier cannot be properly calculated without reference to Mr. Kim's liabilities. For investors, the motto should be: *Invest for a Purpose*. What is conservative for one class of investors will not necessarily be conservative for another class. Investments for college education must be treated differently than for general retirement bills. And, of course the timing of the liabilities must also be considered since the assets which provide higher expected returns are generally more volatile.

The remainder of the report is organized as follows. The next section describes the three alternative models for integrating assets and liabilities. Each of these depends upon the notion of a scenario, and this concept is defined at the beginning. The first model is a direct extension of the classical Markowitz mean/variance quadratic program. Including liabilities causes the efficient frontier to tilt towards that asset category which provides the largest degree of diversification (as a hedge against the NPV of liabilities). The degree of tilting depends upon the investor's aversion to risk.

While the mean/variance (MV) model is easy to understand and has been implemented widely, it suffers from several critical disadvantages. These limitations are listed in Section 2.2. An alternative approach which avoids the MV problems is proposed. The alternative model takes on a multi-stage stochastic program (MSP) with a large network component. In theory, the MSP approach encompasses the most general types of asset-liability problems. While the resulting optimization problems become large quickly, they possess a special structure that can be exploited by parallel algorithms. It is thereby likely that practical methods will be available to *solve* these models using networks of workstations and powerful PCs.

The third model provides an intermediate step between a simplified expected value optimizer, and a full fledged multi-stage stochastic program. The approach is a special case of the notion of "robust optimization" (Mulvey *et al.*, 1991). The basic idea is to provide an investment strategy which will be robust across a set of reasonable outcomes. Here again, the idea of scenarios is key to quantifying the uncertainties. Scenarios are also key to the display of the results so that the decision maker can select the degree of robustness which suits his or her disposition. The model has been successfully implemented by a large U.S. insurance company.

2. THREE PROCEDURES

This section describes three alternative models for assisting an investor in constructing his or her investment portfolio. The basic notion is to model wealth over time (either by means of single or multiple periods), where the wealth calculation depends upon both assets *and* liabilities. To accomplish this goal, we employ the notion of scenarios. A scenario represents a single plausible and discrete path across time for all the relevant uncertainties which are contained in a dynamic decision problem. The time-steps are assumed to coincide with the periods in the multi-stage model. A prominent example in finance involves the time evolution of riskless interest rates – zero coupon government bonds. Much theoretical research has occurred in this area over the past 3-5 years; see Marsh (1992) and Hull (1989). The set of scenarios is defined as:

$$s = \{1, \cdots, S\}$$

where $\|s\|$ depicts the number of scenarios. It is occasionally useful to supply accompanying probabilities – along with the scenarios $p_s = \{p_1, p_2, \cdots, p_S\}$ – to express an estimate of the likelihood of the scenarios. Rather than a strict forecast, the scenarios together depict the full range of uncertainties to be faced by the organization. There are numerous approaches for generating the scenarios. See Marsh (1992) and its references for descriptions of some popular continuous time interest rate models. The scenarios are samples from these continuous time stochastic processes. The optimal number of scenarios remains an open and difficult problem. Dantzig and Infanger describe the use of importance sampling techniques (Dantzig and Infanger, 1991) for addressing this question.

Each of the three models can be used to integrate assets and liabilities. There are pros and cons to be considered by the model builder. The underlying choice of a mathematical model is a multi-dimensional decision problem with all of the ensuing complexities. Mulvey showed that the problem can be posed as a multi-criteria decision, see *Strategies in Modeling* (Mulvey, 1979) for further details.

2.1. *Mean-Variance Investing for Asset/Liability Management*

The Markowitz mean-variance framework provides a simple, elegant solution to the portfolio problem. At its simplest, the model provides a prescription for diversifying one's assets. The task is accomplished by calculating the efficient frontier for expected returns and for risk as measured by variance of returns (as a surrogate for volatility). We define the mean/variance quadratic program as follows:

Maximize	$[\mu^t x + \lambda x^t Q x]$	
subject to	$Ax = b$	(1)
	$1 \leq x \leq u$	(2)
where	x	$(n \times 1)$ vector of asset holdings
	μ	$(n \times 1)$ vector of expected returns
	Q	$(n \times n)$ variance/covariance matrix

where the weighting λ ($0 \leq \lambda \leq 1$) is used to trace out the efficient frontier between the expected return and risk as measured by the variance of returns. The linear constraints (1) and (2) depend upon the investor's circumstances. A planning horizon (τ) is chosen by the investor to fit his or her investment strategy. For example, a natural period is one year for pension plans since the major decisions are made at the annual corporate board of directors meeting. The determination of the input coefficients (μ and Q) has been studied by a number of researchers. We can employ scenarios in this regard:

$\rho^s_{i,t}$ = single period returns (% s), security i, time period t, scenario s.

$$\mu_i = \sum_{s=1}^{S} p_s \times \Upsilon^s_{i,\tau}$$

$$q_{i,j} = \text{covariance}(\Upsilon^s_{i,\tau}, \Upsilon^s_{j,\tau})$$

$$\Upsilon^s_{i,\tau} = \prod_{t=1}^{\tau} (1 + \frac{\rho^s_{i,t}}{100})$$

Note that the length of the planning horizon (τ) affects the computations.

To focus the discussion and show typical mean/variance results, we choose eight popular asset categories. The categories are: 1) Standard and Poor's 500 (large capitalized U.S. stocks); 2) Smaller capitalized U.S. stocks ; 3) the EAFE index (Europe, Australia, and the Far East–non U.S. stocks); 4) Hedged EAFE (EAFE without currency risks); 5) Lipper's Growth stocks; 6) Low PE (price/earnings) U.S. stocks; 7) Cash (money market); and 8) Shearson's government/corporate bond index. These asset categories have been selected based on several factors: 1) each category represents a large and well identified market of securities; 2) there is a recognized index that tracks the performance of the market subset; and 3) clients are interested in watching and ultimately investing in these categories.

The definition of appropriate categories is based upon individual preference. Each organization possesses a set of policy constraints that represent

TABLE I

Historical performance of asset categories – correlation matrix

	Standard deviation of returns	Expected Returns						
S&P 500	18.34	16.11						
SM CAP	22.61	4.65						
EAFE	23.92	23.94						
HGD EAFE	20.83	15.72						
LIPPER G	18.37	13.66						
LOW PE	18.05	10.94						
CASH	0.56	6.97						
G/C BOND	6.1	11.38						
S&P 500	1							
SM CAP	0.926	1						
EAFE	0.618	0.619	1					
HGD EAFE	0.782	0.843	0.8	1				
LIPPER G	0.99	0.952	0.628	0.799	1			
LOW PE	0.969	0.955	0.669	0.839	0.978	1		
CASH	0.109	-0.063	-0.164	-0.136	0.115	-0.008	1	
G/C BOND	0.168	0.107	0.244	0.087	0.222	0.204	0.326	1

legal rules and even tradition. For instance, some pension plans will not invest outside the U.S. despite the lack of rules to prevent this form of diversification. Thus, the first step in any analysis is to decide upon the universe of asset categories. Quantitative methods provide little guidance for answering this important initial question.

Assuming that we have made this decision and have come up with the indicated eight categories, we list in Table I historical information on the expected returns, variances, and correlations. This data is derived from quarterly returns during the twelve-year period: from the first quarter 1979 to the fourth quarter 1990. A graphical view of the information is presented in Figure 1. Here, we have plotted the historical expected returns versus their standard deviation (risk). The latter is often considered as a surrogate for the risk of a portfolio. Note that EAFE had the highest expected value.

Turning to the correlation matrix, we see that seven of the asset categories possess positive coefficients with each other (to various degrees). Cash, as defined by money market accounts, provides the only exception. Simply put, cash has a slight negative correlation with the other asset categories.

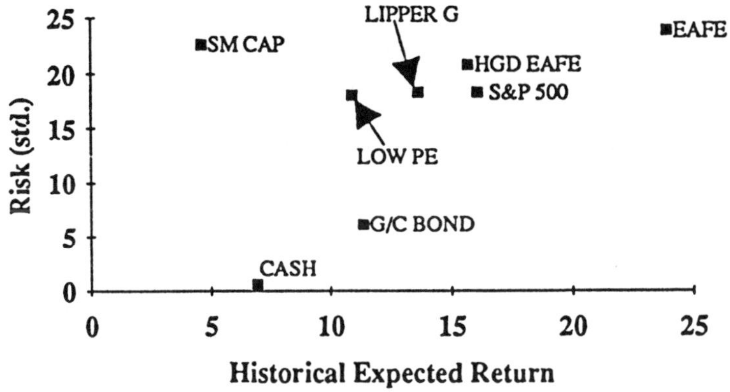

Fig. 1. Historical means and variance for asset categories.

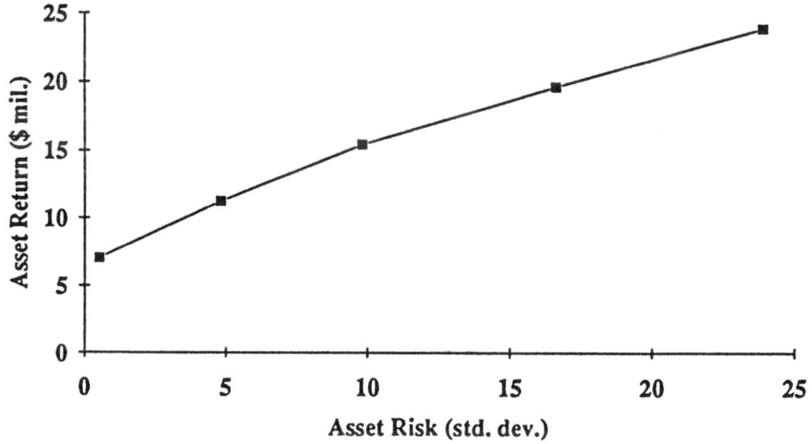

Fig. 2. Unconstrained efficient frontier.

To illustrate the mean/variance approach, we have solved the example asset allocation presented in Table I. We assume that the decision date is 1 January 1991. The MV model has been calibrated by using 24 quarters of historical data (from 1985 to 1990). Each quarter represents a single scenario. The corresponding efficient frontier and the associated recommended asset mixes are depicted in Figure 2 and Table II. Total initial wealth equals $55.5 million for this example.

Next, we placed limits on the model: minimum 5% cash, maximum 10% international EAFE stocks, and maximum 10% smaller stocks. The resulting efficient frontier is shown in Figure 3 and Table III. Many organizations impose restrictions of this type when carrying out an asset allocation procedure.

The efficient frontier provides asset mixes for various degrees of risk aversion. Conservative individuals and companies should focus their attention

TABLE II

Asset mixes for points on frontier

Asset risk	0.55	4.832	9.833	16.659	23.915
Asset return	7.043	11.259	15.477	19.692	23.929
Cash arc	0	0	0	0	0
S&P 500	0	1.45	0.678	0	0
SM CAP	0	0	0	0	0
EAFE	0.204	6.086	18.361	37.261	55.5
HGD EAFE	0.054	0	0	0	0
LIPPER G	0	0	0	0	0
LOW PE	0	0	0	0	0
CASH	55.242	19.388	0	0	0
G/C BOND	0	28.576	36.461	18.239	0

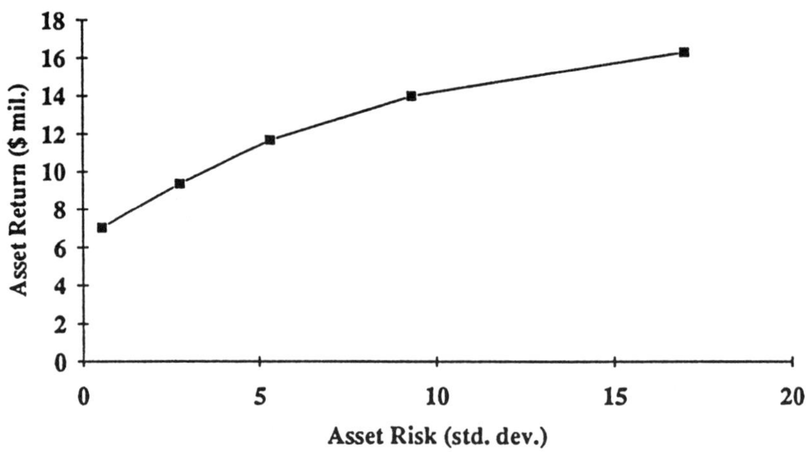

Fig. 3. Constrained efficient frontier.

on the bottom lefthand side of Figures 2 or 3, while the more aggressive investors should be interested in the top right hand side. Unfortunately, the MV model by itself provides little guidance for choosing an acceptable level of risk – a point on the frontier.

We now extend the mean/variance model to handle liabilities. The basic idea is to coordinate the potential changes in the assets with corresponding changes in the Net Present Value (NPV) of the liabilities. Remember that the assets are already measured by means of a market-value. The liabilities must be measured in a similar fashion.

TABLE III

Points on constrained frontier

Asset risk	0.55	2.773	5.333	9.32	17.009
Asset return	7.043	9.373	11.703	14.032	16.363
Cash arc	0	0	0	0	0
S&P 500	0	0.588	2.848	19.863	46.709
SM CAP	0	0	0	0	0
EAFE	0.204	3.713	5.408	5.436	5.463
HGD EAFE	0.054	0	0	0	0
LIPPER G	0	0	0	0	0
LOW PE	0	0	0	0	0
CASH	55.242	35.692	13.519	2.775	2.775
G/C BOND	0	15.506	33.725	27.426	0.553

To accomplish this task, we again employ the concept of "scenarios". Herein, a single scenario provides one possible set of asset *and* liability movements. It acts as a single realization from a multivariate distribution. The generation of the scenarios for the assets is a simple matter. We used previous quarters of historical returns (for instance, 24 quarters), each weighted equally (1/24), to represent 24 possible scenarios. Grauer and Hakkanson (1986) used this simple probability approach for asset only investing with good results.

The liabilities must now be coupled with these 24 scenarios. There are several issues to consider. First, the discount factor must be estimated. Remember that for pension plans, accountants require a market discount value (the FASB87 regulation). We thereby calculate our estimate of the market discount rate for each of the 24 scenarios. In addition, other factors are taken into account, including inflation, workforce changes, and macroeconomic variables. The final result of this process is a vector of 24 numbers for the projected NPV of liabilities, corresponding to the 24 scenarios.

Once these values are determined, we can compute the variance and covariances of the liabilities to the asset categories. Table IV gives a typical example of projected liability cashflows over a 26-year horizon. The NPV of these liabilities depends upon the discount rate: NPV @ 8% = $48.467 million; NPV @ 9% = $40.677 million. Using these cashflows in the context of the scenario analysis, we can compute the correlations of the NPV (liabilities) to the assets. Figure 4 shows the results. Note that we have added a new row to the original variance/covariance matrix Q. This row provides the additional information needed for the Markowitz *surplus* model.

TABLE IV

Correlation of liabilities to assets.

	SP 500	SM CAP	EAFE	HDG EAFE	LIPPER	LOW PE	CASH	G/C BOND
NPV of liabilities	-0.048	-0.131	0.074	-0.176	-0.009	-0.026	0.342	0.687

The extended model has two objectives: maximize the expected wealth, while minimizing the variance of the wealth – as a surrogate for risk. Figure 5 and Table V illustrate a wealth efficient frontier. The overall shape of the frontier has changed very little. The recommended asset mixes can be much different, however, especially on the conservative side of the frontier. For our example, cash has been replaced by the government/corporate bonds. Table V lists the recommended asset mixes for the five points on the wealth frontier. We stress that these results are dependent upon the investor's liability structure.

We call the integrative model a surplus MV optimization, and the overall investment approach: *investing for a purpose*. The primary difference between the two strategies is the role of cash in the conservative investments. In the asset-only approach, cash provides the diversifying asset. It is relatively uncorrelated with the other assets. Thereby, it acts as a hedge to reduce volatility.

In the wealth case, however, the diversifying asset is not cash. It depends upon the uses of the funds. In many cases in which the actual cashflows are not greatly altered under the various scenarios and when the major determinate is the interest rate as in the example discussed above, the diversifying assets are fixed income investments (primarily bonds). Note that in this example bonds are positively correlated with the liabilities (see Figure 4) – but we are subtracting assets from liabilities. Thus, when we attempt to maximize our wealth (Assets - NPV of Liabilities), we add bonds to our portfolio mix as the diversifying asset category. In other instances, the diversifying assets could be other categories, such as commodities – oil or gold – or perhaps real estate.

The major lesson to learn from this discussion is that the wealth model requires more information from the investor – some idea about the intended purpose of future cash flows. But this information provides more accurate estimates of the risk/reward tradeoff as it affects the investor's overall wealth at the end of the planning horizon.

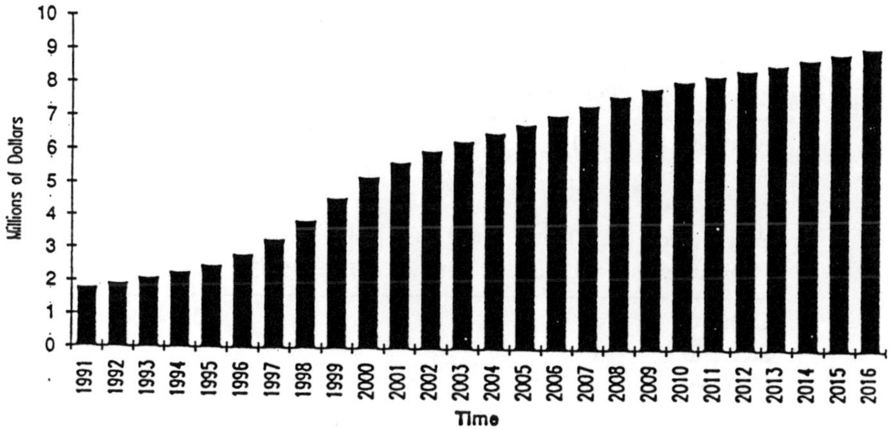

Fig. 4. Projected liability cashflows.

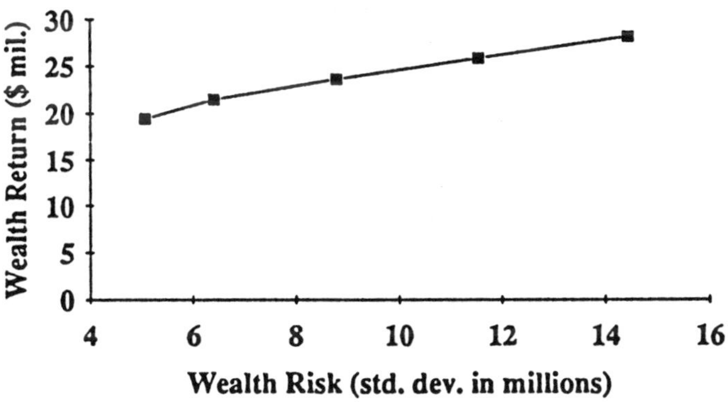

Fig. 5. Wealth efficient frontier.

2.2. *Multi-Stage Stochastic Programs*

The most comprehensive model for integrating assets and liabilities is the multi-stage stochastic program (MSP). Here, the planning horizon is divided into discrete time intervals, such as quarters or years: $t = \{1, \cdots, \tau\}$.

A multi-stage model is partially motivated by the limitations of the Markowitz model. First, the MV model handles transaction and market impact costs in a suboptimal fashion. It has difficulty revising an existing portfolio. Next, this MV model does not recommend a single point on the efficient frontier since a utility curve is left unspecified. The model has difficulty making recommendations concerning the portfolio revision problem without placing ad hoc constraints on portfolio turnover or total transaction costs. Also, the Markowitz model cannot be readily extended to handle multiple periods.

For these and other reasons, we have turned to an alternative model in which the goal is to maximize an expected von Neumann-Morgenstern (V-M)

TABLE V

Points on wealth efficient frontier

Asset risk	6.103	8.485	13.231	18.504	23.915
Asset return	11.375	14.509	17.642	20.776	23.929
Wealth risk	5.079	6.417	8.804	11.556	14.446
Wealth returns	19.386	21.426	23.576	25.836	28.223
Cash arc	0	0	0	0	0
S&P 500	0	0	0	0	0
SM CAP	0	0	0	0	0
EAFE	0	14.275	28.261	41.969	55.5
HGD EAFE	0	0	0	0	0
LIPPER G	0	0	0	0	0
LOW PE	0	0	0	0	0
CASH	0	0	0	0	0
G/C BOND	55.5	41.225	27.239	13.531	0

utility curve. Herein, utility is defined as a function of *wealth* at the end of the planning horizon τ. To develop the V-M model, we define the primary variables as representing the amount of the investor's wealth in each of the assets at the beginning of each time period:

$x_{i,t}^s$ investment in asset category i, time period t, scenario s ($)

Related variables are designated:

$y_{i,t}^s$ purchases of asset i, time period t, scenario s ($)

$z_{i,t}^s$ sales of asset i, time period t, scenario s ($)

The uncertain quantities depend upon the scenario generation process. The primary uncertainties are as follows:

r_t^s interest rate in period t, scenario s

l_t^s liabilities in period t, scenario s

$NPV^s_{t,\Delta t}$	net present value of liabilities at period t, discounting Δt future periods at corresponding interest rates r^s_t for scenario s
$c^s_{i,t}$	cash flows for asset i, time period t, scenario s

We assume that the investor is risk averse with the following iso-elastic V-M utility function:

$$U(\text{wealth}) = \frac{1}{\gamma}(\text{wealth})^{\gamma}$$

where the parameters $\gamma \in$ [-∞,0] denotes the investor's risk aversion.

Thus, given a planning horizon τ, the objective function for the multi-stage stochastic program is:

$$\text{Maximize} \qquad \sum_{s=1}^{S} p_s \times U(\text{wealth}^s_t)$$

where wealth^s_t represents wealth at the beginning of time period t, scenario s.

The [MSP] constraints involve several issues. For example, the projected liabilities l^s_t must be paid in all time periods during the planning horizon. Adequate cash or the availability of borrowing must be possible under all scenarios. Flow balance constraints are needed so that portfolio revision can be carried out at each decision stage. Also, the regulatory and other portfolio mix restrictions must be maintained at each step.

The multi-stage stochastic program (MSP) generates a large-scale problem due to the need for conditional decision variables $x^s_{i,t}$ in the second and subsequent stages. In fact until recently, MSPs have been too large for most practical applications (over 100 scenarios). Remember that the objective function is concave for risk averse decision makers and therefore must be solved as a nonlinear program (NLP).

Two recent developments have changed this situation. First, several new algorithms have been invented for decomposing the MSP problem into relatively independent subproblems. One of the most promising is the DQA method proposed by Mulvey and Ruszczynski (1992). This technique is ideally suited to the use of distributed networks of computers linked by Ethernet or other similar means.

The large improvement in computational resources provides the second development. Workstations and even high performance PC's are now capable of solving relatively large LPs – over 10,000 variables. Thus, a distributed network of these machines provides substantial computational power – almost supercomputer capabilities. Current economics favor this form of computing.

2.3. *Multi-Scenario Analysis*

The previous two methods can be difficult to implement for certain classes of investors, in particular, those who concentrate on the fixed-income marketplace. The required covariance calculations are not easily available for securities in which the cashflows are highly uncertain and contingent on particular economic conditions, such as the state of interest rates. For instance, collaterized mortgage obligations (CMO's) do not easily fit a Markowitz framework. (For some ideas on this topic, see Mulvey and Zenios (1991).)

For these situations, we suggest that a third asset/liability model be considered. We call the approach: "multi-scenario analysis". The basic idea is to develop a small number (handful) of representative scenarios which represent (or cover in a general sense) the range of the uncertainties over the planning horizon. Of course, it is impossible to actually cover all of the possibilities. Rather our intention is to provide a representative but not exhaustive set of scenarios. We call this set the "highlighted scenarios".

Given the representative scenarios, we develop a method for estimating the expected outcome for the individual securities within a portfolio, conditional on scenario s (or the subset represented by scenario s). Again, a planning horizon (τ) is chosen. Since considerable research has been done on the valuation of fixed-income securities, for instance, using binary trees, the basic methodology exists for performing this set of calculations.

The next step is to set up a single-period optimization model in which the investor's wealth is constrained to be above a predetermined threshold ($\text{wealth}_s^{\text{min}}$) for each of the scenarios. This approach is a special case of robust optimization (Mulvey *et al.*, 1991).

There can be a variety of constraints (1) and (2) in the model which limit, for instance, turnover or transaction costs. Under this framework, the primary objective is to guarantee that the portfolio achieves a satisfactory performance (Simon's satisficing idea) over a set of prescribed scenarios. This objective is achieved through the additional constraints.

For many portfolio managers, there is a natural benchmark portfolio which plays a role equivalent to the liabilities. These investors desire a return distribution which falls above the benchmark, over all the proposed scenarios.

The concepts are summarized in Figure 6. Here, there are seven scenarios which depend upon the general level of interest rates. Each rectangle indicates the range of possible outcomes for the portfolio; the highest points represent the maximum that could be attained if all other scenarios were ignored in the objective function. Thus, the portfolio manager should concentrate on the area within the rectangles. The current portfolio and the recommended portfolio (proposed by the optimization model) are also displayed in the figure.

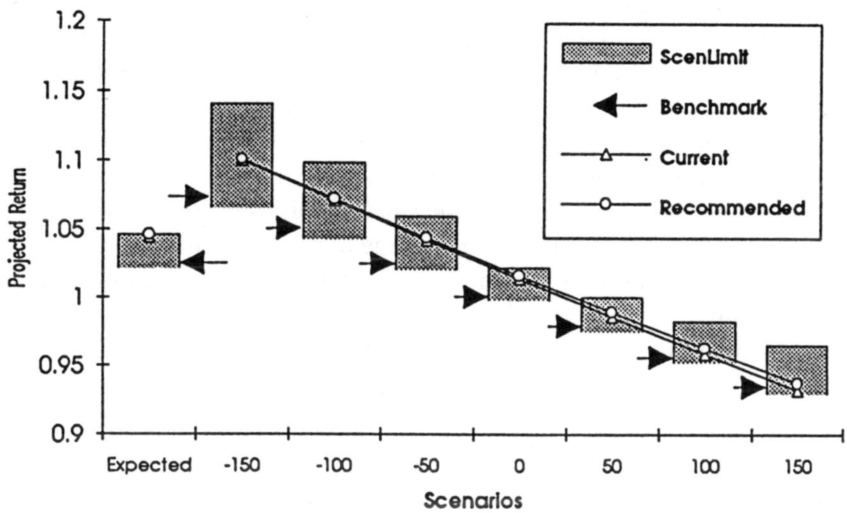

Fig. 6.

Given valuation models for the individual securities, this form of robust optimization model is relatively straightforward to solve. In fact, the model is a linear program which can be solved with standard algorithms.

3. FUTURE WORK

The development of an integrative asset-liability model requires a greater amount of information from the investor than asset-only models, for instance, the liability cashflows for the various scenarios. In most cases, this type of data can be derived from actuarial and econometric studies. One topic which will require further research involves the construction of the investor's preference curve as a function of time. Several ideas can be explored: 1) the use of growth optimal strategies; 2) the nature of changing preferences and its impact on goal satisfaction; and 3) the role of graphical tools for aiding the investor in discovering the possible consequences of alternative decision strategies.

Clearly, another important issue is the design of efficient algorithms for solving multi-stage stochastic programs. These problems become very large as a function of the number of scenarios. Parallel and distributed computers will be critical in this regard.

Another critical aspect of the proposed asset/liability models involves the definition of scenarios. Especially, the number of selected scenarios seems to be important to the model's recommendations. There are various ways to test the number of scenarios: Dantzig and his coworkers at Stanford have used importance sampling with good success (Dantzig and Infanger, 1991). Or an adaptive procedure can be developed in which the number is increased in a progressive fashion – starting slowly and gradually building up the representative set. The process terminates when the key decision variables are consistent from one iteration to the next. In any case, this issue is just beginning to be addressed. Much research is needed.

Ultimately, the integration of assets and liabilities is motivated by the need to find reliable solutions over a wide range of possible futures (scenarios). In Section 2.3, we presented a heuristic for handling this issue in the context of a small number of highlighted scenarios. Other methods for achieving robust recommendations will be needed in the future.

ACKNOWLEDGEMENTS

The research of J. M. Mulvey was funded in part by NSF Grant CCR–91–02660 and IDS Financial Services, Inc.

BIBLIOGRAPHY

Dantzig, G. B. and G. Infanger, 1991, 'Large-scale stochastic linear programs: Importance sampling and Benders decomposition, Report SOL 91–4, Department of Operations Research, Stanford University.

Grauer, R. R. and N. H. Hakansson, 1986, 'A half century of returns on levered and unlevered portfolios of stocks, bonds and bills, with and without small stocks', *Journal of Business* 59(2).

Hull, J., 1989, *Options, Futures, and Other Derivative Securities*, Prentice Hall.

Marsh, T. A., 1992, 'Term structure on interest rates and the pricing of fixed income claims and bonds', in R. Jarrow, M. Maksimovic, and W. Ziemba (Eds), *Handbook in Operations Research and Management Science: Finance*, Amsterdam: North-Holland, forthcoming.

Mulvey, J. M., 1979, 'Strategies in modeling: A personnel scheduling example', *Interfaces* 9(3).

Mulvey, J. M. and A. Ruszczynski, 1992, 'A new scenario decomposition method for large-scale stochastic optimization', Report SOR–91–19, Department of Civil Engineering and Operations Research, Princeton University, Princeton, NJ 08544 (to appear in *Operations Research).*

Mulvey, J. M. and S. A. Zenios, 1991, 'Capturing the correlations of fixed-income instruments', Report SOR–91–29, Department of Civil Engineering and Operations Research, Princeton University, Princeton, NJ 08544 (to appear in *Management Science).*

Mulvey, J. M., R. J. Vanderbei, and S. A. Zenios, 1991, 'Robust optimization of large scale systems: General modeling framework and computations, Report 91–06–04, Decision Sciences Department, The Wharton School, University of Pennsylvania, Philadelphia, PA 19104.

von Neumann, J. and O. Morgenstern, 1953, *Theory of Games and Economic Behavior*, New York: Wiley, third edition.

PART THREE

Economic Modeling and Computational Systems

JAMES C. MOORE, WILLIAM B. RICHMOND, AND ANDREW B. WHINSTON

Economic Decision Theory as a Paradigm for the Construction and Evaluation of Algorithms and Information Systems

ABSTRACT. We present a decision model that can be interpreted as an economic decision model for a decision maker under bounded rationality; as a behavioral decision model where the decision maker makes tradeoffs between the accuracy of the decision and the effort to make the decision; as a general model of computation amenable to both von Neuman computers and parallel computers; as a model for constructing information systems from a library of reusable code or objects; and as a model of organizational decision making. Although the model is general enough to encompass these (plus other) areas, it is powerful enough to achieve interesting results when properly specialized.

1. INTRODUCTION

We present a decision model that can be interpreted as an economic decision model for a decision maker under bounded rationality; as a behavioral decision model where the decision maker makes tradeoffs between the accuracy of the decision and the effort to make the decision; as a general model of computation amenable to both von Neuman computers and parallel computers; as a model for constructing information systems from a library of reusable code or objects; and as a model of organizational decision making. Although the model is general enough to encompass these (plus other) areas, it is powerful enough to achieve interesting results when properly specialized.

Under this decision model, a decision maker faces a problem whose payoff depends on the decision made and the state of the world. The decision maker has the opportunity of acquiring information about the state of the world before making the decision, but only at some cost. Acquiring information is a sequential process of performing experiments. The results of each experiment refines the state space providing the decision maker a better estimate of the true state of the world, thus enabling a better decision. Specializing the model to different domains requires properly defining the state space, the

W.W. Cooper and A.B. Whinston (eds.), New Directions in Computational Economics, 153–173.

payoff function, and the information-acquisition actions and their resulting information structure.

One of the more interesting interpretations of the model is as a general model of computation that enables to construct and evaluate algorithms and information systems. We claim that algorithms and information systems are developed to solve some problem; therefore, the appropriate measure of an algorithm must be related to the net payoff from solving the problem. The tradeoff between the cost and the value of information determines the degree to which a problem is solved. To this end, we view an algorithm as the formalization of a decision strategy, and develop an economic based model for constructing and analyzing algorithms. We use the decision theoretic model developed by Moore and Whinston [8, 9] to look at the cost and the value of computations and select the sequence that maximizes the net payoff. The economic model addresses the issue of how precise an answer or solution should be for any particular problem.

The decision theoretic model highlights the value of using an optimization approach to constructing algorithms. Each parameter of the decision problem influences the optimal decision process. Changing the parameters changes the optimal algorithm, so when an optimization approach is feasible, the algorithm can be designed to match the user's specific characteristics. The optimal algorithm is optimal only for the given state space, experiment set and information partitions. Altering these parameters alters the optimal algorithm. In addition to the final decision process depending on the state space representation, the experiment set and the information partitions, the optimal algorithm depends on the payoff function, the cost function and the probability distribution.

Incorporating all of these parameters enables us to examine, discuss, and sometimes construct optimal algorithms for such problem domains as database retrieval. In database retrieval, the decision theoretic approach is particularly important for very large database systems used by the general public. California and other states are implementing kiosks to provide information to the public, including job matching information. For this case, a tradeoff must be made between finding the ideal job and the cost of searching through the set of available jobs. The various algorithms available for this search process should be evaluated within an economic setting. These kiosk systems are forerunners of multimedia, electronic shopping systems, where the size of the database will necessitate the need to make tradeoffs between the cost and value of search. These systems will open a new distribution channel that will depend on the underlying algorithm used to support the system.

From an economic viewpoint, incorporating the cost of information acquisition into the choice process should bring the normative, economic choice models and the descriptive, psychological choice models closer together. It will allow us to investigate the conditions under which the psychological choice models are optimal, while opening the field of constructive economics. It can enable us to embed rational (optimal) strategies within information retrieval and decision support systems.

In Section 2, we present the decision model. Section 3 presents an example and discusses the model as a model for human decision making. It then shows how the model can be used to model computer supported choice processes. Section 4 shows that the model can be used for algorithm construction and evaluation. We conclude in Section 5 with a discussion of the implications of the model and future research.

2. DECISION MODEL

We propose using the Moore and Whinston [8, 9] decision model as a normative Model of decision making with bounded rationality and for the construction and evaluation of algorithms. Under this decision model, a decision maker faces a problem whose payoff depends on the decision made and the state of the world. The decision maker has the opportunity of acquiring information about the state of the world before making the decision, but only at some cost. Acquiring information is a sequential process of performing experiments. The results of each experiment refines the state space providing the decision maker a better estimate of the true state of the world, thus enabling a better decision.

As an example, consider a person who wants to purchase a car. The utility to this person will depend on the car chosen and environmental factors, such as the cost of gasoline. Before buying the car, the consumer has the opportunity to obtain information on the set of available cars and to obtain forecasts on such factors as the future price of gasoline. The process of acquiring the information and making the decision, is called the decision strategy.

In this decision model, a decision is a function of eight parameters.

$$D = \langle X, \phi, \omega, D, A, \{\mathbf{M}_a \mid a \in A\}, c, r \rangle$$

where:

X is the state space. It represents all the possible states of the world, and it embodies all the relevant aspects of the decision about which the decision maker is uncertain. In the car selection example, a state would represent a set of possible cars, plus relevant aspects of the environment, such as the price of gas, oil, tires, and service mechanics. It also may include dimensions on such things as political instability that could affect the desirability of bulletproof glass, etc.

ϕ is a probability distribution over the set of possible states of the world, X. $\phi(x)$ represents the probability that x is the true state.

$\omega = \omega^*(x, d, c)$ is the net payoff function. We use $\omega^*(x, d, c)$ as part of the objective function for evaluating the different decision strategies available to the decision maker. By altering $\omega^*(x, d, c)$ we can reflect the priorities of the decision maker. We will frequently assume that the payoff function is separable, so that $\omega^*(x, d, c) = \omega^*(x, d) - c$. In this case, $\omega^*(x, d)$ is the gross payoff resulting from decision d when x is the true state of the world. In the car selection example, $\omega^*(x, d)$ is the utility the decision maker would receive from purchasing car d from the set of cars and under the environmental conditions represented by state x.

D is the set of possible final decisions or choices. In the example, it is the set of all possible cars.

$A = \{a_0, a_1, \ldots, a_n\}$ is the set of available experiments or computations. The experiment a_0 is the null experiment – do nothing, and we represent the set of non-null experiments as $A^* = \{a_1, \ldots, a_n\}$. Each experiment partitions the state space and reduces the set of possible true states of the world.

Depending on the decision problem and the issues under investigation, each $a \in A^*$ can be a machine instruction for a computer, a module of code, a linear program for a decision support system, or an entire computer system. For an individual decision maker, each experiment could be an elementary information process as in Johnson and Payne [5], or a step in Tversky's Elimination by Aspects Model [22]. For an organization, A could be partitioned into $A_1, \ldots, A_k$ where A_i represents the actions available to the ith member of the organization. These various interpretations provide the flexibility to use the decision model to investigate problems in computer science, economics and psychology.

For the selection of a car, reading *Road and Track*, test driving a car, talking to a current owner are all experiments designed to identify the set of available cars. Executing simulations on gas prices and talking to friends at the United Nations are experiments for determining the relevant environmental conditions.

$\mathbf{M}_a = \{M_{a1}, \ldots, M_{a,\eta(a)}\}$ is the partition of the state space resulting from experiment a. Each experiment results in the decision maker receiving some signal (e.g., test driving the Dodge Caravan reveals that it is comfortable, roomy, has plenty of pickup, etc.). Associated with each possible signal is a set of states (e.g., the Dodge Caravan has a certain set of attributes). Once a signal is received, the decision maker knows which set of states contains the true state.

c is the cost function. A common assumption when evaluating algorithms is that the cost of each experiment is constant for all experiments; $c(a) =$ c for all $a \in A^*$ and $c(0) = 0$. For other problems, such as searching for a car, the cost of each experiment may differ.

r is the maximum number of experiments allowed. We frequently require $r \geq n$ to ensure that the resulting decision strategy can obtain complete information if doing so is justified.

In this model, a decision strategy is defined as follows:

Definition 2.1. *A decision strategy s is represented by a sequence of r + 1 pairs.* $\sigma = <(\mathbf{B}_1, a_1), \ldots, (\mathbf{B}_r, a_r), (\mathbf{B}_{r+1}, \delta)>$, *where:*

$\mathbf{B}_t$ *is a partition of the state space and is termed an information structure* $(\mathbf{B}_t = \{B_1, B_2, \ldots, B_k\})$.

$\mathbf{B}_1$ *is the entire state space.*

α_t *defines the action taken at the tth step on each element of the partition* $\mathbf{B}_t$. α_t: $\mathbf{B}_t \rightarrow A$. *For example, let* $\mathbf{B}_t = \{B_1, B_2, B_3\}$ *and let the function* $\alpha_t(\mathbf{B}_t)$ *be given by* $\alpha_t(B_1) = 0$, $\alpha_t(B_2) = 0$, $\alpha_t(B_3) = 3$. *The* $\alpha_t(\mathbf{B}_t)$ *corresponds to taking no information-acquisition action at step t if the true state is an element of* B_1 *or* B_2*, and taking experiment 3 if the true state in an element of* B_3.

δ *defines the final decision made at the end of the information gathering process.* δ: $\mathbf{B}_{r+1} \rightarrow D$.

The goal is to determine an information and decision strategy, σ, that maximizes $\Omega(\sigma) - \Gamma(\sigma)$, where

σ defines a sequence of actions that partition the state space. At each element of a partition a (possibly different) action is specified. For each element of the final partition, $\mathbf{B}_r + 1$, σ determines the decision (choice) to be made.

Ω is the gross expected value of the strategy σ. $\Omega = \Sigma_B \in \mathbf{B}_{r+1} \Sigma_{x \in B} \phi(x)$ $\omega(x, d)$, where d is the decision taken when the information-gathering strategy ends in partition element B.

Γ is the gross expected cost of the strategy σ. $\Gamma = \Sigma_B \in \mathbf{B}_{r+1} \pi(B) C(B)$, where $C(B)$ is the cost of executing the experiments that result in partition element B, and $\pi(B)$ is the probability of the true state being in partition element B.

Graphically, the decision strategy, σ, can be represented by a tree. Each node of the tree represents a set of states of the world, $B \subseteq X$. Each arc of the tree represents the possible signals of the experiment, $\alpha_t(B)$, taken on the node (subset B) from which the arc emanates. The nodes at the end of the arc represent the refinement of B induced by $\alpha_t(B)$. Each level of the tree represents a partition, B, of X. Note that for each level of the tree to represent a partition of X, when the null experiment, $a = 0$, is taken a single signal is possible, so a single arc emanates from B and the node B is repeated at the end of the arc.

3. MODEL OF HUMAN CHOICE

The decision model presented in Section 2 is a model of human decision making that explicitly incorporates bounded rationality. Traditional economic search models with complete recall, including those proposed by Weitzman [27], Morgan and Manning [15] and Manning and Morgan [6] are all special cases of this model. The model also conforms to the behavioral choice theory proposed by Johnson and Payne [5] that explicitly assumes that people conserve their mental resources and intuitively make tradeoffs between the optimality of the choice and the amount of mental processing used. Using this model, we can mimic behavioral decision strategies examined by Johnson and Payne, and other strategies, such as Tversky's Elimination by Aspects [22] and Tversky and Sattath's Hierarchical Elimination Method [23]. By formalizing the notion of the tradeoff between the cost of information and the value of the choice, we believe that inconsistencies in choices can, at least in part, be explained by incomplete information about the alternatives, and that the gap between economic, rational choice behavior and human choice behavior can be narrowed.

In this choice model, the choice mechanism may be either probabilistic or deterministic. Probabilistic choice occurs when the decision maker does not have enough information about the alternatives to distinguish the unique alternative that will maximize utility. The probability of any alternative, x_i, being selected depends entirely on the strategy the decision maker uses to make the choice – not on the decision maker's preferences – we assume, however, that the decision maker will use a strategy that results in choices that reflect his or her preferences, and when describing an economically rational agent, the strategy maximizes expected utility.

3.1. Example

As an example, consider an individual who wants to purchase a car, and assume that Table 1 represents the alternatives and their attributes. The decision maker knows the different possible attributes that are relevant to his or her choice, and he or she knows that the ideal car has a price less than \$10,000, has four seats, gets more than 40 miles per gallon, is a convertible, and has manual transmission. The decision maker also realizes that this combination is unlikely to exist. In general, the decision maker knows what he or she wants in a car, but does not know which attribute combinations exist or the attributes that any particular car embodies.

To determine which cars are available, the decision maker must gather information (perform experiments in our terminology). The decision maker goes to a car lot and drives a Honda to find that it has great suspension. He or she reads *Car and Track* magazine to find that Buicks are reliable, but Fiats are not. As the decision maker gathers information, he or she fills in the information matrix, Z. At some point, the decision maker makes a decision – usually before the matrix is completely filled in.

Where:

Attributes A, B, C and D represent different price levels with

A $\leq$ \$10,000
B = \$ 10–15,000
C = \$ 15–20,000
D $\geq$ \$ 20,000.

Attributes E, F, G and H represent different number of seats, with

E = 2
F = 4
G = 5
H = 6.

Attributes I, J, K and L represent different miles-per-gallon ratings, with

I $\leq$ 20 mpg
J = 20–25 mpg
K = 25–30 mpg
L $\geq$ 30 mpg.

Attributes M and N represent the type of roof, with

M being a convertible
N being a hardtop.

Attributes O and P represent the type of transmission, with

O being manual transmission
P being automatic transmission.

Let the decision maker's preferences be represented by the linearutility function:

$$\begin{aligned} u(x) &= 30A + 15B + 5C + 0D \\ &\quad + 5E + 10F + 0G + 0H \\ &\quad + 0I + 0J + 25K + 45L \\ &\quad + 10M + 20N + 20O + 0P. \end{aligned}$$

TABLE I
Available cars

Car	Price				No. of seats				MPG				Roof		Transmission	
	A	B	C	D	E	F	G	H	I	J	K	L	M	N	O	P
Honda Accord	0	1	0	0	0	1	0	0	0	0	0	1	0	1	1	0
Yugo	1	0	0	0	0	1	0	0	0	0	1	0	0	1	1	0
BMW 320i	0	0	0	1	0	1	0	0	0	1	0	0	0	1	0	1
Corvette	0	0	0	1	1	0	0	0	1	0	0	0	1	0	1	0
Chevette	1	0	0	0	0	1	0	0	0	0	1	0	0	1	1	0
Roadmaster	0	0	1	0	0	0	0	1	1	0	0	0	0	1	0	1
Fiero	0	1	0	0	1	0	0	0	0	1	0	0	0	1	0	1

Under the decision model, the probability of choosing any of the cars is unknown at this point (or can be considered random), because the probability depends on the information that the decision maker has about the alternatives. The probability of choosing any alternative will depend on the information acquisition and decision strategy. In the car example, let the consumer use a decision function that selects the alternative with the highest utility.

A (not necessarily optimal) strategy of testing the columns in decreasing order of their weights results in the following choice probabilities:

After one experiment (column L)

P(Honda) = 1

After two experiments (column L and K)

P(Honda) = 1

After three experiments (columns L, K, A)

P(Honda) = 0
P(Yugo) = 1/2
P(Chevette) = 1/2.

For a utility maximizing individual, the probability of selecting an alternative changes with the information on the alternatives. It is no wonder, then, that people show inconsistencies in making choices, since their information rarely stays constant. Note that in each case, the probability of choosing an alternative, x, given the known information, will always be either 0 or $1/k$, where k is the number of alternatives that have the same, maximum expected utility. This symmetry in the choice probabilities results from our assumption that an individual will use an economic evaluation and selection model and will select the alternative that maximizes his or her expected utility. We could obtain choice probabilities similar to the choice probabilities derived from descriptive models by using a probability distribution over different strategies (especially over the maximum allowable number of experiments, r). Since we do not have a rationale for any probability distribution, however, imposing one would be artificial.

Using this model, we can identify optimal decision strategies under various conditions. As mentioned above, we can use the decision model to duplicate the traditional economic search strategies. To do this, let $X = D$ = the set of alternatives. $\omega(x, d)$ is the searcher's utility function and c is the cost of search. Different experiment sets result in different models of search. If $a_i \in A$ examines i alternatives and $r = 1$, then we have the search strategy proposed by DeGroot [2]. If $a_i \in A$ represents examining alternative i, then we duplicate the search process proposed by Weitzman [27]; and if $a_i \in A$ represents examining i alternatives, then we duplicate the search process examined in Morgan and Manning [15].

We can advance the economic search literature and integrate it with behavioral psychology, marketing's consumer choice theory and computer science by altering the definition of the state space and the experiment set, for example, by defining the experiments to examine attributes rather than alternatives, we flip economic search theory upside down. Defining $X = D$ = the set of alternatives and eliminating all states that do not have a particular attribute results in the behavioral decision strategy Elimination By Aspects [22].

Alternatively, we can define the state space as the set of possible $m \times n$ matrices where each row of the matrix represents an alternative. Each column of the matrix represents an attribute and a cell, (i, j), of the matrix has a 1 if row i has attribute j. The experiments work toward revealing the true set of available alternatives. Moore *et al.* [13] show that when the probability an alternative has an attribute is 1/2 and is independent of the other attributes the alternative has and the attributes that other alternatives have, and when the consumer's utility function is a linear function of the attributes, then the optimal search strategy is to examine the attributes in descending order of their weight. The experiments used in this strategy resemble the commands and responses found in relational database queries, which naturally leads to the issue of computer supported consumer search.

3.2. Database Search

Relational database query languages allow the user to select all records that have a particular attribute. In these database systems, the decision maker and the database system are separate entities. The original decision problem, the basis for the retrieval, is separate from the retrieval process. The decision maker is forced to translate his or her preferences into a test of feasibility that the database system can answer. He must construct his own search strategy by first translating his preferences into characterizations of feasible sets of alternatives.

A characterization of the feasible set acts as a query. The response to the query may be:

1. an acceptable (small) set of alternatives,
2. an unacceptable (large) set of alternatives, and
3. the null set.

Depending upon the type of response, the decision maker takes one of two actions. If the response is acceptable, then the search is complete and the decision maker makes the final choice. If the response set is either the null set or too large, then the decision maker must recast his or her preferences into a new characterization of a feasible set of alternatives and repeat the search process. Both the efficacy and efficiency of this method depend upon users' knowledge of the contents of the database and upon users' willingness to spend their mental resources.

Moore *et al.* [11, 14] propose viewing information retrieval as a choice problem where the decision maker wants to find the record that represents the best available alternative. This approach takes advantage of the results on optimal consumer search and allows the decision maker to use his preference function as a query. Retrieval systems that support choice problems exist for gemstones [25], used cars [26] and aviation parts [24], and we expect that these electronic markets will become more pervasive in the near future. For these systems to be widely adopted, however, they must reduce the customers' search costs by better facilitating the customer's search process. We believe that the integration of the users' preferences into the retrieval algorithm is one way of accomplishing this.

The existence of computer supported choice processes has numerous economic implications. The different choice process implies that consumers will make different choices. This will affect issues ranging from the optimal degree of product differentiation and the products produced to the type and amount of advertising. It also raises issues about the relationship between the producer, the consumer and the provider of the search service, and the impact of these relationships on the retrieval algorithm. For example, if the search service is owned by a producer, the search service may return alternatives that it produces, even if they are not the best available. This is similar to what consumers faced with the airline reservation systems. American Airlines always returned its flights on the first screen, causing customers to choose American Airlines even when there was a choice that was better for them. Finally, there are issues related to competition among suppliers of the search service and how to structure the price for search – payment for each referral or based on the quantity purchased?

4. ECONOMICS AND ALGORITHM CONSTRUCTION

Although developed as a model of human decision making, we propose using the decision model as a general model of computation for applying economic principles to the construction and evaluation of computer algorithms and information systems. According to Rogers [19], "An algorithm is a deterministic, bookkeeping procedure which can be applied to any of a certain class of symbolic inputs and which will yield, for each such input, a corresponding symbolic output." Given this definition of an algorithm, several features are essential, including:

1. An algorithm is given as a finite set of instructions.
2. There is a computing agent.

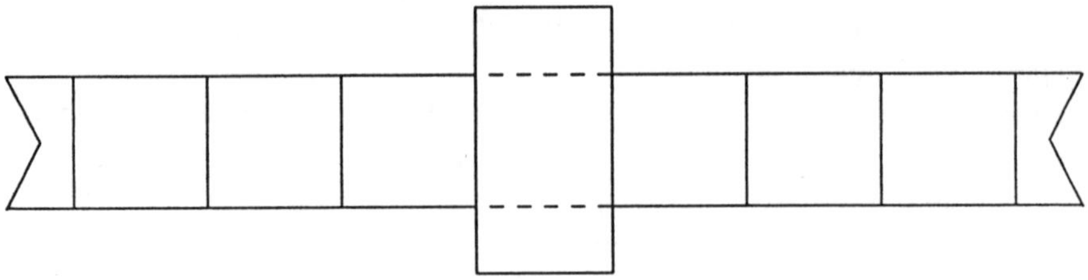

Fig. 1. Turing machine.

3. There is a way to make, store and retrieve the steps in the algorithm.
4. The agent performs the algorithmic instructions in discrete steps.
5. The agent performs the steps in the algorithm deterministically.

In the decision model, the algorithm is represented by the decision strategy, which contains a finite set of statements. The computing agent is the decision maker, and can be represented by either a human or a computer. The steps of the algorithm are stored in the nodes of the decision tree and retrieving the next step consists of following the appropriate path to the next node in the tree. The decision maker executes the decision strategy by executing a series of experiments – each of which is discrete, and deterministic. Thus, the decision strategy generated by the decision model fits with the informal idea of an algorithm.

In more formal investigations [1, 16, 19], an algorithm is equated with a model of a computer, which is shown to compute exactly the partial recursive functions, and the computer model most commonly used is the Turing machine. The Turing Machine (Figure 1) has a tape of infinite length in both directions. The tape is divided into equal size cells, which just fit into the machine. The cell in the machine is being examined by the machine. The tape can move left or right, one cell at a time. At each step, the machine can:

1. write a 1 on the cell being examined, or
2. erase the cell being examined, or
3. move the tape 1 cell to the right, or
4. move the tape 1 cell to the left.

At the end of each step, the machine takes on one of a finite set of internal states, $q_0, q_1, q_2, \ldots$ The internal state and the contents of the cell being examined determine the next operation and internal state according to a finite set of rules. Each rule is represented by a quadruple (i, ii, iii, iv) where

i. is the initial internal state,
ii. is the current cell value,
iii. is the operation to be performed, and
iv. is the next internal state.

Any two distinct quadruples must have different i and ii. A Turing machine is represented by any finite set of quadruples, and each stage in a Turing Machine's calculations is given by:

i. the condition of the tape
ii. the internal state of the Turing Machine
iii. the location of the cell being examined.

This is called an instantaneous description of the Turing Machine.

Ideally, we would like to prove the following assertion by showing that the decision model is equivalent to the Turing Machine.

Assertion 4.1. *The set of partial recursive functions can be computed by decision strategies generated from the Moore and Whinston decision model.*

Technically, this assertion is true, since the set of actions could be made equivalent to a Turing machine, but for the analysis of algorithms that would defeat the purpose. Because the decision strategies generated by the decision model are represented by a tree of finite depth, it is impossible to represent all occasions where the Turing Machine would not stop. However, we can prove the following assertion:

Assertion 4.2. *Any (partial) function whose solution can be generated by a Turing Machine in N steps can be generated from the Moore and Whinston decision model. This is true for arbitrary N.*

Start by numbering the cells in the tape from $-\infty$ to ∞, where cell 0 is the start of the tape, and define the range of cells examined by the Turing Machine during its operations as L. Define T to be the set of possible tape configurations that can occur during the operation of the Turing Machine. Using these terms, we define the parameters of the decision model as:

$X \subset Q \times L \times T$. X is a subset, since not all possible combinations will occur. Each element of the state space represents an instantaneous description of the Turing Machine for some input.

D is the set of all possible responses that the Turing Machine can make when operating for N steps.

$A = \{a_1, \ldots, a_n\}$ where a_1 checks the input to the machine and $a_2, \ldots, a_n$ are the rules defining the Turing Machine.

$\mathbf{M}_a$ depends on the experiment. For a_1, $\mathbf{M}_a = \{M_{a1}, \ldots, M_{ak}\}$ where $M_{ai} = \{x \in X \mid x$ could be generated by the Turing Machine operating on the given input }. For a_i, $i = 2, \ldots, n$, $\mathbf{M}_a = \{M_{a1}, M_{a2}\}$ where $M_{a1} = \{\emptyset\}$ or $\{x\}$ where x is a single element of X, and x is such that the Turing Machine rule can validly be applied to it. M_{a2} is $\{X\}$ or $\{X \backslash x\}$ depending on the value of M_{a1}.

r equals $N + 1$. If r experiments have been executed, then the Turing Machine could not solve the problem in N steps.

The other parameters are not relevant for this analysis.

Given this description of the decision problem, we can construct a strategy that mimics the Turing Machine. The first step of the decision strategy identifies the input, and partitions the state space. Each partition of the state space contains the instantaneous descriptions of the Turing Machine that occur when it processes the given input. Each subsequent experiment eliminates one instantaneous description and continues until the problem is solved or the maximum allowable number of experiments has been executed. The decision strategy mimics the Turing Machine by executing the experiments in the same order as the Turing Machine.

The assertion implies that for any problem that can be solved via an algorithm, a corresponding decision strategy can be constructed and evaluated within the framework of this model. Under certain circumstances, constructing an optimal algorithm is feasible. The resulting algorithm will be optimal with respect to all the parameters of the decision model. Changing any of the parameter values may change the optimal algorithm. Moore and Whinston [9] show that an additively separable payoff function is a sufficient condition for using dynamic programming to construct an optimal decision strategy. Due to the combinatorial explosion of the subproblems, however, the dynamic programming algorithm may be to complex to solve. Moore *et al.* [10] show that a linear ordering over the experiment set is a sufficient condition for dynamic programming to be an effective approach for obtaining an optimal decision strategy or algorithm. A linear ordering over the experiment set is defined as:

Definition 4.1. *A linear ordering exists over an experiment set, A, if either:*

1. *For every $a \in A$, $\mathbf{M}_a = \{M_{a1}, M_{a2}\}$ (a is called a binary experiment) and for every pair of experiments a_i, a_j, $M_{ai,1} \subseteq M_{aj,1}$ or $M_{aj,1} \subseteq M_{ai,1}$;*
2. *For every $a \in A$, $\mathbf{M}_a = \{M_{a1}, M_{a2}, M_{a3}\}$ (a is called a trinary experiment) and for every pair of experiments a_i, a_j, $M_{ai,1} \cup M_{ai,2} \subseteq M_{aj,1}$ or $M_{aj,1} \cup M_{aj,2} \subseteq M_{ai,1}$.*

The linear ordering over the experiment enables the simple identification of the feasible subproblems and for each subproblem the set of efficient experiments. It also reduces the number of subproblems from $X!$ to 1/2 $|X||X+1|$. The computer file search is one example of a problem that can be formulated in the decision model so that the experiments satisfy the linear ordering condition. Moore and Whinston [9] and Moore *et al.* [10] analyze this problem in detail.

The linear ordering over the experiment set is a sufficient, but not necessary condition for using dynamic programming to develop optimal algorithms. Moore *et al.* [12] and Richmond and Whinston [18] develop several optimal algorithms where the linear ordering condition is not satisfied. They show that if each experiment in A can be broken down into primary experiments from sets $A_1, \ldots, A_k$ and there is a linear ordering over each set of primary experiments A_i, and A can be defined as $A = A_1 \cup \ldots \cup A_k$ or $A = A_1 \times \ldots \times A_k$ then the decision problem can be reformulated and an optimal algorithm developed. They use this approach to improve an existing algorithm and to develop several new algorithms. They term the experiments in A composite experiments.

Decision strategies based on composite experiments can be interpreted as organizational decision strategies or as parallel algorithms. Interpreting them as organizational decision strategies associates each member of the organization with an experiment set A_i. The members of the organization are a team, and the cost of communication is 0. The conditions for developing optimal decision strategies with multiple experiment sets are conditions for optimal delegation of duties. Alternatively, interpreting the decision strategies as a parallel algorithm associates each processor with an experiment set, A_i, with the additional assumption of free communication costs.

For parallel algorithms and distributed computer systems as well as for organizations, communication costs constitute a significant portions of the total costs. Kofman and Ratliff [4] explore communication algorithms for a two person team where each person knows a real valued parameter value that is within some interval. The team must make a common decision, whose value depends on both member's parameter values. The designer's goal is to construct a communication algorithm that will minimize the worst-case communication cost and the worst-case decision error.

4.1. Algorithm evaluation

Although the set of problems for which we can efficiently construct optimal algorithms and information systems is important, it is relatively small. Due to assertion 4.2, however, we can use the decision model to evaluate any algorithm or information system. In the traditional approach to algorithm construction, a problem is identified and an algorithm is developed to solve the problem. An algorithm, A, is superior to another algorithm, B, if in the limit as the size of the problem goes to infinity, A requires fewer computations than does B for the worst possible case. This worst-case, order-of measure is pervasive because it is machine independent and relatively easy to calculate.

The purpose of the worst-case-order-of measure is to effectively evaluate and rank algorithms, and therefore prescribe the algorithms that are good for certain classes of problems. As a ranking measure it is independent of the idiosyncrasies of computation, but it is not highly discriminatory. Also, its use implicitly assumes that an algorithm's purpose is to solve the problem exactly. Traub and Wozniakowski [21] relax the assumption that an algorithm should solve a problem exactly. They have introduced the idea of e-complexity, where e is the radius of information and measures how close the provided solution is to the exact solution. The e-complexity measure identifies the cost of solving the problem to within e of the true or exact solution. How to define the optimal radius of information, however, is omitted. Evaluating an algorithm or information system requires specifying the payoff function and the cost function.

Obtaining the traditional worst case results from computer science, requires $c(a) = 1$ for all $a \in A^*$ and

$$\omega^*(x, d, c) = \begin{cases} w - \max\limits_{B \in Br+1} \{C(B)\} & \text{if the correct decision is made} \\ \\ -C(B) & \text{otherwise} \end{cases} \quad (1)$$

Extending the traditional analysis requires identifying the appropriate payoff and cost functions. The worst-case-cost payoff function is unacceptable. Practitioners implicitly acknowledge its inappropriateness by using algorithms, such as quick sort, that are suboptimal under this ranking procedure. Algorithm theorists implicitly acknowledge that the worst-case-order-of analysis is too simplistic, through their use of probabilistic and heuristic algorithms. They explicitly acknowledge its drawbacks in the development of new complexity measures. For example, Karp (see [3]) advocates using average case analysis; Tarjan and Sleator [20] propose amortized complexity; and Traub and Wozniakowski [21] support e-complexity.

The payoff function in Equation (1) assumes that an approximate answer has no value and that the correct answers for all inputs have the same value. We know that this is not the case in the real world. For years, people have been using systems that produce erroneous outputs, such as banking systems that charge too much or too little on floating-rate loans [17], and executive information systems where the executive prefers current information with 60% accuracy to completely accurate information in four weeks time. (This according to a private communication with Michael DeWoody, Special Projects Manager at Eastman Kodak.)

The payoff function in Equation (1) may be appropriate if the value of any correct answer is so high that any two efficient algorithms solving the same problem will provide the same answer. This is what algorithm theorists implicitly assume, when they assume that complete information will be obtained (i.e., the exact solution will always be found). In this case, the algorithms should be compared based on their costs; however, an expected cost evaluation may be more appropriate than a worst-case evaluation.

Identifying an appropriate payoff function has immediate implications in at least three areas:

1. design and evaluation of heuristics for NP-complete problems,
2. design of computer-aided software engineering tools supporting code reuse, and
3. redesigning algorithms and information systems that currently obtain complete information.

The decision theoretic framework provides a formalism for constructing and evaluating heuristics that to date has been lacking. Since many NP-complete problems are naturally formulated as optimization problems [7], these problems and their associated algorithms naturally lend themselves to economic evaluation. Because of the problems' complexity, approximation algorithms are usually used to compute solutions that are nearly optimal at a low cost. For these algorithms, the natural payoff function is the optimization problem's objective function, and for a general purpose computer, the cost function can be $c(a) = 1$ for all $a \in A^*$. Under these circumstances, the best algorithm will be the one that gives the appropriate tradeoff between a better solution and lower costs.

For example, consider the traveling salesman problem. This problem is NP-complete, but there are heuristics whose solution approximate the exact answer. One of these heuristics is an 1-approximate algorithm with worst-case cost of $O(n^2)$. Another heuristic is an 1/2-approximate algorithm with worst-case cost $O(n^4)$ [7]. The optimal algorithm has a worst-case cost of $O(n^2 2^n)$. The question is which algorithm should be used in which situations? By using an economic paradigm, we can address this question.

Computer-aided software engineering tools supporting code reuse are a new technology with surging interest due to the high cost of software development, the high probability of software failure, and the advent of object-oriented languages. These tools must take a library of modules and a problem and select the set of modules and integrate them into a system for solving the problem. The economic model from Section 2 provides a framework for addressing this problem, once the appropriate payoff function, state space and experiment set are specified. One possibility would be for the state space to represent the power set of the set of modules. The goal would be to choose the best element of the state space. Alternatively, the modules could be experiments and the resulting strategy would represent the final information system.

Redesigning "optimal" algorithms requires reassessing the tradeoff between the cost of computation and the value of the problem solution. Redesigned algorithms and information systems will obtain complete information only if the value of the information exceeds the cost. For these problems, a potential payoff function would relate the value of the answer provided by the system to the true answer. The closer the answer provided, the higher the payoff. One area where this approach is particularly suited is file and database search. For file search, changing the payoff function to

$$\omega(x, d) = 1/(|\omega_u - \omega_d| + 1)$$

where ω_d is the index of the element chosen by the search process and ω_u is the index value of the best available alternative changes the traditional file search problem to the common index problem.

The common index problem is defined as follows: Given a random individual, find the element in a set that maximizes the individual's utility, where utility is a function of the index. Several information systems have been developed along these lines including AUCNET, a system for the wholesale trading of used automobiles in Japan. In AUCNET, the index is a measure of the cars' quality.

To formalize the common index problem, define Z as the characteristic space. For $z \in Z$, $z = (z_1, \ldots, z_n)$, where z_i represents the degree of characteristic i embodied in the alternative z. Define the universal set from which the file is drawn at $T \subset Z$, and define the set of available alternatives from which a best element can be chosen as $S = \{s_1, \ldots, s_n\} \subset T$. S can be thought of as a relational database where $z \in S$ is a record in the database with attribute i having value z_i.

Define W as the common index on T where $W \subseteq \mathcal{R}_+$ such that $w \in W$, $0 \leq w \leq w^\perp$ and where the function γ, γ: $T \rightarrow W$, assigns the index value to each element in the set T. The function γ may or may not be known, but $\gamma(s)$ is known for all $s \in S$. The set of indices on the available elements, S, is termed $W^* = \{w \in W : \exists s \in S : (w = g(s))\} = \{w_1^*, \ldots, w_n^*\}$.

The set of potential users is designated by U and each user is identified by his or her utility function $u \in U$. The utility functions are a function of the index, so $\forall t_1, t_2 \in T)$: $\gamma(t_1) = \gamma(t_2) \Rightarrow u(t_1) = u(t_2)$. We also restrict the set of utility functions to single-peaked symmetric functions that are strictly decreasing away from the maximum, so each user's preferences differ only in their choice of the ideal point.

Given the restriction on the utility functions, the best available element will always be the element $w^* \in W^*$ closest to the ideal element w^{**}. The goal in the common index problem is to determine an optimal decision strategy for searching the database of the given form, and although it is very similar to the file search problem, but the new payoff function requires a modified state space, probability distribution and experiment set.

Formulating the common index in the framework of the decision model gives:

$$X = Y \cup V; \quad Y = \{y_1, \ldots, y_{n-1}\}; \quad V = \{v_1, \ldots, v_n\},$$

where each y_i represents the value of the index midway between the index values of records in the database. We interpret the state y_j as:

$$x = y_j \Leftrightarrow y^* = 1/2(w_j^* + w_{j+1}^*),$$

where y^* is the index of the best available alternative, and each v_i represents the set of index values that fall between y_{j-1} and y_j with $y_0 = 0$ and $y_n = w^\perp$.

The probability distribution over the state space is ϕ, where $\phi(x)$ is the probability that a random customer's ideal alternative is in state x. The set of final decisions is $D = \{d_1, \ldots, d_n\}$ where d_i is the decision that the best available record is the ith record in the database.

As identified earlier, the gross payoff function for the searcher is

$$\omega(x, d) = 1/(|w_u - w_d| + 1)$$

where w_d is the index of the element chosen by the search process and w_u is the index value of the best available alternative. This is equivalent to the user paying the search intermediary on a sliding scale based on the quality of the alternative selected. Other payoff functions are feasible and will be discussed in future research. Note that we cannot use the value of the user's ideal alternative, since it is not part of the state space. It's use would require a reformulation of the problem. The cost of each experiment is c for $a \in \{1, \ldots, n-1\}$ and is 0 for $a = 0$.

The set of available experiments is $A = \{a_0, \ldots, a_{n-1}\}$, where a_0 represents the null experiment, do nothing, and a_i represents comparing the ideal point, u^* with the ith element of Y, and each experiment results in a partitioning of the state space into $\mathbf{M}_a = (M_{a1}, M_{a2}, M_{a3})$ where:

$$\begin{aligned} M_{a1} &= \{v_1, y_1, \ldots, v_{a-1}\} \\ M_{a2} &= \{y_a\} \\ M_{a3} &= \{v_{a+1}, y_{a+1}, \ldots, v_n\}. \end{aligned}$$

Because there is a linear ordering over the set of experiments, we can effectively use dynamic programming to construct an optimal algorithm.

The common index problem completes the circle and returns us to the problem of consumer choice. Unlike the consumer choice problem, however, in the common index problem, all people using the system will share a common search algorithm. This raises anew the issues of the impact of such a system on product diversity, advertising and search service ownership.

5. CONCLUSIONS

We have proposed using an economic decision model as a model of computing. Drawing on information economics, decision theory and algorithm theory provides a powerful approach for investigating optimal algorithms or decision processes. By coupling decision theory with algorithm theory, we can include the characteristics of the users' environment into algorithm construction. The users' preferences, their payoff function and their time priorities can all be incorporated into the computer algorithm. By coupling algorithm theory with the economics of information, we can direct the allocation of the computer's resources toward producing the most valuable information. We can account for the tradeoff between more accurate and precise information and the cost of producing that information.

BIBLIOGRAPHY

1. Aho, A. V., J. E. Hopcroft, and J. Ullman, 1974, *The Design and Analysis of Computer Algorithms*, Reading, MA: Addison-Wesley Publishing Company.
2. DeGroot, M. H., 1970, *Optimal Statistical Decisions*, McGraw-Hill.
3. Frenkel, K. A., 1986, 'Complexity and parallel processing: An interview with Richard Karp', *Communications of the ACM* 29(2), 112–117.
4. Kofman, F. and J. Ratliff, 1991, 'Johnny Carson vs. the Smothers Brothers: Monolog vs dialogue in costly bilateral communication', Slaon Graduate School of Management, Massachusetts Institute of Technology, Working Paper.
5. Johnson, E. J. and J. W. Payne, 1985, 'Effort and accuracy in choice', *Management Science* 31(4), 395–414.
6. Manning, R. and P. B. Morgan, 1982, 'Search and consumer theory', *Review of Economic Studies* 49, 203–216.
7. Melhorn, K., 1984, *Data Structures and Algorithms 2: Graph Algorithms and NP-Completeness*, Berlin: Springer-Verlag.
8. Moore, J. C. and A. B. Whinston, 1986, 'A model for decision making with sequential information-acquisition – Part 1', *Decision Support Systems* 2, 285–307.
9. Moore, J. C. and A. B. Whinston, 1987, 'A model for decision making with sequential information-acquisition – Part 2', *Decision Support Systems* 3, 47–72.
10. Moore, J. C., W. B. Richmond, and A. B. Whinston, 1988, 'A decision theoretic approach to file search', *Computer Science in Economics and Management* 1(1), 3–20.
11. Moore, J. C, W. B. Richmond, and A. B. Whinston, 1990a, 'A decision theoretic approach to information retrieval', *ACM Transactions on Database Management Systems* 15(3), 311-340.
12. Moore, J. C, W. B. Richmond, and A. B. Whinston, 1990b, 'Optimal decision processes and algorithms', *Journal of Economic Dynamics and Control* 14, 375–417.
13. Moore, J. C, W. B. Richmond, and A. B. Whinston, 1992a, 'Search for a consumer durable – an optimal strategy', William E. Simon Graduate School of Business Adminsitration, University of Rochester, Rochester, New York, Working Paper.

14. Moore, J. C, W. B. Richmond, and A. B. Whinston, 1992b, 'An optimal search strategy based on user preferences for choice oriented databases', William E. Simon Graduate School of Business Adminsitration, University of Rochester, Rochester, New York, Working Paper.
15. Morgan, P. and R. Manning, 1985, 'Optimal search', *Econometrica* 53(4), 923–944.
16. Peter, R., 1981, *Recursive Functions in Computer Theory*, London: Ellis Horwood Limited.
17. Quinn, J. B., 1992. 'Banks often charge too much, too little on floating-rate loans', *The Rochester, NY, Democrat and Chronicle*, May 12.
18. Richmond, W. B. and A. B. Whinston, 1992, 'Optimal algorithms with composite experiments', William E. Simon Graduate School of Business Adminsitration, University of Rochester, Rochester, New York, Working Paper.
19. Rogers, H., 1967, *Theory of Recursive Functions and Effective Computability*, New York: McGraw-Hill.
20. Tarjan, R. E. and D. D. Sleator, 1985, 'Self-adjusting binary search trees', *Journal of the ACM* 32(3), 652–686.
21. Traub, J. F. and H. Wozniakowski, 1984, 'Information and computation', *Advances in Computers* 23, 35–92.
22. Tversky, A., 1972, 'Elimination by aspects: A theory of choice', *Psychological Review* 79, 281–299.
23. Tversky, A. and S. Sattath, 1979, 'Preference trees', *Psychological Review* 86(6) 542–573.
24. Warbelow, A. and B. Konsynski, 1991, 'Inventory locator service', Cambridge, MA: Harvard Business School, Case #9–191–008.
25. Warbelow, A. and B. Konsynski, 1988, 'American Gem market system', Cambridge, MA: Harvard Business School, Case #9–189–088.
26. Warbelow, A. and J. Kokuryo, 1989, 'Aucnet', Cambridge, MA: Harvard Business School, Case # 9–190–001.
27. Weitzman, M. L., 1979. 'Optimal search for the best alternative', *Econometrica* 47(3), 641–654.

DALE O. STAHL AND ANDREW B. WHINSTON

A General Economic Equilibrium Model of Distributed Computing *

ABSTRACT. The operation of a distributed computing system such as Internet can be viewed as a resource allocation problem, and thereby becomes amenable to analysis using the techniques of mathematical economics. We define a general distributed computing system and translate that setup into a model of an economy. In this model, the preferences of users are taken as primitives, and processing units (PU) are viewed as productive firms with input queues. Each PU charges a rental price for its services. In order to avoid the difficulties associated with modelling discrete choices of users over the set of possible programs, we assume that a user benefits depend on the average flow of services and that user choices can be modeled as a stochastic arrival process. This representation may be a more realistic model of a group of users than the more straightforward discrete choice model. Within the context of this model, we characterize optimal system allocations, and prove the existence of stochastic equilibrium rental prices such that total expected demand does not exceed optimal system capacity utilization. The profit measures for each PU can be used to guide the evolution of the distributed computing system. We also propose a tatonnement process for guiding the system towards equilibrium. Since only limited general convergence theorems are available, we propose simulation testing of the dynamic properties. Future research will explore the performance of the pricing mechanism in experimental environments and eventually in actual usage.

1. INTRODUCTION

Distributed Computing Systems (DCSs) offer the potential for harnessing the power of thousands of computers linked through a network, dwarfing the power of any single supercomputer. Already the scientific community is exploring the development of a nationwide network of processors with unique software to enhance the opportunities for scientific research. Companies are also currently rationalizing their investment in a vast array of computers by creating a network to support the concept of cooperative or client-server processing. A major challenge in this process is how to effectively coordinate the users and processing units in a diverse and changing environment. Since this coordination task is essentially a resource allocation problem, economic

* This research was funded in part by the National Science Foundation #IRI–9005969, but does not necessary reflect the views of the NSF.

W.W. Cooper and A.B. Whinston (eds.), New Directions in Computational Economics, 175–189.

theory has the potential to help solve the problem (e.g. Chaudhury *et al.* 1994; Hogg 1990; Ferguson *et al.* 1989).

Noting the analogy between millions of buyers and sellers in a market economy and the users and processing unit in the computing network, the natural tendency has been to model a DCS in a manner that mimics the workings of real markets. Processing Units (PUs) on the network are viewed as agents who bid for jobs and obtain unfinished inputs and/or subcontract for certain tasks. In applying this analogy, numerous ad hoc specifications are made, and simulation tests are run. The SPAWN mechanism (Waldspurger *et al. 1990*) is an example of this approach. Unfortunately, there is no formal general theory of an entire economy with such agents.[1]

Our approach is to build a DCS model from the basis of established general economic equilibrium theory. Rather than modelling PUs as strategic price-setting agents, we view PUs as elements of the production technology of an economy. Given factor prices, decisions regarding how to use PUs are based on (passive) cost-minimization criteria. Dividing a large-scale computation problem into numerous tasks, delegating to PUs, and adjusting to improve performance is analogous to allocating resources among firms in an economy for the purpose of achieving the maximal net value of output. The economic solution is a price system with free entry and exit of firms based on profitability. (For a graduate-level introduction, see Varian (1984); for more advanced reference material see Arrow and Intriligator (1982)).

To apply the general economic equilibrium approach to DCSs, we first develop a formal model of a DCS that lends itself to economic analysis. A DCS is defined as a network of PUs which can perform a variety of potential services. Examples of services could be movies on demand, home shopping, news services, as well as numerical based computations. We envision user-interface software that generates DCS code to deliver the services, and predicts the throughput time and cost for the services. To each PU is attached a stack that stores new input until the PU is ready to process the new input; hence, asynchronous user inputs will lead to stochastic queues and delays. (Mendelson (1985) used a similar approach to analyze optimal pricing of the single PU case.)

We recognize that a DCS does not exist in isolation, and users of the DCS are not the only agents in the economy. Accordingly, we view the demands for DCS services as arising from their usefulness outside the DCS environment. For example, organizations need services such as issuing financial statements, calculating bridge loads, simulating guidance systems, etc. Viewing a DCS user as an organization with a variety of DCS service needs, we model

---

[1] While real markets often have independent bidding agents, the game-theoretic nature of an entire economy composed of price-setting agents, and the fundamental non-computability of such a game (Binmore 1987), casts doubts on the appropriateness of this mimicry approach.

the demand for services as a stochastic flow. Of course, individuals in the organization will choose services and programs to execute and thus their individual choices are discrete-valued variables. However, it is reasonable to assume that collectively their behavior can be described by a Poisson process with a specific arrival rate (or "average flow" rate). Further, we assume that the net user benefits depend only on the average flow rates, expected throughput times and monetary costs. This combination of stochastic flows, queues, and user preferences, overcomes the troublesome integer (or indivisibility) aspect of individual computation tasks.

A rental price and an expected waiting time are associated with each PU. Given this data, a user (or user-interface software) evaluates and selects cost-minimizing programs. The demand (flow rate) of service requests from a user depends on the service benefits to the user and the costs. Optimal service demands are then translated into demands on individual PUs. These demands are aggregated over all users.

With a system of queues, there is a trade-off between greater throughput and longer waiting times. We characterize the optimal allocation of resources. We prove that there is a generically unique welfare-maximizing allocation, and we derive the rental prices that support this optimum as a "stochastic equilibrium". That is, (i) user flow rates are optimal for each user given the rental prices and anticipated waiting times, (ii) the anticipated waiting times are the correct ex ante expected waiting times given the average flow rates, and (iii) the aggregate average flow rates are equal to the welfare-maximizing rates.

Next, we turn to the question of implementing this solution. That is, how do we find the equilibrium rental prices? One answer is the direct method of computing them. An alternative approach to finding equilibrium rental prices is motivated by the classic tatonnement process (Hahn 1982). Our proposed tatonnement process also has the advantage of permitting considerable decentralization of the pricing computation. We suggest that further simulation testing of the tatonnement process should be pursued in future research.

Finally, assuming successfully implementation of equilibrium pricing, DCS managers can use the profitability of each PU (based on rental prices) to guide investment and design decisions. The ratio of expected profits to the capital cost of the PU can be used to decide whether to invest in another PU of that type or to remove that PU from the network, analogous to entry and exit in real free-enterprise economies. In this manner, a DCS can evolve over time to more effectively serve the users.

The paper is organized as follows. Section 2 presents the formal model of the DCS that lends itself to economic analysis. Section 3 describes the users' preferences, and choice of optimal computation plans. Section 4 derives our main theorems and shows how a welfare optimum can be supported as a stochastic equilibrium. All proofs are relegated to an Appendix. Section 5 presents implementation methods, and Section 6 discusses capital investment and design issues. Finally, Section 7 concludes with an assessment of the power and practicality of our economic approach to the design and management of large-scale DCSs, and a brief indication of areas for future research.

2. DESCRIPTION OF THE DCS

We consider a DCS consisting of a finite number of hardware units, called processing units (PUs), with well-defined, commonly known, possibly diverse capabilities. For instance, some PUs may be particular personal computers with a specific finite set of application programs. Other examples of specialized PUs would be an ethernet system, multi-server queues that route services to the next available PU, external disk storage devices and controllers, and output interfaces. Additionally, in the Internet, PUs would supply consumer and business services.

In any real-world DCS, one must be able to handle conflicting demands on the system, such as a program arriving at a PU before that PU is free to execute a new program. To resolve such conflicts, we assume that each PU is equipped with an input stack that functions as a waiting-line queue. For simplicity, we assume the FIFO queue discipline, although our approach can be modified to permit priority systems. Also for analytical simplicity, we assume unlimited queue capacity. We hasten to point out, however, that in equilibrium the expected queue lengths are finite, so for practical purposes, sufficient finite queue capacity would suffice and yield qualitatively similar results.

Let P denote the set of all finite "programs" in the language of the DCS. We assume that programs are partitioned into two distinguishable parts: instructions and data. A PU reads the instructions and then carries out whatever operations are called for on the data (and instructions). PUs may pass instructions through to the output which are then carried out by successor PUs. Thus, inputs to PUs are viewed as "batch" programs complete with all relevant data and output disposition instructions.

Let M denote a finite set of PUs; let $m \in M$ denote a specific PU. A PU m can be represented by a production function f_m: $P \to P$; a processing speed of v_m cycles per second; and a load function: q_m: $P \to Z$ (the set of positive integers). Given input $p \in P$, $f_m(p)$ gives the output, $q_m(p)$ gives the number of cycles required to process p, and $q_m(p)/v_m$ is the execution time of m.

The PUs are connected with each other through a network. By modelling shared communication devices (such as data bases and ethernets) as distinct PUs, the network will consist of direct connections only; that is, if m and m' are directly connected in the network representation, then there exists a dedicated physical linkage between m and m' that is not shared by any other PUs. Let A_m denote the set of PUs from which m can receive direct input, and let B_m denote the set of PUs to which m can send direct output. If A_m is empty, then m receives input from the external environment only. If B_m is empty, then m sends output to the external environment only. PUs with their A_m or B_m sets empty are the only PUs with direct connection to the external environment. We formally represent the network as $\mathcal{N} \equiv \{(A_m, B_m), m \in M\}$.

In the next section, we will introduce user preferences for employing the DCS, but for now let us take as given that a user wants a "service" $s \in S$, where S is the class of services potentially provided by the DCS. We assume that s is a sufficient description so a DCS-programmer[2] can write DCS program code that will deliver the service to the user. Let $P(s)$ denote the set of programs that will successfully deliver service s.

Computational services can be viewed as "subroutines" which operate on the specific user-designed data, provided that the characteristics of the data (such as size and format) are compatible with the subroutine. Accordingly, we assume that the service is sufficiently defined so the DCS-programmer (or an automated compiler) can accurately estimate the load that program $p \in P(s)$ will place on the DCS.

Since a DCS is a deterministic system, given a time path of all user inputs (from some initial state), the entire evolution of the DCS is determined: in particular, the demands on every PU (the number of cycles of processing required by all the "jobs" in its input queue plus the remaining cycles required by its current job). Let $Q_m(p)$ denote the incremental load imposed by program p on PU m. Given a stationary stochastic arrival process for services, let $w \equiv \{w_m, m \in M\}$ denote the vector of expected queue waiting times at the PUs. A program may access a given PU several times in the course of executing. Let $\mu_m(p)$ be defined as the number of distinct times program p accesses m (i.e. go through m's queue). Thus, program p has an expected waiting time of $w_m\mu_m(p)$ at PU m.

The total expected throughput time for program p is the sum of the processing time and the waiting time:

$$\tau(p, w) \equiv \Sigma_m[Q_m(p)/v_m + w_m\mu_m(p)]. \tag{1}$$

---

[2] We envision that this DCS-programmer function could be an automated feature of the user-interface software of a well-developed DCS.

3. USER PREFERENCES AND DEMANDS

Recall that we view a DCS user i as an organization with a variety of DCS service needs, which we can model as a Poisson process with a specific arrival rate (or "average flow" rate). Further, we assume that the benefits of DCS services depend on the average flow rate. Accordingly, we represent the instantaneous value to user i of service s at an average flow rate x by a strictly concave and continuously differentiable function $V_{is}(x)$.

The net benefit to the user is less than $V_{is}(x)$ because the service takes time to execute and it costs money to use the DCS. Different programs in $P(s)$ may have different costs, so consider each program $p \in P(s)$ separately. The expected throughput time of p is $\tau(p, w)$, as defined in Equation (1). Let δ_{is} denote user i's delay cost per unit time for service s, so $\delta_{is}\tau(p, w)$ is the total cost of delay of using program p.

Money costs are determined by the load imposed by p and the rental prices of the PUs. Let $r \equiv \{r_m, m \in M\}$, where r_m is the rental price per cycle for use of m. Then, the monetary cost of p is $\Sigma_m r_m Q_m(p)$. Clearly, the user prefers the program $p \in P(s)$ that minimizes total expected costs. Accordingly, we define

$$c^*_{is}(r, w) \equiv \min \left\{\delta_{is}\tau(p, w) + \Sigma_m r_m Q_m(p) \mid p \subset P(s)\right\}. \tag{2}$$

This task of finding the minimum-cost program could be subsumed by the programmer function in an automated user interface.[3] We assume there is a unique cost-minimizing program for service s, denoted $p_{is}(r, w)$.[4] By standard arguments, $c^*_{is}(r, w)$ is a continuous function. Given the sensitivity of current computer service users to peak-load pricing schemes, we believe that this cost-minimization stage will have a very significant impact on the efficiency of DCS resource utilization.

The net benefit to user i of an average flow rate, x_{is}, is

$$u_{is}(x_{is}, r, w) \equiv V_{is}(x_{is}) - x_{is}c^*_{is}(r, w). \tag{3}$$

[3] While this appears to be an infinite dimensional problem, under mild conditions it reduces to a finite dimensional problem. To see this, observe that by continuous differentiability of V_{is}, the instantaneous marginal value of any output is bounded, while the completion time and/or cost of p is unbounded, so infinitely long programs will never be optimal. Hence, there will be a finite limit, L, for the length of programs such that if $p > L$, then p is never considered. Under these circumstances, P can be replaced by the finite set PL of programs of length L or less. Finally, for practical purposes, any single programmer is likely to be knowledgeable about a small subset of $P(s) \subset PL$, so the cost minimization problem is finite.

[4] There will be a unique cost-minimizing program for almost every (r, w), but for some (r, w) there may be several cost-minimizing programs. In mathematical economics (see, for example, Debreu 1959), there are standard methods for handling these rare multiplicities, and the qualitative results of this paper would hold, so we spare the reader unnecessary technical complications by making this simplifying assumption.

The user is assumed to choose x_{is} to maximize $u_{is}(x_{is}, r, w)$, and we let $x_{is}(r, w)$ denote the optimal demand. A standard argument from mathematical economics establishes that $x_{is}(r, w)$ exists and is finite, single-valued, and continuous for all non-negative (r, w). Specifically, $x_{is}(r, w)$ is the unique solution to

$$V'_{is}(x_{is} = c^*_{is}(r, w).^5 \tag{4}$$

We pause to interpret the act of choosing flow rates x_{is}. We envision a world in which questions (that might require DCS services) arise from some natural process (for example, manager's request for some special financial report, an engineer needs some design calculation, etc.). These questions, in turn can be translated into requests for DCS services. Thus, we model the arrival of potential DCS service requests as an exogenous stochastic process that is independent of the pricing of the DCS. A user who receives one of these questions and is contemplating whether or not to actually request DCS service, say s, undertakes a two-stage decision. First, he queries his programmer function for the cost $c^*_{is}(r, w)$. Second, he compares this cost with the marginal benefit V'_{is}. If the marginal benefit exceeds the cost, he submits the request; if the cost exceeds the marginal benefit, he rejects the request; and if the marginal benefit and cost are equal, he can decide randomly.

Suppose the exogenous arrival rate of questions requiring DCS-service s is X_0, with the interpretation that if the minimum cost of delivering s were 0, then X_0, would be the average flow demand for service s. Given the actual cost $c^*_{is}(r, w)$, the user must decide whether to accept the question and submit the request. Let λ_{is} denote the probability of accepting the question and submitting service request s. Given the exogenous arrival rate X_0, the average flow demand for s from this user will be $x_{is} = \lambda_{is} X_0$. Thus, the choice of λ_{is} is equivalent to the choice of an average flow rate x_{is}. The optimal choice maximizes $u_{is}(x_{is}, r, w)$.

Figure 1 illustrates this optimization graphically. The downward-sloping "demand" curve gives the marginal benefit of service s as a function of the average flow rate of service s. For example, the marginal benefit of quarterly financial reports may be \$500 each, while the marginal benefit of monthly reports may be only \$200 each. The horizontal "supply" curve gives the cost c^*_{is}. An exogenous change in X_0 would cause a change in the optimal λ_{is}, and hence x_{is}.

Observe that we have resolved the well-known integer nature of computation problems. While each service s is an indivisible entity, we have treated the demand choice as if it could be subdivided in any matter to accommodate the certainty-equivalent flow rate of x_{is}. However, in actual implementation,

[5] We assume that user i when maximizing $u_{is}(\cdot r, w)$ takes rental prices and waiting times as fixed, and does not anticipate how his service demand may ultimately affect r and w.

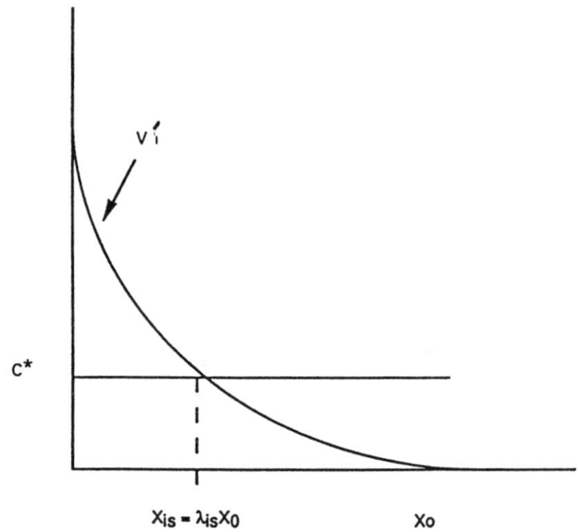

Fig. 1. Determination of arrival rate.

the service requests enter the DCS as indivisible units. We accommodate this integer requirement by modelling the arrival process as a stochastic process with arrival rate x_{is}, and we hold input in the PU queues until ready to be processed. The resulting delays are reflected in the waiting times w.

The aggregate load on PU m from all users is

$$z_m(r, w) \equiv \Sigma_s \Sigma_i x_{is}(r, w) Q_m[p_{is}(r, w)], \tag{5}$$

In other words, $z_m(r, w)$ is the demand flow (measured in cycles per second) to m resulting from a stochastic arrival process of user service requests. Let $z(r, w)$ denote the vector $\{z_m, m \in M\}$. Given the results of Cinlar (1972), it is reasonable to assume that $z(r, w)$ is the arrival rate of a Poisson process.

4. OPTIMAL RESOURCE ALLOCATION AND STOCHASTIC EQUILIBRIUM

The most natural definition of an equilibrium would be that average demand z_m at each m equal the "supply" v_m. However, with a Poisson arrival process, equality of the arrival rate and the service rate yields infinite expected queue waiting times. But if queue waiting times are infinite, then there is no value to computation services, so demand would sink to zero, an inconsistency. Clearly, we want to have consistency between expected waiting times, demands, and actual waiting times.

We assume that the expected waiting time at m is a function of the average flow rate and the capacity:

$$w_m = \Omega(z_m; v_m), \tag{6}$$

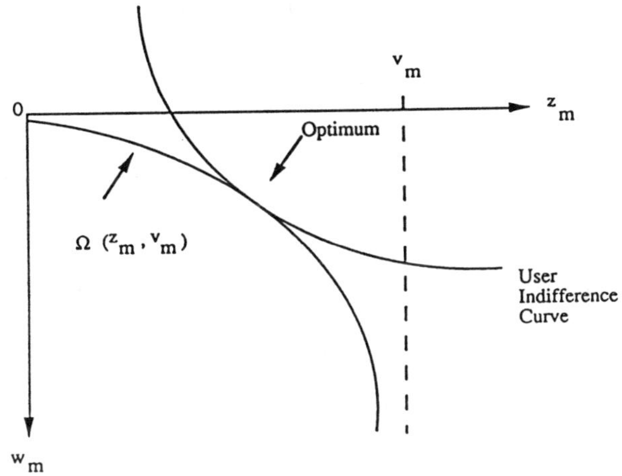

Fig. 2. Optimal determination of waiting time.

where $\Omega(\cdot; v_m)$ is continuously differentiable, strictly increasing and convex for all $z_m < v_m$, $\Omega(0; v_m) = 0$, and $\lim_{z_m \to v_m} \Omega(z_m; v_m) = \infty$.[6] $\Omega(z_m; v_m)$ gives the physical tradeoff between waiting time and throughput, as illustrated in Figure 2, where w_m is plotted in the downward direction. Users prefer points to the northeast of this convex boundary; i.e. they prefer more throughput and less waiting time.

To derive the optimal trade-off we need to define a system-wide welfare function. It is natural to take the sum of non-pecuniary user benefits:

$$W(x, w) \equiv \Sigma_i \Sigma_s [V_{is}(\Sigma_p x_{isp}) - \delta_{is} \Sigma_p x_{isp} \tau(p, w)]. \tag{7}$$

We then seek an allocation of demands, $x \equiv \{x_{isp}, s \in S, p \in P(s)\}$, and waiting times w, that maximize $W(x, w)$ subject to Equations (5) and (6). (Note that in Equation (7), the sum over p is confined to $P(s)$.) Substituting Equation (5) into Equation (6), the Kuhn-Tucker conditions of this welfare maximization are:

$$V'_{is} - \delta_{is} \tau(p, w) \leq \Sigma_m \Omega_z \gamma_m Q_m(p); \tag{8}$$

and

$$\gamma_m = \Sigma_i \Sigma_s \Sigma_p \delta_{is} x_{isp} \mu_m(p), \tag{9}$$

where γ_m is the Lagrangian multiplier for Equation (6), and $\Omega_z \equiv \partial\Omega(z_m; v_m)/\partial z_m$. Equation (9) defines the shadow price of waiting time at m; let $\gamma \equiv \{\gamma_m, m \in M\}$. Equation (8) requires the marginal net benefit of service

[6] For example, given an M/G/1 queue system, the expected waiting time is given by the Pollaczek-Khintchine formula: $\Omega(z_m; v_m) = z_m v_m / [2(v_m - z_m)]$.

s to be less than or equal to the total shadow cost of the induced incremental waiting times; if less, then the optimal $x_{isp} = 0$.

Theorem 1. *There exists a generically unique* (x^*, w^*, γ^*) *that maximizes* $W(x, w)$ *subject to Equations (5–6), and, further, satisfies Equations (8–9).*

When will the vector of user demand functions, $x(r, w) \equiv \{x_{is}(r, w)\}$, which optimize each $u_{is}(x_{is}, r, w)$, also optimize $W(x, w)$? Recall from Section 3 that if $x_{is}(r, w) > 0$, then $V'_{is} = c^*_{is}(r, w) = \gamma_{is}\tau(p_{is}, w) + \Sigma_m r_m Q_m$. Then, $x_{is}(r, w)$ will satisfy Equation (8) iff $\Sigma_m r_m Q_m = \Sigma_m \Omega_z \gamma_m Q_m$. The obvious solution is to set $r_m = \Omega_z \gamma_m$, or equivalently:

$$r_m = \Sigma_i \Sigma_s \delta_{is} x_{is}(r, w) \mu_m(p_{is}) \Omega_z(z_m; v_m). \tag{10}$$

In other words, the welfare maximizing rental price for m must equal the aggregate cost of delays multiplied by the waiting-time/throughput trade-off at m. The number $\mu_m(p_{is})$ of times a service program p_{is} accesses m appears in the formula, because additional delay is suffered by all other users that many times.

However, Equation (10) is not an "explicit" formula for r_m, since r_m enters the right-hand side via $x_{is}(r, w)$ and $z_m(r, w)$.

Theorem 2. *There exists an* (r^*, w^*) *such that* x_{is} (r^*, w^*) *maximizes* u_{is} (x_{is}, r, w), $(x(r^*, w^*), w^*)$ *maximizes* $W(x, w)$, *and* $w^*_m = \Omega[z_m(r^*, w^*); v_m]$ *for all* $m \in M$.

In other words, given (r^*, w^*), individual users choose demands $x_{is}(r^*, w^*)$, which aggregate to $z_m(r^*, w^*)$ according to Equation (5), which in turn generate expected waiting-times w^* satisfying Equation (6). Furthermore, these demands and waiting times maximize welfare $W(x, w)$.

An alternative interpretation in terms of competitive equilibrium can be made. Let z^*_m denote the welfare-maximizing aggregate flows from Theorem 1. Then, Theorem 2 asserts the existence of rental prices r^* and expected waiting times w^* so (i) demand $z_m(r^*, w^*)$ equals optimal flows z^*_m at every m, and (ii) these demands via the queues, Equation (6), generate expected waiting times w^*.

We can call this interpretation a "stochastic equilibrium" in that expected waiting times are correct and "excess demand" in terms of flow rates $(z_m - z^*_m)$ is zero.

5. IMPLEMENTATION: PRICE DETERMINATION

The solution to the DCS resource allocation problem we propose is to charge welfare-maximizing rental prices for the PUs in the DCS. Given such prices, the charges could be easily implemented by adding to each user's DCS interface software the capability of computing the appropriate charge for each service, or to dedicate a central DCS PU to the task of billing.

The task of determining the welfare-maximizing prices requires information about (i) the flow rates, $x_{is}(r, w)$, (ii) the expected waiting times, w_m, and (iii) the user's cost of delay parameters δ_{is}. Given this information, we can take several approaches to calculating the welfare-maximizing r^*: a direct computation method, or a tatonnement method.

5.1 The Direct Computation Method

Let $x_{is}(r, w; \theta)$ denote a family of demand functions, where θ is a vector of parameters. Econometric techniques could be used to estimate θ. Next, we would need to know the user delay costs δ_{is}. Based on demand revelation mechanisms for priority queues (e.g. Dolan, 1978; and Mendelson and Whang 1990), the delay costs could be obtained as part of the input from users.

Given estimated demand functions and $\{\delta_{is}\}$, Equations (5), (6), and (10) can be solved for (r^*, w^*). There is an extensive literature describing computable general equilibrium models in which researchers have explored numerous algorithms for this task (Codsi and Pearson 1988; Manne 1985; and Talman and van der Laan 1987). Periodically, the estimate of θ could be updated, and the rental prices and waiting times re-computed and made available to all users.

5.2. A Tatonnement Method

An alternative approach to finding equilibrium prices is motivated by the classic tatonnement process (Hahn 1982). Heuristically, one wants to raise the rental price when the social costs of delays at a queue are excessive, and vice versa. We first describe the method of obtaining the required information for the tatonnement process. In lieu of estimating (or knowing) the demand functions, we suggest measuring the average flows. Given the processing speed v_m, knowing the capacity utilization rate $\rho_m \equiv z_m/v_m$ is equivalent to knowing z_m. Noting that $(1 - \rho_m)$ is the fraction of time that m is idle, it is a simple statistic to measure. Let $\tilde{\rho}_m(t)$ be the current time-averaged estimate of ρ_m. Then, using Equation (6), let $\tilde{w}_m(t) \equiv \Omega[\tilde{\rho}_m(t)/v_m; v_m]$ serve as the current estimate of expected waiting times.

It is also useful to define a new quantity that permits an insightful rewriting of Equation (10). Let $y_{ism} \equiv x_{is}\mu_m(p_s)$, the flow rate of is-type "jobs" at m – counting each time program p_{is} accesses m as a "job". Then, Equation (10) becomes

$$r_m = \Sigma_i \Sigma_s \delta_{is} y_{ism} \Omega_z. \tag{11}$$

From Equation (11), we see that it will suffice to measure the flow rates y_{ism} at each PU. The measurement of $\tilde{\rho}_m(t), \tilde{w}_m(t)$, and $\tilde{y}_{sm}(t)$ could be decentralized to each PU. An estimate of δ_{is} could be obtained from a sampling of inputs to the DCS; call such an estimate $\tilde{\delta}_{is}(t)$. Then, let $\tilde{r}_m(t)$ denote the current value of the right-hand side of Equation (11) using the above estimates. To lessen the chances for instabilities due to over-responsiveness, we suggest a partial adjustment. Let $r_m(t)$ denote the rental prices in "period" t, and let $\alpha \in (0, 1)$; then, set

$$r_m(t+1) = \alpha \tilde{r}_m(t) + (1-\alpha) r_m(t). \tag{12}$$

It is natural to begin with $r_m(1) = 0$, and let the DCS run for one period. Then, take the measurements, $\tilde{\rho}_m(1), \tilde{w}_m(1)$, and $\tilde{y}_{sm}(1)$, and compute $\tilde{r}_m(1)$ from Equation (11) and $r_m(2)$ from Equation (12). The continuation of these steps for every period defines a stochastic dynamic process.

The central issue for future research and development is to determine the convergence and stability properties of this dynamic system. Specifically, will $r(t)$ tend towards a small neighborhood of r^* sufficiently rapidly and stay there? How do the methods of estimating $\tilde{\rho}_m(t), \tilde{w}_m(t)$ and $\tilde{y}_{sm}(t)$, the adjustment parameter α, and the period length affect dynamic stability?

To ensure stability, the time required to measure accurately the statistics of the stochastic flows and queues should be small relative to the time between rental price adjustments, which in turn should be small relative to changes in the external environment (e.g. exogenous changes in DCS services demanded).

We suggest simulation testing in specific environments to explore these stability issues. Although stability is more likely to be attainable for stationary environments (users and services), simulation testing could be employed to experiment with gradually changing environments. There will be a trade-off between rapid adjustment to the equilibrium on the one hand, and the stability of the process on the other. In addition, simulations would provide evidence of the potential gains in DCS efficiency from optimal rental prices.

6. CAPITAL INVESTMENT

Finally, we turn to longer run considerations about the design of the DCS. The rental prices can be to evaluate incremental changes. For example, the profits earned by each PU, $r_m z_m$, can be used to evaluate whether additional PUs would be beneficial or not. If K_m is the capital cost of an additional m, then, $r_m z_m / K_m$ is the expected rate of return to the investment. All the PUs can be ranked by this rate-of-return measure. Then it would be prudent to invest first in the PUs with the highest expected rate-of-return, provided that their rate-of-return exceeds the economy-wide rate-of-return for investments of similar riskiness. PUs that fall considerably below the acceptable rate-of-return could be eliminated from the DCS.

As another example, consider the choice of capacity v_m. If $K_m(v_m)$ is the cost of capacity at m, then the optimal capacity is defined by $dK_m/dv_m = -r_m\,(\partial\Omega/\partial v_m)/\Omega_z$. In other words, the marginal throughput improvement (holding waiting time fixed) should be evaluated at the rental price r_m and compared with the marginal cost of capacity.

To investigate other design changes such as adding entirely new PUs or re-configuring the connections, we advocate economic benefit-cost analysis of trial (or simulated) design changes. Since system profits, $\Sigma_m r_m z_m$, are a first-order approximation to welfare, a 'small' DCS design change would be desirable if and only if it increases the gross profits of the DCS.

7. CONCLUSIONS

The coordination of users of a DCS to achieve efficient utilization of the resource is a complex and important problem. With the expected growth of DCS an inefficient coordination mechanism will cause significant economic losses. Computer scientists have considerable experience in creating coordinating mechanisms that are part of a distributed operating system. While the mechanisms do coordinate the different processors there has been no attempt to develop optimal solutions. The issue we explored is the design of a mechanism that can potentially achieve the highest level of resource allocation. To achieve this goal, we have successfully modelled a DCS as an economic resource allocation problem. The key conceptual innovation was to treat the program code (a string in the DCS language) as the label of a distinct commodity (like apples or shirts). Then the "production technology" defines the DCS resources required for successful execution of a program (production of the commodity). To solve the indivisibility problem, we modeled the demands as being driven by a stochastic arrival process and specified a queuing system.

The social welfare maximization problem was specified and solved to define the optimal allocation of services. We then derived rental prices for each PU that would support the optimal allocation as a decentralized stochastic equilibrium. Given optimal expected queue waiting times w^* and optimal rental prices r^*, user-programmers independently choose when and how many services to submit. The aggregation of these submittals constitutes a stochastic process that generates queue waiting times w^*. Moreover, the average flow rates and queue waiting times maximize social welfare.

We suggested several methods for implementing this pricing solution to the resource allocation problem, including direct computation and a dynamic tatonnement process. Further study involving simulations are needed to determine the best method in practice.

Our economic approach has the added benefit of providing a sound basis for evaluating DCS investment alternatives, using a process analogous to free entry and exit in free-enterprise economies. All of these theoretical advantages motivate further study.

In future research we will extend the theoretical model to take account of organizational constraints such as the need to set prices to recover the cost of operating the network. Introducing additional constraints to the welfare optimization of Equation (7) will lead to a different expression for the rental prices and raise questions about the role of these prices and their determination. There are many issues yet to be explored before a pricing mechanism can be successfully integrated into a distributed operating system environment. Some of these issues deal with the determination of prices, and the development of adequate software support for users to enable them to quickly price alternatives. Once we have an operational system we can compare, using simulation techniques, the performance of a DCS using our coordination mechanism with other allocative mechanisms. Clearly, the discovery and validation of a superior mechanism would have great significance.

BIBLIOGRAPHY

Arrow, K. and M. Intriligator (Eds.), 1982, *Handbook of Mathematical Economics*, Volumes I–II, Amsterdam: North-Holland.

Binmore, K., 1987, 'Modeling rational players, I and I', *Economics and Philosophy* 3, 179–214, and 4, 9–55.

Chaudhury, A., D. Stahl, and A. Whinston, 1994, 'The economic theory foundation for neural computing systems', in A. Whinston and J. Johnson (Eds.), *Advances in Artificial Intelligence in Economics, Finance and Management*, J.A.I. Press.

Cinlar, E., 1972, 'Superposition of point processes', in P. Lewis (Ed.), *Stochastic Point Processes: Statistical Analysis, Theory and Applications*, New York: Wiley, pp. 549–606.

Codsi, G. and K. Pearson, 1988, 'GEMPACK: General purpose software for applied general equilibrium and other economic applications', *Computer Science in Economics and Management* 1, 189–208.

Debreu, G., 1959, *The Theory of Value*, New Haven: Yale University Press.

Dolan, R. J., 1978, 'Incentive mechanisms for priority queueing problems', *Bell J. of Economics* 9, 421–436.

Ferguson, D., Y. Yemini, and C. Nikalson, 1989, 'Microeconomic algorithms for load balancing in distributed computer systems', T.J. Watson Research Center, Yorktown Heights, New York, research report.

Hahn, F., 1982, 'Stability', in K. Arrow and M. Intriligator (Eds.), *Handbook of Mathematical Economics II*, Amsterdam: North–Holland, Chapter 16.

Hogg, T., 1990, 'Primed for performance', *Byte* June, 241–250.

Manne, A., 1985, 'On the formulation and solution of economic equilibrium models', *Mathematical Programming Study* 23.

Mendelson, H., 1985, 'Pricing computer services: queuing effects', *Commun. ACM* 28, 312–321.

Mendelson, H. and S. Whang, 1990, 'Optimal incentive-compatible priority pricing for the M/M/1 queue', *Operations Research* 38, 870–883.

Talman, A. and G. van der Laan, G., 1987, *The Computation and Modeling of Economic Equilibria*, Amsterdam: North-Holland.

Varian, H., 1984, *Microeconomic Analysis*, New York: Norton.

Waldspurger, C., T. Hogg, B. Huberman, J. Kephart, and S. Stornetta, 1990, 'SPAWN: A distributed computational economy', Working Paper, Xerox Palo Alto Research Center, Palo Alto, CA.

ALAN S. MANNE AND THOMAS F. RUTHERFORD

International Trade, Capital Flows and Sectoral Analysis: Formulation and Solution of Intertemporal Equilibrium Models*

ABSTRACT. This paper examines international trade and capital flows within a five-region intertemporal equilibrium model. The paper reports on the use of sequential joint maximization to solve a specific class of AGE (applied general equilibrium) problems – those in which each agent may be characterized by a homothetic utility function.

The paper also considers issues related to the formulation of intertemporal AGE models that are focussed upon an individual sector. The balance of the economy is then described in terms of a numéraire good. With either static or recursive models, this form of aggregation seems appropriate. However, with *intertemporal* AGE models (that is, with dated commodities), difficulties are encountered unless the rate of return is identical in all regions. We explore the implications in terms of international trade and capital flows.

1. INTRODUCTION

This paper examines trade and capital flows within a five-region intertemporal equilibrium model. Each region is viewed as a single agent with an infinite life. The regional and intertemporal features are identical to those employed in Global 2100, an energy-environmental analysis described by Manne and Richels (1992). They employed an informal decomposition procedure to examine interregional trade linkages. Here we report on a formal AGE (applied general equilibrium) solution method, but exclude all aspects related to energy and the environment. There are capital flows, savings, investment and international trade in the numéraire good.

To compute an equilibrium through a technique that may be extended directly to much larger problems, we employ Negishi weights and a sequential joint maximization (SJM) algorithm. For the theory underlying this general

* For presentation at Conference on Computational Economics, Austin, May 1992. This research was funded by the Electric Power Research Institute (EPRI). The views presented here are solely those of the individual authors, and do not necessarily represent the views of EPRI or its members. For helpful suggestions on earlier drafts, we are indebted to Lars Mathiesen and John Rowse.

W.W. Cooper and A.B. Whinston (eds.), New Directions in Computational Economics, 191–205.

approach, see Negishi (1972). Dixon (1975) and Ginsburgh and Waelbroeck (1981) have shown that trial-and-error (tâtonnement) techniques are effective ways to solve for these weights in medium-sized models of international trade.

The SJM procedure is based upon the assumption of constant-returns utility functions for each region. The basic idea can be illustrated by an example in which there is one unit of a single divisible good to be allocated between several regions. Let U_r (the utility attained by region r) be proportional to the quantity that it receives. We then have:

$$\sum_r U_r = 1.$$

For each region r, there is a positive Negishi weight ω_r. These weights are normalized so that their sum is unity. A "global welfare function" is defined as the following weighted sum of the *logarithm* of each region's utility function:

$$\text{GWF} = \sum_r \omega_r \log U_r.$$

In order to maximize the GWF subject to the constraint on the global resource endowment, it is both necessary and sufficient to set $U_r = \omega_r$. That is, the equilibrium values of the Negishi weights may be interpreted as *shares* in the global endowment of economic resources. This greatly simplifies the iterative process for the determination of Negishi weights. To our knowledge, Rutherford was the first to propose the procedure, and this paper represents its initial application. For technical details, see Rutherford (1992).

When embedding a single sector within a model of the economy as a whole, it is customary to analyze the sector in considerable detail. Typically, the balance of the economy is described in terms of a single numéraire good, e.g. dollars of constant purchasing power. Real prices, e.g. those of oil or wheat, may then be expressed in terms of dollars per ton. A similar convention is often adopted when there is international trade. With either static or recursive models, this form of aggregation seems appropriate. However, with *intertemporal* AGE models (that is, with dated commodities), difficulties are encountered unless the rate of return is identical in all regions.

To illustrate the problem, assume that there are two regions called North and South (abbreviated N and S, respectively). Let the initial period's prices $p_{N1} = p_{S1} = 1$, and let p_{rt} be the present-value price of the numéraire good in region r during period t. If, for example, the marginal productivity of capital is 5% per year, the present value price in the following year will be 0.95. Now if the rate of return on capital is higher in the South than in the North, $p_{N2} > p_{S2}$. The terms of trade have moved in favor of the North and against the South. The converse would hold if $p_{N2} < p_{S2}$. There is no way to define an international numéraire unless we assume that the rate of return on capital is identical in all regions. If there were differences in the rates of return, capital movements and arbitrage would tend to reduce them to zero.

The Walras law implies that capital flows may be positive in some periods and negative in others, but the sum of their present values is zero for each individual region over the planning horizon. It does not ensure that there will be a realistic pattern from one period to the next. To allow for differential rates of return within an AGE framework, the most straightforward approach is to assume period-by-period constraints on capital flows. These constraints may be interpreted as a rule-of-thumb to allow for risks such as expropriation, repudiation or debt rescheduling.

With constraints on international capital flows, there are foreign exchange premia. Over time, these lead to systematic changes in the relative prices of each region's output. There are North-South policy issues for which it is appropriate to allow for constraints on capital flows and for endogenous changes in the terms of trade. The idea is straightforward, but it presents a major challenge – both from an empirical and a computational viewpoint. For purposes of *sectoral* analysis, it is far more convenient to assume that there is an international numéraire, and that there is therefore a uniform rate of return on capital in all regions.

The balance of this paper is organized as follows. We begin by formulating a single-good intertemporal model of international trade and capital flows. We show how this joint maximization problem may be employed iteratively for solving the AGE problem. With a model based on a single tradeable good during each time period, there are no computational difficulties in imposing constraints on capital flows. The results may easily be compared in two polar cases – one with and the other without capital flows. We also check for "end effects" by solving the model with alternative horizon dates.

2. FORMULATING THE SINGLE-GOOD MODEL

In Global 2100, the world is divided into five major geopolitical regions: the United States, other OECD nations, the former USSR, China, and the rest of the world. These are abbreviated, respectively, USA, OOECD, USSR, China and ROW. The model is benchmarked for a base year of 1990, and the projections cover ten-year time intervals extending from 2000 through 2100.

In general, the same macroeconomic parameters are employed as in Global 2100. The GDP growth rates are significantly different between regions, but – just as in the original model – the rates of return are equal. Under base case assumptions, there can be capital flows from one region to another, but overall their impact is negligible.

For each region, there is a single representative producer-consumer. Supplies and demands are equilibrated within each individual time period, but there are "look-ahead" features to allow for savings and investment interactions between periods. Capital is fully malleable, but in a more realistic example it would be straightforward to allow for adjustment costs, e.g. through "putty-clay" assumptions.

Expectations affect the accumulation of capital over time. Savings and investment decisions are modeled through the maximization of discounted utility. As in the Ramsey model of optimal economic growth, consumers receive equal benefits from an additional dollar's worth of current consumption and the future consumption generated by an additional dollar's worth of investment.

Within each region, aggregate output is determined by a Cobb-Douglas function of the inputs of labor and capital. Two polar cases are compared. In one, capital is immobile. In the other, it is fully mobile. That is, it may be exported to other regions or imported from them. In all cases, labor is immobile. To allow for increases in productivity, the growth rate of the labor force is measured in "efficiency units". At constant labor-capital price ratios, these assumptions determine the potential rate of GDP growth within each region. Depending upon the pattern of capital accumulation, the realized growth may exceed or fall short of these potential rates. These rates differ from one region to another, and they constitute some of the key input data.

The model is written in GAMS, a generalized algebraic modeling system (Brooke *et al.* 1988). With the GAMS language, it is natural to begin by describing the sets, then the decision variables, and the data tables. In this case, there are only two sets. These identify, respectively, the five regions (indexed by r) and the time periods (indexed by t).

Among the decision variables, the single-region maximand UTILITY_r is a scalar. All other variables are indexed both by region and by time period. Base year values are denoted by $t = 0$ (1990). The projection periods are $t =$ 1 (2000), 2 (2010), ..., T (2100). The variables are as follows:

UTILITY_r Single-region maximand

The following variables are *flows* measured in \$ trillions per year (expressed in dollars of constant 1990 purchasing power):

C_{rt} Consumption
I_{rt} Investment
X_{rt} Exports
M_{rt} Imports
Y_{rt} Production

The following variables are *stocks* measured in \$ trillions (also expressed in dollars of constant 1990 purchasing power):

K_{rt} Capital stock

TABLE I

Macroeconomic parameters

		USA	OOECD	USSR	CHINA	ROW
gdp0	initial GDP ($ trillions)	5.6	10.2	2.68	1.1	3.34
kgdp	initial capital-GDP ratio	2.4	2.8	3.0	3.0	3.0
depr	annual percent depreciation	5.0	5.0	5.0	5.0	5.0
kpvs	capital value share parameter	0.24	0.28	0.30	0.30	0.30

N.B. As part of the benchmarking procedure, this data set is calibrated so that there will be a uniform rate of return on capital. That is, kpvs/(kgdp) - depr = 5% in all regions. E.g., for the USA, we have 0.24/2.4 - 5% = 5%.

In formulating the constraints, all parameters are indicated by lowercase letters. These values are specified either directly or indirectly through Table I (macro parameters) and through the potential GDP growth rates described by Figure 1. Note that the growth rates are identical for all three industrialized regions: the USA, other OECD and the former USSR. To ensure that the system approaches a steady-state during the post-horizon years, we adopt lower values than those used by Manne and Richels to describe the growth potential for China and the ROW during the years 2060–2100.

For each region, there is a single equation defining the maximand and a single constraint referring to the terminal period. All other constraints are indexed by region and time period. They are identified as follows:

UTIL_r	Discounted utility, summed over all projection periods
GDP_{rt}	Gross domestic production
GDE_{rt}	Gross domestic expenditures
CAP_{rt}	Capital accumulation equation
TC_r	Terminal condition on investment and capital stock

The single-region utility maximand depends upon the consumption sequence, and is based upon the assumption that there is unitary elasticity of substitution between consumption at each point of time:

$$\text{UTIL}_r: \quad \log\ \text{UTILITY}_r = \sum_{t=1}^{T} udf_{rt} \log C_{rt}$$

where the utility discount rate for region r and period $t = \text{udr}_{rt} = (\text{kpvs}_r/\text{kgdp}_r)$ - depr_r - grow_{rt}. For periods $t = 1, 2, \ldots, T-1$, the utility discount factor is

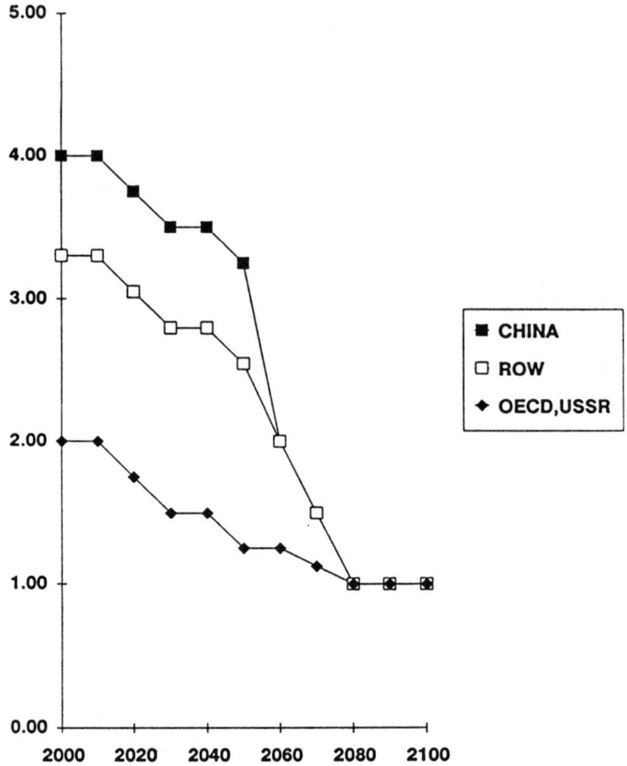

Fig. 1. Potential GDP growth rate, % per year.

$$\prod_{\tau=1}^{t-1} (1 + \mathrm{udr}_{r\tau})^{-10}.$$

The exponents of 10 allow for the fact that the first $T - 1$ periods are each 10 years in length.

For period T, the utility discount factor is

$$\prod_{\tau=1}^{T} (1 + \mathrm{udr}_{r\tau})^{-10} / [1 - (1 + \mathrm{udr}_{rT})^{-10}].$$

The terminal period extends an infinite length of time after the terminal date. The sum of this infinite geometric series is provided by the final square-bracketed factor. Note that the utility discount factors may be normalized so that $\mathrm{UTILITY}_r$ is a linearly homogeneous function of its arguments C_{rt}. This is a special case of homotheticity – an assumption that is typically employed in AGE models.

A numerical example shows how the utility discount rate is determined if the following parameter values are adopted. Omitting the subscripts for region r, we have:

kpvs	= capital's value share	= 24%
kgdp	= initial ratio of capital to GDP	= 2.4 years
depr	= depreciation rate	= 5% per year

net rate of return on capital		
	= (24%/2.4 years) - 5% per year	= 5% per year
grow_t	= potential growth rate	= 2% per year
$\therefore \text{udr}_t$	= utility discount rate	= 3% per year

The utility discount rates are chosen for descriptive rather than normative purposes. These values ensure that the optimal steady-state growth rate coincides with that assumed for the potential GDP. Along an optimal path, the rate of decline in the present value of the marginal utility of consumption equals the net marginal productivity of capital. (For a calculus-of-variations proof of this proposition, see Chakravarty (1969, p. 65). Moreover, these discount rates mean that the economy-wide savings rate adjusts downward (upward) automatically if there is a drop (rise) in the potential GDP growth rate.

The production function is written in a standard Cobb-Douglas form:

$$\text{GDP}_{rt}: \quad Y_{rt} = a_r(K_{rt})^{\alpha}(L_{rt})^{(1-\alpha)}$$

where the parameter α (= kpvs) denotes capital's value share in the GDP of region r, and a_r is an "efficiency" parameter determined by benchmarking to a first-order optimality condition for the base year. The labor force (measured in efficiency units) is an exogenously specified index number, L_{rt}. Its values are

$$L_{r0} = 1, \quad \text{and} \quad L_{r,t+1} = (1 + \text{grow}_{rt})^{10} L_{rt}.$$

The GDE_{rt} equations specify that the gross value of production is divided among the following expenditure categories: current consumption, investment for building up the domestic stock of capital, and exports minus imports (net foreign investment):

$$\text{GDE}_{rt}: \quad Y_{rt} = C_{rt} + I_{rt} + X_{rt} - M_{rt}.$$

Since the variable C_{rt} enters only into the single-region objective function and into constraint GDE_{rt}, the dual variable for this constraint represents the present value of the marginal utility of consumption during period t. First-order optimality conditions lead to the Ramsey rule for the optimal allocation over time among savings, investment, and consumption. That is, the marginal productivity of capital determines the rate of decline of these dual variables from one period to the next. All other dual variables for period t have a similar interpretation; they are present value prices. In order to convert them into future values, they must be divided by π_{rt}, the dual variables for the GDE_{rt} constraints.

In Global 2100, the net marginal productivity of capital is 5 percent, and the dual variables for the GDE_{rt} constraints decline by about 5 percent annually in all regions. Suppose that we identify the numéraire with the output of region 1 during the initial time period. For short, we define π_{1t} as π_t, the present-value price of this good.

The CAP_{rt} equations describe the dynamics of capital accumulation. Since investment is measured as an annual flow, an accumulation factor of 5 is applied to the beginning and ending rate of investment to determine net new capital formation during the decade as a whole. Within each 10-year period, net new capital formation is determined by cumulating the average of the beginning and ending rate of gross investment less depreciation:

$$\begin{aligned}\mathrm{CAP}_{r,t+1}: \qquad K_{r,t+1} &= (1+\mathrm{depr}_r)^{-10} K_{r,t} \\ &+ 5[(1+\mathrm{depr}_r)^{-10} I_{rt} + I_{r,t+1}] \quad t = 0, \ldots, T-1,\end{aligned}$$

where

$$\begin{aligned} K_{r0} &= (\mathrm{kgdp}_r)(\mathrm{gdp0}_r), \quad \text{and} \\ I_{r0} &= (\mathrm{grow}_{r0} + \mathrm{depr}_r)(\mathrm{kgdp}_r)(\mathrm{gdp0}_r). \end{aligned}$$

At the end of the planning horizon, a terminal constraint is applied to ensure that the rate of investment is adequate to provide for replacement and net growth of the capital stock during the subsequent periods. This reduces horizon effects, but is not guaranteed to eliminate them entirely. For a more complete discussion of terminal conditions, see Svoronos (1985):

$$\mathrm{TC}_r: \quad K_{rT}(\mathrm{grow}_{rT} + \mathrm{depr}_r) \le I_{rT}.$$

If capital is immobile, there are no interregional flows. That is, $X_{rt} = M_{rt} = 0$ (for all r and t). In this special case, we solve five independent optimization problems – one for each of the regions. If, however, there are trade and capital flows, we must ensure that they are balanced between all regions within each time period. A period-by-period global balance is provided by the following equations:

$$\mathrm{BAL}_t: \quad \sum_r (X_{rt} - M_{rt}) = 0.$$

3. SOLUTION BY NEGISHI WEIGHTS

The SJM solution procedure is based upon the idea that there is a "utility possibility frontier" – that is, a set of efficient points so that one region's utility cannot be improved without a decline in that of another region. See Dixon (1975, Chapter 1). In virtually all joint maximization methods, an equilibrium is characterized by a positive weight ω_r for each region r. An optimal solution is based upon a "global welfare function". This optimization may be obtained through a standard nonlinear programming algorithm. Without loss of generality, the Negishi weights may be normalized so that their sum is unity. Their numerical values must be determined so that the present value of each region's consumption is consistent with the present value of its endowments. In the specific case of Global 2100, we may write the global welfare function (GWF) as:

$$\text{GLOBAL}: \quad \text{GWF} = \sum_r \omega_r \log \text{ UTILITY}_r.$$

In this expression, a crucial role is played by the logarithmic transformations. Since the utility functions for each region are linearly homogeneous (and therefore homothetic), the equilibrium value of the weight ω_r may be interpreted as the *share* of region r in the present value of global resource endowments. This interpretation is the key to Rutherford's sequential optimization procedure. For a given set of weights, we solve a nonlinear programming problem in which all regions' decision variables are chosen simultaneously so as to maximize the GWF subject to the constraints listed in the preceding section.

When there is the possibility of trade or capital flows, there is no reason to expect that an arbitrary set of weights will lead to an optimal solution that satisfies the region-by-region intertemporal budget constraints. Accordingly, we recall the gross domestic expenditure equations GDE_{rt}, noting that the endowment of region r (that is, its capital and labor income) during period t is the value of its gross output less its investment. This endowment is available for current consumption and for net foreign capital formation. With π_t as the present value price of the international numéraire, we may define the present value of region r's endowment as follows. This definition does *not* enter directly into the formulation of the constrained maximization problem. It involves both the primal and dual solution values, and it is employed in the SJM procedure for determination of the Negishi weights:

$$\text{PVE}_r = \sum_t \pi_t (Y_{rt} - I_{rt}).$$

For an intertemporal economic equilibrium, the weights must be chosen so that the present value of each region's consumption will equal that of its endowment for the planning horizon taken as a whole. That is:

$$\sum_t \pi_t C_{rt} = \text{PVE}_r.$$

International capital flows may be positive in some periods and negative in others, but their net present value must be zero. In view of the gross domestic expenditure equations GDE_{rt}, these conditions are equivalent to the following version of the Walras law.

$$\sum_t \pi_{rt}(X_{rt} - M_{rt}) = 0.$$

Now consider an iterative procedure in which we solve the equilibrium problem through a sequence of nonlinear optimizations. At iteration k, the values of the Negishi weights are $\omega_{r,k}$. Measured in terms of the numéraire, the endowment values are $\text{PVE}_{r,k}$. At iteration $k+1$, the revised value of the weights is:

$$\omega_{r,k+1} = \text{PVE}_{r,k} / \sum_r \text{PVE}_{r,k}.$$

Typically, this process leads to positive value shares that sum to unity, and convergence is rapid. We have, however, constructed a counter-example to demonstrate that the algorithm will not always converge. This can occur when relative prices are highly sensitive to the distribution of endowment values.

4. BASE CASE NUMERICAL RESULTS – NO CONSTRAINTS ON CAPITAL MOBILITY

In this example, there are 187 constraints and 291 variables. To generate and to solve two cases (e.g., with and without international capital mobility), it takes eight minutes on a 25 MHz desktop 486 computer. The Negishi weights converge quite rapidly to their equilibrium values. According to Table II, the first nonlinear programming problem requires the bulk of the computing time. Thereafter, the only data changes are in the objective function. The successive optimization problems are immediately feasible, and the computing time declines progressively. With a sequence of only four successive optimizations, the values of $\omega_{r,k}$ converge to three decimal places.

In order to initialize the weights, it is recommended that they be chosen proportional to gdp0_r, the initial year's GDP in region r. These initial values tend to understate the equilibrium values for those regions (China and

TABLE II

Performance of the sequential optimization procedure

Iteration k	1	2	3	4
Negishi weights, $\omega_{r,k}$:				
USA	0.200	0.223	0.224	0.224
OOECD	0.200	0.402	0.403	0.403
USSR	0.200	0.102	0.102	0.102
CHINA	0.200	0.081	0.081	0.081
ROW	0.200	0.191	0.191	0.191
Solution time excluding problem generation (seconds on 25 MHz 486 desk-top computer)	78	51	27	2

Base case; no constraints on capital mobility.

ROW) that are growing more rapidly than the global average. Conversely, they overstate the equilibrium values of the weights in the other three regions (USA, OOECD and the former USSR). Table II shows that the SJM algorithm performs quite effectively even when there is a poor choice of the initial weights.

5. THE GAINS FROM CAPITAL MOBILITY

The base case was designed so that a sectoral analysis may easily be embedded within a macro framework. The rates of return on capital are virtually identical in all regions, and the terms of trade remain constant. This explains why the interregional trade and capital flows are a negligibly small percent of each region's GDP. The utility values and the present value prices are independent of the presence or absence of constraints upon trade and capital flows. With other numerical assumptions, these constraints could become significant. Nonetheless the algorithm converges quite rapidly. Its performance does *not* depend upon the assumption of uniform rates of return in all regions.

In the two following examples, we maintain all the base case parameters but vary the initial or the terminal conditions. Suppose, for example, that the planning horizon is shortened from 2100 to 2050. This means that China and the ROW are growing faster than the other three regions at the terminal date. (Recall Figure 1.) In turn, this means that they have lower utility discount rates than the other regions at that point.

TABLE III

Comparison of the values of log UTILITY$_r$ – with and without constraints on capital mobility – termination in 2050 (instead of 2100)

Regions r	With constraints	No constraints
USA	2.177	2.179
OOECD	2.764	2.766
USSR	1.393	1.395
CHINA	1.460	1.494
ROW	2.159	2.164

The result is a counter-intuitive pattern of interregional trade and capital flows. China and the ROW *export* capital to the other three regions during the initial years, and they import capital during the terminal period. Under this scenario, there would be utility gains for China and the ROW, but we should not impute any policy significance to these gains (see Table III). This is a case in which horizon effects clearly dominate the solution. It is easy to obtain dubious results if the planning horizon is truncated prior to a date at which the economies of all regions are growing at approximately the same rate.

Our second example illustrates the impact of trade and capital flows in a somewhat more realistic context. Here we vary the *initial* conditions. Suppose, for example, that the ROW's initial capital stock is arbitrarily halved. This means that the net marginal productivity of capital in that region is raised from 5% to 15% annually during the initial years of the planning horizon. All other parameters (e.g., the utility discount rates) remain unchanged from those employed in the base case.

As can be seen from Figure 2, this change provides a strong incentive for a rapid increase in the rate of investment. If capital is mobile, some of the ROW's investment can be financed by imports from the other four regions. There is an improvement in economic efficiency, but only a small gain in the ROW's maximand. (The value of log UTILITY increases from 2.195 to 2.197). The UTILITY values are virtually unchanged in the other four regions. It takes only one or two decades for the rate of return on capital to drop back to 5%.

When we impose a constraint on capital transfers by setting trade flows at zero, there is a premium on foreign exchange in the ROW region. That is, the present value of the numéraire good is systematically higher in the USA than in the ROW. Figure 3 shows that the foreign exchange premium changes

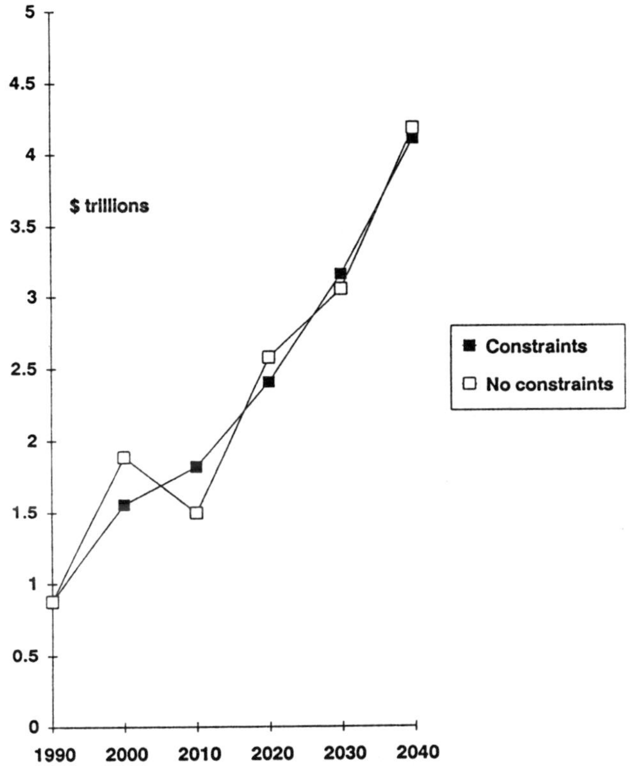

Fig. 2. ROW Investment, 15% initial marginal productivity of capital (instead of 5%).

only moderately over time, and there is therefore little difference between the rate of return on capital in the two regions.

Why does this numerical example seem to differ so much from those that are frequently reported in North-South policy analyses? Here there is only a modest effect of capital inflows upon the ROW's growth potential, and there is no need to impose "absorptive capacity" constraints in order to avoid a rapid buildup in the region's investment rate. We conjecture that these results are due primarily to the assumption that each region's numéraire good is a perfect substitute for that of the other regions. This is qualitatively different from the imperfect substitutes view of the world that is often embodied in the development planning literature. See e.g., the classic paper by Chenery and MacEwan (1966).

In order to analyze North-South policy issues (trade, aid and development), one must employ a different type of model than that presented here. For an illustration of capital flow constraints in a multi-commodity model with imperfect substitution between the outputs of individual regions, see Manne and Preckel (1984). Alternatively, one could introduce foreign capital supply

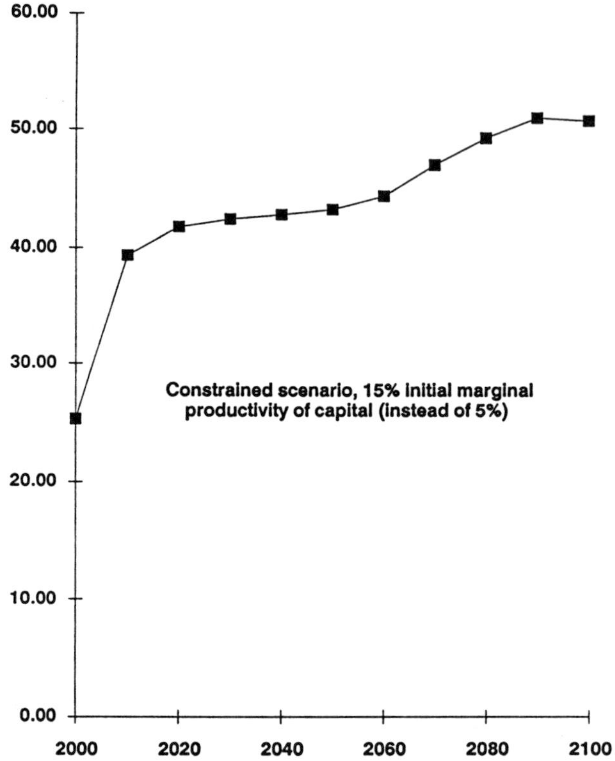

Fig. 3. Foreign exchange premium in ROW relative to USA, %.

curves as a surrogate to represent the possibility of defaults on international debts and the risks of capital expropriation. These considerations go well beyond those that are usually considered appropriate for international sectoral analyses.

6. CONCLUDING COMMENTS

In an applied general equilibrium framework, one adopts some general principles, e.g. the importance of economic efficiency and of price-guided decentralization. Within the AGE paradigm, many different assumptions may be explored, and these will depend upon the policy issues to be addressed. In some cases, it may be essential to include capital market imperfections. These imperfections are central to debates over, say, the design of tax rates or electricity pricing within a single country. They are also central to North-South dialogue over capital flows between countries. For this type of analysis, we cannot make much progress if we restrict ourselves to models implying that all agents are confronted by the identical rate of return on capital.

By contrast, it may be a tolerably good approximation to assume a uniform rate of return within sectoral analyses of international trade. Otherwise, with non-uniform rates, we would imply that there are profitable possibilities for arbitrage in the numéraire good. We would also encounter arbitrage possibilities for goods that can be both stored and traded, e.g. a ton of oil resources or a ton's worth of carbon emission rights.

Provided that it is acceptable to assume homothetic utility functions, we have found that sequential joint maximization is a practical way to solve large-scale intertemporal AGE models. Such models need not be restricted to continuously differentiable production and utility functions. They may also include activity analysis – and therefore the possibility of zero prices or zero activity levels. To date, there have been no general methods available for large problems when the solution procedure must deal with complementary slackness conditions – that is, to determine which prices and activity levels are at zero level, and which are positive. In a forthcoming paper, we will show that the Negishi-Rutherford approach provides an effective way to compute an intertemporal equilibrium problems that involve the simultaneous determination of several thousand prices and activity levels.

BIBLIOGRAPHY

Brooke, A., D. Kendrick, and A. Meeraus, 1988, *GAMS: A User's Guide.*, Redwood City, CA: Scientific Press.

Chakravarty, S., 1969, *Capital and Development Planning*, Cambridge, MA: MIT Press.

Chenery H. and A. MacEwan, 1966, 'Optimal patterns of growth and aid: the case of Pakistan', in I. Adelman and E. Thorbecke (Eds.), *The Theory and Design of Economic Development*, Chapter 6, Baltimore, MD: Johns Hopkins Press.

Dixon, P., 1975, *The Theory of Joint Maximization*, Amsterdam: North-Holland.

Ginsburgh V. and J. Waelbroeck, 1981, *Activity Analysis and General Equilibrium Modelling*, Amsterdam: North-Holland.

Manne A. and P. Preckel, 1984, 'North-South trade, capital flows, and economic growth: An almost neoclassical model', in M. Syrquin, L. Taylor, and L. Westphal (Eds.), *Economic Structure and Performance*, New York: Academic Press, pp. 409–427.

Manne A. and R. Richels, 1992, *Buying Greenhouse Insurance – the Economic Costs of Carbon Dioxide Emission Limits*, Cambridge, MA: MIT Press.

Negishi, T., 1972, *General Equilibrium Theory and International Trade*, Amsterdam: North-Holland.

Rutherford, T., 1992, 'A sequential joint maximization algorithm for applied general equilibrium problems', Working Paper, University of Western Ontario.

Svoronos, A., 1985, *Duality Theory and Finite Horizon Approximations for Discrete Time Infinite Horizon Convex Programs*. Ph.D. Thesis, Stanford University, Department of Operations Research.

REINHARD NECK AND JOSEF MATULKA

Stochastic Control of Nonlinear Economic Models*

ABSTRACT. In this paper we discuss some solutions of stochastic optimum control problems for nonlinear economic systems, emphasizing algorithmic and computational aspects. Several algorithms for this purpose have been implemented in FORTRAN programs, mostly for use with a mainframe computer. We point out some problems associated with such programs and propose an implementation in the package GAUSS to be run on personal computers. Our algorithm, called OPTCON, has the additional advantage of being able to deal with the optimal control of nonlinear economic systems where some or all of the parameters may be stochastic. An outline of the structure of this algorithm is given, and applications to small econometric models of the Austrian economy are described. The next step of research, apart from extending this algorithm, should be directed towards embedding it into a decision support system in order to make it more accesible to potential users and to make possible its application to real-world economic policy problems.

1. INTRODUCTION

It is generally acknowledged that decision-making by managers for a firm or by policy-makers for an economy should be supported by a careful analysis of their objectives, the constraints they are confronted with, and the possibilities of achieving an outcome which is in some well-defined sense "better" than other available alternatives. Operations research and economics have produced a vast array of theoretical models in order to provide guidelines to arrive at "optimal" solutions for decision problems on the microeconomic and the macroeconomic level. Mathematical models for the systems under consideration are especially helpful in structuring decision problems and guiding

* An earlier version of this paper was presented at the Conference on Computational Economics, Austin, Texas, May 17–19, 1992. Helpful comments from the participants of this conference and financial support from the Austrian "Fonds zur Foerderung der wissenschaftlichen Forschung" (research project no. P7966-SOZ) are gratefully acknowledged. Reinhard Neck is with the Department of Economics, University of Bielefeld, Bielefeld, Germany; work on this paper was done during his stay as Schumpeter Research Fellow at the John F. Kennedy School of Government, Harvard University, Cambridge, MA, USA. Josef Matulka is with the Department of Applied Computer Science, Vienna University of Economics and Business Administration, Vienna, Austria.

W. W. Cooper and A.B. Whinston (eds.), New Directions in Computational Economics, 207–226.

the search for "better" solutions. However, if one tries to build a model which gives a realistic picture for an actual decision problem, the limits of analytical tractability are reached very soon. Obstacles which tend to preclude analytical solutions of decision problems include, among others, the intertemporal nature of the decision process, the presence of uncertainty and of imperfect information, the fact that even in a relatively simple model the interactions among a large number of variables must be considered, and the nonlinearities and other complications which are inevitable in all but the simplest models. Hence it turns out that explicit qualitative results can be obtained only for very simple models, while more sophisticated theoretical approaches often give ambiguous results or results which depend on a large number of additional assumptions not necessarily justified by the real-world problem.

These difficulties can be illustrated by the attempts to apply methods and tools of stochastic control theory to economics and management science. In principle, stochastic optimum control theory is an appropriate instrument for the solution of economic decision problems: It takes into account the intertemporal nature of decision-makers' preferences and the dynamics of the changing environment they are confronted with, and it models explicitly the uncertainty under which decisions have to be made by introducing random variables into the system description. Although some theoretical studies using stochastic control theory have succeeded in obtaining results for dynamic stochastic optimization problems both for the firm and the national economy, the impact of this work on actual decision-making has been fairly limited. The main reason for this is the extremly complicated structure of the solution for a fully stochastic optimum control problem, which prevents an analytical solution even in very simple cases. One obvious way out of this dilemma consists in deriving numerical solutions for decision problems whose parameters are estimated from empirical data or assigned some plausible values. This approach, however, so far has suffered from the lack of available software and the mathematical difficulties of deriving algorithms which deliver approximately optimal solutions for numerically specified stochastic control problems. Thus it is not surprising that most actual decision problems in firms or in government are still solved by ad hoc methods, which rarely lead to optimal decisions, or by algorithms based on linear (or nonlinear) programming, which mostly neglect the dynamics and uncertainty inherent in decision-making.

With the availability of powerful computing facilities, however, this situation ought to be changed. Even if it must be acknowledged that a mathematical solution to a fully specified stochastic optimum control problem is not likely to be achieved in the near future, numerical solutions for such problems should be a practicable alternative. In order to derive such solutions and to make them accessible to actual decision-makers, two requirements have to be fulfilled. First, algorithms have to be developed that deliver approximately optimal solutions to stochastic control problems with numerically specified multivariable nonlinear economic models. Second, these algorithms must be implemented in such a way that they can be used by advisers of managers and policy-makers in an interactive way without requiring much mathematical knowledge, programming effort or extensive data manipulation by the user. So far, some progress has been achieved with respect to the first requirement, whereas the second task is still largely open for research by specialists in computational economics and applied computer science. In this paper, we give an overview of the state of the art in the development of algorithms for the stochastic control of nonlinear economic models and suggest some directions for future research, particularly with the aim of making these algorithms more user-friendly. We avoid mathematical notation completely and emphasize algorithmic and computational issues. Moreover, we do not attempt at providing a comprehensive survey of the literature on stochastic control algorithms for economic models, but concentrate on dynamic-programming approaches and neglect algorithms based on different solution methods.

2. FORTRAN PROGRAMS FOR STOCHASTIC OPTIMUM CONTROL OF DYNAMIC ECONOMIC MODELS

Although some algorithms and software for stochastic optimum control problems are available in the engineering literature, they are not always suited to economic applications. For instance, numerical economic models in general are formulated in discrete time whereas continuous-time models prevail in the engineering literature, state space representations used in economics are sometimes different from those used by engineers, etc. Therefore several economists have developed their own algorithms and computer programs for deriving optimal solutions to stochastic control problems. In this section we give a brief description of three algorithms which have been implemented in FORTRAN computer programs: OPTNL, DUAL, and PLEM. Apart from using FORTRAN, their common features are the assumption of a quadratic objective function, the use of a dynamic multivariable model as constraint, and the introduction of additive error terms in the dynamic model. Approximately optimal solutions are derived by stochastic dynamic programming in each of them, and the problem formulation comes from economic policy problems encountered in the theory of quantitative economic policy, although their applicability is not confined to this area. These algorithms are selected as examples because they are readily available, relatively well documented, and seem to be the most general ones among those developed so far which base their solution procedure upon a dynamic-programming approach instead of "stacking" the model variables to avoid stagewise optimization. The latter solution alternative is not discussed here as it amounts to suppressing some essential aspects of intertemporal decision-making under uncertainty by concentrating on open-loop policies.

A. The Algorithm of OPTNL

Chow [1, 2] developed an algorithm which can solve optimum control problems for nonlinear systems with additive disturbances under a quadratic objective function. This algorithm is implemented in the FORTRAN66 computer program OPTNL. The parameters of the dynamic model are assumed to be known with certainty. The problem to be solved consists in determining a trajectory of control variables over a given finite time horizon which minimizes an intertemporal objective function defined in the deviations of the state variables from their desired values with time-dependent weights of the target variables, subject to a nonlinear first-order vector difference equation for the state vector, which includes exogenous variables and additive disturbances assumed to be serially uncorrelated. The functional form of the system equations, the initial state, the desired values of the state variables (which may be time-dependent), the values of the exogenous variables, the weighting matrices in the objective function and the variance-covariance matrix of the error term are assumed given and have to be supplied by the user of the computer program. Although in Chow's formulation only state variables enter the objective function, control variables' deviations from their desired values can be penalized, too, by including control variables in the state vector. In a similar way the state vector has to be augmented and identities have to be added to the dynamic model if the model contains lags of length more than one. The time structure in the discrete-time formulation of the problem is such that the decision-maker knows only the lagged and not the current value of the state when deciding upon the optimal control for each period, which in turn affects the current value of the state.

The optimization procedure in the OPTNL algorithm is based on iteratively solving time-varying linear approximations to the nonlinear system via dynamic programming. First, the user has to specify an initial time path for the control variables over the planning horizon, which may consist of historical or predicted values for these variables. Next, the path of the state variables resulting from applying this initial control path to the state equations is calculated using the Gauss-Seidel iterative algorithm, using the given values for the exogenous variables and the initial state variables and the calculated values for the lagged state variables in each period; the disturbances are set equal to zero. This creates a reference path for the state vector and the control vector, around which the nonlinear system is linearized to result in a time-varying linear system. Then the resulting linear-quadratic optimum control problem is solved using matrix Riccati equations obtained from dynamic programming backwards in time. From given terminal conditions, one obtains time-varying Riccati matrices and feedback matrices for the optimal linear decision rule linking the optimal control vector to the lagged state vector for all periods as well as the minimum cost expected at the initial time over the entire planning horizon under the optimal policy as a function of the initial state; the expected minimum cost consists of a deterministic and a stochastic component. Then the optimal control and state vectors are calculated upwards in time, using the linear feedback equations and the nonlinear system equations, respectively, where again the Gauss-Seidel algorithm is applied. The resulting time path for the state variables is compared to the reference path. If the relative difference between these values of the state variables stay within some given small number, then the values calculated for the control and state variables are regarded to be approximately optimal; otherwise, these values are taken as new reference paths and another iteration is started until the algorithm converges. The optimal state vectors are stochastic variables due to the presence of the additive error term, hence the "optimal" state trajectory eventually arrived at has to be interpreted as path of expected values of the (approximately) optimal state. The algorithm also calculates the variance-covariance matrices of the optimal states.

The combination of the dynamic optimization procedure with the iterative Gauss-Seidel solution procedure for nonlinear systems makes it possible to apply the algorithm OPTNL to a fairly broad class of economic models. Although it does not really start from a general structural form for a nonlinear econometric model, because it requires the state vector to be given as an explicit function in the system equation, most practically occuring nonlinearities can be transformed into this form. On the other hand, this algorithm results in a solution which is only approximately optimal. Convergence is not guaranteed, although practical experience shows that it usually is obtained unless the model deviates too far from the reference path during the planning horizon.

The computer program OPTNL, which has been written by Chow and Butters, is implemented in FORTRAN66. Its code consists of the optimization program proper and the supporting matrix- and I/O-subroutines. It is documented in a user's manual (reprinted in [2, Chapter 5]), a programmer's manual and a description of the subroutines. Using the program requires at least a rudimentary knowledge of FORTRAN, because the user has to supply (via NAMELIST) not only the dimensions of the problem (number of state variables, number of exogenous variables, etc.), some options and the input data (variance-covariance matrices, initial state vector, etc.), but he (she) also has to code the FORTRAN functions MODELS and MODELI containing the economic model. Apart from this, the documentation is relatively detailed;

the user-friendliness of the program is also enhanced by the documentation of a coded example (the Klein-Goldberger model) with program output, which can easily be reproduced.

B. The Algorithms of DUAL

Several algorithms have been derived by Kendrick [3] for the optimum control of dynamic systems where not only disturbances in the reduced-form equations of the econometric model ("additive uncertainty"), but also stochastic parameters ("multiplicative uncertainty") are considered. They can deal with linear-quadratic problems, i.e., the objective function has to be quadratic (as with Chow) and the economic system has to be linear, which is much more restictive than in the Chow-algorithm. Some versions of these algorithms have been implemented in the computer program DUAL, written in FORTRAN77, which has been modified in recent years to be capable of running on different computers (including PCs). Originally the program was designed to solve only "small" problems (with only a few state and control variables), but possibilities of re-dimensioning for larger problems are now provided.

The algorithms implemented in DUAL determine the values of the control variables for a finite planning horizon which minimize a quadratic objective function, defined in the deviations of the state and control variables from their desired values, with symmetric, time-varying weighting matrices, subject to a dynamic system given by a linear vector difference equation, with the initial value of the state vector being given. Exogenous variables may be present, as is a vector of stochastic disturbances. In addition, and in contrast to Chow, the matrices of parameters (coefficients) of the dynamic system may be stochastic. Here the state space representation assumes a time structure different from that in Chow's algorithm: At the end of each period the current state is known to the decision-maker, who has to decide on the value of the control vector; hence the latter cannot directly affect the current state. The additive error terms are assumed to be serially uncorrelated, with zero mean and constant given variance-covariance matrix. The stochastic parameters in the system matrices are put together in random vectors, which may or may not be time-dependent. In a model for constant but unknown parameters it is assumed that the random parameters are serially uncorrelated with known expected values and variance-covariance matrix. Defining the objective function in terms of deviations from desired values (for a "tracking problem") is not really restrictive, as such a problem can easily be reformulated as a problem with a general quadratic objective function. Also the requirement of the weighting matrices in the objective function to be symmetric implies no loss of generality as one can solve problems with asymmetric weighting matrices by suitable substitutions without changing the results of the calculations.

The transformed linear-quadratic intertemporal optimization problem has been solved analytically in [3] by dynamic programming, resulting again in a linear feedback decision rule linking the optimal control to the current value of the state vector. If one assumes the distribution (the first two moments) of the stochastic parameters to be known, the Riccati matrices can be determined for all periods backwards in time from the Riccati equations; then the parameter matrices of the optimal decision rule can be computed for all periods. For a given initial state the initial-period control vector can then be determined, and for known realizations of the system parameters the state equations can be solved forwards in time to calculate the alternating sequence of states and controls up to the final period of the planning horizon.

Taking into account the presence of the stochastic system parameters considerably complicates the determination of the optimal control sequence; exact solutions for problems with general information patterns are not available. The existing algorithms use various approximation schemes to deal with the problems arising from the interactions between control and uncertainties. In DUAL, apart from a simple certainty-equivalence algorithm, two schemes are implemented, namely open-loop feedback ("passive learning"), where potential learning effects of control actions are neglected, but state variables (when measurement errors are present) and parameters are re-estimated for each period, and closed-loop or adaptive (dual) control ("active learning"), where the control in each period takes also into account its effects on future parameter estimation besides its direct effects on the objective function.

For the open-loop feedback solution with "passive learning", the initial-period optimal control is calculated according to the linear-quadratic problem-solving algorithm described above, taking the expected values of the stochastic parameters as constant for all periods and assuming the exogenous variables to be given for all time periods. The expected values of the stochastic parameters are taken from the the given initial values of the parameter vector. The first-period value of the state is then obtained from inserting into the state equation the initial-period optimal control and a realization of the stochastic disturbance term for the initial period, which is provided by a Monte Carlo random number generator. This value of the state for the first period is used to update the distribution of the stochastic parameters using a second-order Kalman filter algorithm; this gives a new expected value and a new variance-covariance matrix for the stochastic parameters. With these results the linear-quadratic optimization problem is solved again for the remaining time periods, with new expected values for the stochastic system coefficients and given exogenous variables, to yield the optimal control for the first period. Then the second-period value of the state variable is generated from the first-period optimal control and a realization of the first-period stochastic disturbance, and so on until the value of the state vector in the final period is obtained. Finally the value of the objective function obtained from the specific Monte Carlo run used is calculated. Apart from the system and objective function parameters, the user of the program has to specify only the initial values for the first two moments of the stochastic parameters, which may come from an estimation of the economic model, the initial value of the state variables, and the values for the exogenous variables for all time periods. Thus the open-loop feedback algorithm contains an "ordinary" non-learning optimum control algorithm for a linear-quadratic control problem, but it is more general as this "ordinary" optimization procedure is applied several times with different inputs and shrinking control horizon.

In addition to the idea of re-estimating the parameters of the model (and, with measurement errors, also the state) contained in the "passive learning" algorithm, "active learning" also takes account of the effects of changes in a control variable on future measurements and hence the information to be obtained in future periods. Present control inputs into the system may serve to provide more accurate estimates of the parameters and the states in the future, which in turn will improve the control performance for future periods. Various algorithms have been developed in the engineering literature to give approximately optimal solutions to adaptive control problems where "active learning" is present. In DUAL, a version of the algorithm proposed by Tse, Bar-Shalom, and Meier [4] has been implemented for this purpose. The linear dynamic system under consideration may contain additive errors in the equations, measurement errors in the state variables, and stochastic parameters, with given first and second moments for all of them.

The algorithm embeds the dynamic optimization problem into a Monte Carlo procedure; the dynamic optimization problem in turn contains a static optimization problem. In each Monte Carlo run the required random terms are generated, and the problem is solved for these realizations of the stochastic variables. The solution of the dynamic optimization problem starts by solving, in each time period, the certainty-equivalence problem for the remaining time periods. The control obtained in this way is then modified in the static optimization problem, where the approximate cost-to-go for the remaining periods is evaluated iteratively. After determining the optimal control for any period, that control is applied to the system along with the random elements to obtain new states and estimates of the means and the variance-covariance matrix of the random elements for the next period.

The program DUAL was written in FORTRAN77 by Kendrick and Coomes; a discussion paper by the authors is available [5] which serves as manual for the program. The program code consists of the routines for the optimization, a collection of matrix- and I/O-subroutines and some subroutines from the IMSL library. The logic of the program is documented in the manual by flowcharts, listings of all routines and of the most important input and output parameters. Two reference examples are also provided which can be reproduced by the user. Although the documentation of the matrix- and I/O-subroutines is less extensive than for OPTNL, the user-friendliness of the two programs can be judged to be roughly equal.

C. The Algorithm of PLEM

The computer program PLEM developed by Coomes [6] is similar to DUAL as it computes also open-loop feedback solutions for formally analogous stochastic control problems. It does not allow for measurement errors and active learning; on the other hand, it can solve larger problems than DUAL. Instead of using a random number generator to update the estimates for the first and second moments of the distribution of the stochastic parameters, the user has to supply actual data for this purpose. This serves to allow for comparisons between actual historical policies and approximately optimal open-loop feedback policies, which is often desirable in economic applications. The exogenous variables are regarded as random and can be updated using actual data. The updating algorithm is also different from that used in DUAL: Instead of a Kalman filter, PLEM uses the Bayesian method of MacRae [7], which treats the original estimates of the reduced-form coefficients as priors and updates their means, variances and covariances when new observations are added. This procedure is intended to simulate the process of re-estimating the econometric model with the advent of additional data. As the reduced form itself is updated, there is no need for re-estimating the structural form of the econometric model. Apart from these modifications, the PLEM algorithm is essentially the same as the open-loop feedback algorithm of DUAL. PLEM is easier to handle, but DUAL can be applied to models with a richer stochastic structure. Also for PLEM a discussion paper serving as manual, a reference example, and a version for the PC are available.

Both DUAL and PLEM can be applied to problems with longer than one-period lags for the state or the control variables in the state equation. In this case the model has to be changed to the standard state space representation by augmenting the state vector; this has to be done by the user by hand. Such a conversion is also required if the econometric model is given in the structural instead of the reduced form. Although calculation of the reduced form from the structural form is relatively easy for a linear model, such a procedure ought to be appended to the control program as well. In the PLEM algorithm the transformation of the structural into the reduced form has to be done only once, because re-estimation of the structural form is not necessary under the MacRae updating procedure. The major drawback of both DUAL and PLEM, on the other hand, is their restriction to linear dynamic models. The theoretical approach to nonlinear active-learning stochastic control contained in [3] is not incorporated in either of the two programs. As it is rather difficult to avoid nonlinearities even in very simple economic models, some linearization algorithm for nonlinear econometric models should be added to the stochastic control algorithms of DUAL and PLEM. On the other hand, the program OPTNL, which does contain such linearization procedures, does not allow for either "active" or "passive" learning or for the updating of states and parameters, although the algorithms for determining optimal policies and state variables contained in all three programs are very similar.

D. Comparison and Evaluation of the FORTRAN Programs

The structure of the three algorithms implemented in the FORTRAN programs OPTNL, DUAL and PLEM suggests that they should be equivalent in the sense of producing identical optimal policies (apart from numerical inaccuracies) for the class of problems to which each of them can be applied, namely optimum stochastic control problems for linear systems with known parameters, no measurement errors, with additive disturbances in the equations, under a quadratic objective function, with no learning taking place. For this class of problems the certainty-equivalence theorem holds, i.e., the optimal policy rules are the same as in the deterministic case. For DUAL and PLEM, this equivalence is obvious, because these two programs differ only with respect to the updating procedure in the open-loop feedback algorithm and to the possibility of "active learning", which are not relevant to the class of problems without learning. Elsewhere [8] we have shown that there is also a one-to-one correspondence between the state space representations, the objective functions and the feedback rules for optimal policies between OPTNL on the one hand and DUAL and PLEM on the other. Any linear-quadratic optimum control problem with deterministic parameters and additive stochastic disturbances can therefore be solved by either of the three algorithms, and the same results are obtained. We have verified this also by using each of the three programs for solving several optimum control problems, such as those delivered with DUAL and an economic policy problem for Austria. It turned out that all values of control and state variables for each period were virtually identical across the programs, showing that the implementation of the different algorithms in the three computer programs preserves their equivalence.

As for the implementation of the three programs, it can be noticed that FORTRAN77 used for DUAL and PLEM provides more possibilities, e.g. for the storage of strings. Both DUAL and OPTNL use GOTOs extensively in their subroutines, which makes the code sometimes nearly incomprehensible; this is not the case for the main routines. Storage of matrices is performed in different ways in the programs: OPTNL has one single big one-dimensional array for that purpose, parts of which are transferred to the matrix-subroutines and interpreted as two-dimensional arrays there. This saves storage capacity and allows confining oneself to changing one single dimension when redimensioning is required. In DUAL and PLEM, on the other hand, each matrix is stored in a separate two-dimensional array; hence if the user wants to solve a problem of larger dimension, he (she) has to change dimensions for all the matrices occurring in the program, i.e. to recompile the entire program. Obviously the solution chosen for OPTNL has to be preferred in this respect. Finally, the programs differ in the amount of output they produce and in the possibilities of editing this output: DUAL has a much greater variety of options for the user to change the extent of output produced. This corresponds with the degree of complexity of the programs: DUAL is much more complex than OPTNL, as it offers three algorithms, embedded into a Monte Carlo simulation, with the active learning algorithm being particularly elaborate. The complexity of PLEM lies slightly below that of the open-loop feedback version of DUAL, as it does not allow for measurement errors.

All the algorithms discussed so far are implemented in FORTRAN. This relatively old programming language has the advantage of being fast; in addition, it provides the possibility of writing subroutines that can be used for a variety of purposes. However, some drawbacks of FORTRAN detract from the usefulness of the programs under consideration. For instance, variable names are confined to six characters at most, preventing self-explanatory labels. Variables do not have to be declared in FORTRAN, which easily leads to coding errors. Some "dirty tricks" made possible in FORTRAN and GOTOs make it difficult to grasp the code quickly. FORTRAN also does not support the specification of abstract data types or any elaborate module concept. Input data have to be provided in fixed format, and coding errors are not checked. Also the output consists of numbers, without providing possibilities for user-friendly graphics. If stochastic control algorithms are to be implemented in a conventional programming language, now there exist alternatives to FORTRAN making a simpler, more elegant and more secure implementation possible, such as MODULA-2. On the other hand, it is questionable whether an implementation in a conventional programming language is an optimal solution at all. For the purpose of applying the algorithms the most important point seems to be the requirement of transferring (usually large amounts of) data from an econometric software package to the control algorithm. In particular, the GAUSS package, which has applications for many statistical and econometric problems, combines this advantage with programming capabilities nearly equivalent to a programming language, or even superior as far as matrix operations are concerned. GAUSS is coded directly in assembler language and exploits the PC's mathematical coprocessor. GAUSS applications thus can run with high speed. Therefore we decided to implement our own stochastic control algorithm in GAUSS.

3. THE GAUSS PROGRAM OPTCON

In designing the algorithm OPTCON we started from one of the extensions to the OPTNL algorithm suggested in Chapter 3 of [2]. The suggested algorithm chosen was simplified and modified and then mathematically derived in a way which should ease its interpretation and its implementation in GAUSS. Also an exact specification of the problem is provided that is essentially independent of the programming language and may be helpful for implementations in other languages and as a documentation of the program. In this section, we give a short description of the algorithm OPTCON and of some test results. Mathematical details of the algorithm are reported in [9], and more details about the applications can be found in [10].

A. The Algorithm OPTCON

OPTCON gives approximate solutions to stochastic optimum control problems with a quadratic objective function and a nonlinear multivariable dynamic model under additive and parameter uncertainties. Thus it combines the nonlinearity element of OPTNL with the stochastic-parameter element of DUAL. The objective function is again quadratic in the deviations of the state and control variables from their respective desired values, but can easily be transformed to the "general quadratic" form. Symmetry of the possibly time-varying weighting matrices is assumed without loss of generality. The dynamic system is assumed to be given in a state space representation analogous to that of Chow, which is more suited to econometric applications than the form used in DUAL. Apart from the additive error term, a constant vector of unknown (hence stochastic) parameters enters the system equation. Parameter and additive disturbance vectors are assumed to be independent with known expectations and variance-covariance matrices. Although the dynamic system is formulated as a first-order system of difference equations, longer lags can be easily handled by augmentation of the state vector as in the Chow algorithm.

As an input for the algorithm, the user has to supply the system function, the initial value of the state vector, a tentative path for the control variables, the path of the exogenous non-controlled variables, the expected value and the variance-covariance matrix of the stochastic parameter vector, the variance-covariance matrix of the additive system noise, the weighting matrices of the objective function, and the desired paths for the state and control variables. The algorithm starts by computing a tentative path of the state vector from the system equations with the tentative path for the control variables, using the Gauss-Seidel algorithm. Then it linearizes the system equations at the reference values obtained before, replacing the nonlinear time-invariant system by a linear time-varying one. The parameter matrices of the linearized system equations are (in general nonlinear) functions of the random parameter vector; these functions are approximated by linear functions by computing the derivatives of the parameters of the linearized system with respect to the parameter vector, which are also used to evaluate the variance-covariance matrices of the parameters of the linearized system equations and some expected values needed for the Riccati equations and expressing the influence of the stochastic parameters. Using dynamic programming, we can derive linear feedback policy rules linking the control variables to the lagged state variables, where the feedback matrices are computed from Riccati matrices calculated backwards in time, given terminal conditions from the objective function. Using the feedback rules and the state equations, the sequence of controls and states is computed forwards in time. The resulting values for the state and control variables are used as tentative paths, and another iteration is started by linearizing the system along these values etc., until convergence is reached, i.e., until the approximately optimal control and state variables calculated do not change more than a prespecified small number from one iteration to the next. Also the expected welfare loss is computed in each iteration. The procedure is similar to that used in OPTNL, but we introduce another linearization for the influence of the stochastic parameters on the parameter matrices of the linearized system equation.

As it is impossible to derive an exact solution for the nonlinear stochastic optimum control problem with random parameters, in designing the algorithm OPTCON we had to introduce simplifying assumptions. The linearizations of the system along the reference paths and of the relation between the parameter matrices and the random parameter vector have already been mentioned. An even more drastic simplification consists in substituting for the expectations and the variance-covariance matrices conditional on the information available in the previous period those conditional on the initial period, because this rules out any learning about the parameters of the model. "Passive learning" could be incorporated to some extent by repeatedly applying OPTCON to successively re-estimated econometric models over the planning horizon and using only the respective first-period controls for actual implementation. "Active learning", on the other hand, so far cannot be done by using OPTCON; thus, with respect to the possibility of exerting influence upon the control variables in order to obtain more informations about the parameters our algorithm has lower capabilities as compared to DUAL.

The implementation of the algorithm OPTCON in the program package GAUSS has been done in two steps. First, an algorithm equivalent to that of OPTNL was implemented and tested. Both the Klein-Goldberger model and the Austrian model used for the comparisons between the FORTRAN programs were run under this algorithm and produced virtually identical results as with the existing programs. Running time provides some concern, at least on a PC with a 286/287 processor, which was mainly due to the Gauss-Seidel iterations and not to the solution of the Riccati equations; the latter was efficiently supported by the powerful matrix operations implemented in GAUSS. In a second step, this algorithm was extended to include parameter uncertainty. Thus, for the first time there is an algorithm available which calculates approximately optimal controls for nonlinear models under additive and parameter disturbances according to a quadratic objective function. The results of this algorithm can be presented on the screen and printed, using the excellent graphics facilities provided by GAUSS.

The implementation of OPTCON in GAUSS showed several advantages as compared to an implementation in a procedural language, such as FORTRAN or even MODULA–2. Programming was much easier, and the source code is considerably shorter and hence more easily comprehensible. The GAUSS program is much closer to the mathematical notation of the algorithm; hence it is easier for a control theorist not being a computer specialist to read the program and to check the code. As GAUSS is relatively widely used among statisticians and econometricians, results of OPTCON can be transferred to other GAUSS procedures, and data from other GAUSS procedures (e.g., procedures for estimating econometric models) can be used as inputs for OPTCON more easily. GAUSS generally enhances the programmer's and the user's flexibility. On the other hand, one drawback of GAUSS consists in the impossibility of generating a compiled stand-alone application. Nevertheless, the advantages of GAUSS outweigh the drawbacks of an implementation in a procedural programming language. Instead, one could consider using a language providing still more powerful operators instead of GAUSS, such as APL. This would help avoiding the high programming efforts necessary to create higher-dimensional arrays and operations with them. Although an implementation in APL would thus have been easier than in GAUSS, APL is notoriously difficult to read and accessible only to a small number of programmers.

B. Applications of the Algorithm OPTCON

In order to test the algorithm OPTCON and its implementation in GAUSS, we have applied it to some macroeconomic policy problems. Two small demand-side econometric models for the Austrian economy were estimated, which we called AUSTRIA1 and AUSTRIA2. AUSTRIA1 is a nonlinear model estimated by ordinary least squares; AUSTRIA2 is a linear model estimated by three stage least squares. Although the estimations could have been performed in GAUSSX, a collection of GAUSS procedures for econometric methods, we decided to use the software system IAS, because this has very easy access to the database of the Austrian Institute of Economic Research from which all our data were taken. The theoretical basis for both models is a Keynesian one in the sense of textbook IS-LM models. The controls are fiscal and monetary policy instrument variables, the states are macroeconomic target variables, and the objective function is intended to express either "social welfare" in the sense of the theory of quantitative economic policy or a policy-maker's objectives. All behavioral equations of both models are formulated according to the partial-adjustment hypothesis. The estimation period was 1965 to 1988.

Model AUSTRIA1 has eight endogenous or state variables (real private consumption, real fixed investment, real imports of goods and services, the nominal rate of interest, real GDP at market prices, real total aggregate demand, the general price level, and the rate of inflation); the first six of them are also the state variables of model AUSTRIA2. AUSTRIA1 has three control variables (the net tax rate, real public consumption, and the nominal stock of money supply) and three exogenous non-controlled variables (the import price level, real autonomous expenditures (including exports of goods and services), and the domestic price level). AUSTRIA2 has also three control variables (real net tax revenues, real public consumption, and the real stock of money supply) and two exogenous non-controlled variables (the relative price of imports, and real autonomous expenditures). The structures of the two models are very similar; in both cases, real private consumption, real fixed investment, real imports of goods and services, and the nominal rate of interest are explained by estimated behavioral equations; the other state variables are determined by identities.

For the optimization experiments, a planning horizon from 1971 to 1988 was chosen; thus we are considering evaluations of historical policies in the past. For the desired values of the state and control variables in the objective function we assume historical values for all variables to be given for 1970 and postulate constant growth rates for all level variables and constant values for all rate variables. The weighting matrices are assumed to be constant; their off-diagonal elements are set equal to zero, and the main diagonal elements get weights determined (after some trial and error) to express the idea of "balanced growth" for all real variables, with real GDP being regarded as the main objective variable.

For the model AUSTRIA1, three control experiments are performed: In the first experiment, all parameters of the model are regarded as known with certainty. The only stochastic influences considered are the additive error terms in the behavioral equations. The variance-covariance matrix of the additive error terms is assumed to be diagonal with the squared estimated standard errors of the behavioral equations in the main diagonal. For the other two experiments performed with AUSTRIA1, we tentatively introduce some stochastic parameters. Here we assume the variance-covariance matrix of the parameters to be diagonal and select only some diagonal elements of this matrix to be non-zero. In the second experiment those parameters whose estimates have the lowest t-values are regarded as stochastic; these happen to be those which are crucial for the monetary policy multiplier. In the third experiment, the marginal propensity to consume, which determines the fiscal policy multipliers, is made stochastic in addition. This allows us to study the effects of uncertainty on the optimal conduct of monetary and fiscal policy.

For model AUSTRIA2, two experiments have been run. The first experiment is analogous to the first experiment for model AUSTRIA1 in assuming all parameters to be known for certain. Here the entire estimated variance-covariance matrix of the behavioral equations' additive disturbances is available as the model has been estimated by three stage least squares. In the second experiment with AUSTRIA2, the stochastic nature of all the parameters of the model (the coefficients and the constants) is taken into account by assuming the estimated values of the parameters to be their expected values and the variance-covariance matrix of the coefficients of the model to be the variance-covariance matrix of the parameters.

The five optimum control experiments described above were carried out on an IBM compatible 12 MHz PC-AT with an 80287 mathematical coprocessor. The running time of the GAUSS program of OPTCON ranged from 5 min. 5 sec. to 24 min. 37 sec. All the experiments indicate that fluctuations of the main objective variables can be stabilized to some extent by optimal policies. The optimal values of the control variables, especially those of fiscal policies, exhibit counter-cyclical behavior. Optimal values of most real state variables are lower than historical ones until the end of the seventies and higher during the eighties, showing that optimal policies in this model can to some extent overcome the lower historical growth rates of the period after the two oil price shocks.

Introducing stochastic parameters has the following effects on optimal policies for model AUSTRIA1: In the second experiment the differences to the results of the first experiment are minor. On the other hand, for the third experiment the differences to the first are more pronounced. It seems that optimal fiscal policies become more active (i.e., the absolute deviations from the desired values of these variables become larger on average) if their effects are uncertain, which is somewhat counterintuitive and not in line with results obtained from analytical models in the theory of quantitative economic policy.

From the experiments with model AUSTRIA2, we get the following results: In the first experiment, the optimal control values for most variables appearing in both models are rather close to the optimal values from the analogous (first) experiment with AUSTRIA1, which shows that both models embody similar trade-offs. The second experiment gives the somewhat surprising result that optimal values for all objective variables are very close to those obtained in the first experiment. Control variables show slightly more active behavior, but in general it seems that in this model taking fully account of stochastic parameters does not have a strong influence upon the optimal policies. It remains an open question whether this result generalizes to models with different kinds of nonlinearities.

Although it would be premature to base strong conclusions on the few experiments we have run with OPTCON, at least the feasibility of the algorithm has been established. Some of the results obtained open up interesting lines of further research in the theory of quantitative economic policy, which can be pursued by using OPTCON or more general algorithms to be developed out of OPTCON. For instance, it would be interesting to know whether the minor differences in the course of economic policies between a linear and a nonlinear model of similar structure carry over to more complicated models. Also the results concerning the influence of stochastic parameters on optimal policies (marked differences as compared to the deterministic or certainty-equivalence policies in the case of the nonlinear model with a few parameters being stochastic, minor differences in the case of the linear model with all parameters being stochastic) deserve further scrutiny. Many more experiments are required to check whether these outcomes remain true for different models, too.

4. EVALUATION AND OBJECTIVES FOR FURTHER RESEARCH

The earlier algorithms for the optimum control of stochastic dynamic economic systems seem to have been implemented with a concern for running time, quick implementation of the elaborate algorithm, and to some extent numerical accuracy. Therefore FORTRAN was chosen as a well-established programming language for numerical problems. In our view, more care should be taken of the transformation of the mathematical description of the algorithm into an informatical description. Using GAUSS, the gap between the description of the algorithm and that of the program could be narrowed: The algorithm has been implemented as a GAUSS procedure in a similar way as the GAUSS routines implementing econometric methods. Input data are transmitted to this procedure as parameters and checked for plausibility. The form of the system equation used is the one due to Chow, which is best suited for applications to econometric models. For the first time, the computer program allows for an explicit treatment of parameter uncertainty in the control of nonlinear economic models. The output of OPTCON is provided as matrices and data sets in GAUSS, which allows for an efficient use by other GAUSS routines, particularly the graphics routines. The documentation giving the mathematical description of the formulas and the code written for GAUSS variable names are relatively closely linked. Thus the implementation of OPTCON in GAUSS can be regarded as a true improvement as compared to the FORTRAN programs. It facilitates the application of stochastic control algorithms to economic models by taking into account nonlinearities and parameter uncertainty.

For the practical use of stochastic control methods in areas like economic policy, however, not a one-time access to an optimization program is required. Instead, usually an interactive approach is chosen, where several runs with different parameters are performed to arrive at the eventual decision. Not only the algorithm, but also this interactive approach has to be represented in a useful computer program. Decision support systems aim at applying computer-based technology to enhance the quality of decision-making in such semi-structured tasks. These systems are intended to bridge the gap between real-world problems and solution algorithms. Algorithms like those in stochastic control theory deliver solutions for highly structured mathematical problems. Practical problems like those in management and economic policy, however, are not structured a priori. Introducing economic models as descriptions of real economic systems and condensating policy preferences into an objective function in operations research and in the theory of quantitative economic policy can be interpreted as devices for structuring these problems at least partially; hence a decision support system could be applied. This would provide "soft" interactive approaches for solving the problem to the user, which nevertheless rely on "hard" methods, data, and models. Such an approach could help to improve the quality of decisions in a real application, even if the result is not characterized as "optimal" in a strict, mathematical sense.

For example, such an interactive approach using stochastic control theory to support economic policy decisions could start from specifying and estimating an econometric model (or improving one that is already available). The values of the non-controlled exogenous variables have to be forecast for some planning horizon. The actual policy-maker has to specify a proposal for his (her) policy instruments over the planning horizon. Simulations of the model give information about the effects of the proposed policies on economic variables. The results can be used to check the plausibility of the model and the forecasts, possibly leading to re-estimations, and to formulate new proposals for policies. This simulation approach, which often alternatively is regarded as a method for solving policy problems in itself, serves to improve the quality of the model and the data within the control-theoretic approach. Next, a quantitative objective function has to be specified by interactions with the decision-maker. Applying a control algorithm gives an "optimal" path for economic policies. This "optimal" policy is proposed to the decision-maker, possibly necessitating a re-specification of the objective function (changing weights, desired values, etc.). The results of the optimization algorithm may also lead to re-specifications or re-estimations of the model if they are considered implausible. Another run of the algorithm can be performed, and so on.

Such an iterative and interactive process may help improving actual decisions. Most important in designing a decision support system of this kind would be its user-friendliness. Mathematical symbols and expressions have to be translated into the language of the decision-maker. For the user, the decision support system must be easily accessible. Such a system consists not only of the stochastic control algorithm but must contain procedures for econometric estimations, tests, forecasting and for simulations. Apart from these methods, a data base must be provided which stores all necessary data, including those obtained as results of applications of the methods to the original data. Finally, the models used have to be defined in a descriptive language that is independent of the methods and have to be stored. Transformations of the models to representations needed for the different models must be provided. Similar proposals are discussed in [11].

Obviously it is still a long way from the present situation, where a few control-theoretic algorithms are available in a form more or less inaccessible to potential users, to a decision support system of the kind outlined above. While GAUSS improves on the representation of the algorithm, implementing a decision support system in GAUSS is somewhat awkward. Such a system has to include a modeling language capable of describing the different forms of models encountered, a data base component for the storage of inputs and outputs of various algorithms, as well as a standardized interface to the algorithms themselves. For example, GAMS represents an interesting first step in this direction, covering, however, only parts of the functionality required. In any case, this task must be taken up to make the results of previous, current and future research in stochastic control theory and in the algorithmic developments resulting from it useful for the actual problems of decision-makers in economic policy and management, which ultimately should help making decisions in economic affairs more "rational" than they have been hitherto. This provides a challenge for control theorists, computer scientists, and economists, especially for those active in the emerging field of computational economics.

BIBLIOGRAPHY

1. Chow, G. C., 1975, *Analysis and Control of Dynamic Economic Systems*, New York: John Wiley & Sons.
2. Chow, G. C., 1981, *Econometric Analysis by Control Methods*, New York: John Wiley & Sons.
3. Kendrick, D., 1981, *Stochastic Control for Economic Models*, New York: McGraw-Hill.
4. Tse, E., Y. Bar-Shalom, and L. Meier, 1973, 'Wide sense adaptive dual control for nonlinear stochastic systems', *IEEE Transactions on Automatic Control* AC–18, 98–108.
5. Kendrick D. and P. Coomes, 1984, 'DUAL. A program for quadratic-linear stochastic control problems', Center for Economic Research, University of Texas, Austin, discussion paper No. 84–15.
6. Coomes, P. A., 1987, 'PLEM: A computer program for passive learning, stochastic control experiments', *Journal of Economic Dynamics and Control* 11, 223–227.
7. MacRae, E. C., 1975, 'An adaptive learning rule for multiperiod decision problems', *Econometrica* 43, 893–906.
8. Neck R. and J. Matulka, 1989, 'Optimal control of dynamic economic models: a comparison of three computer programs', in P. Borne *et al.* (Eds.), *Computing and Computers for Control Systems*, Basel: J. C. Baltzer AG, pp. 63–68.
9. Matulka J. and R. Neck, 1992, 'OPTCON: An algorithm for the optimal control of nonlinear stochastic models', *Annals of Operations Research* 37, 375–401.
10. Neck R. and J. Matulka, 1991, 'Stochastic optimum control of macroeconometric models using the algorithm OPTCON', Vienna University of Economics and Business Administration, Vienna, working paper.
11. Kendrick D. (Ed.), 1991, 'Research Opportunities in Computational Economics', Center for Economic Research, University of Texas, Austin, report R–91–1.

Index

Advances in Computational Economics

1. A. Nagurney: *Network Economics.* A Variational Inequality Approach. 1993 ISBN 0-7923-9293-0
2. A.K. Duraiappah: *Global Warming and Economic Development.* A Holistic Approach to International Policy Co-operation and Co-ordination. 1993 ISBN 0-7923-2149-9
3. D.A. Belsley (ed.): *Computational Techniques for Econometrics and Economic Analysis.* 1993 ISBN 0-7923-2356-4
4. W.W. Cooper and A.B. Whinston (eds.): *New Directions in Computational Economics.* 1994 ISBN 0-7923-2539-7

KLUWER ACADEMIC PUBLISHERS – DORDRECHT / BOSTON / LONDON